The Top Ten Algorithms in Data Mining

Chapman & Hall/CRC
Data Mining and Knowledge Discovery Series

SERIES EDITOR

Vipin Kumar

University of Minnesota

Department of Computer Science and Engineering

Minneapolis, Minnesota, U.S.A

AIMS AND SCOPE

This series aims to capture new developments and applications in data mining and knowledge discovery, while summarizing the computational tools and techniques useful in data analysis. This series encourages the integration of mathematical, statistical, and computational methods and techniques through the publication of a broad range of textbooks, reference works, and handbooks. The inclusion of concrete examples and applications is highly encouraged. The scope of the series includes, but is not limited to, titles in the areas of data mining and knowledge discovery methods and applications, modeling, algorithms, theory and foundations, data and knowledge visualization, data mining systems and tools, and privacy and security issues.

PUBLISHED TITLES

UNDERSTANDING COMPLEX DATASETS: Data Mining with Matrix Decompositions
David Skillicorn

COMPUTATIONAL METHODS OF FEATURE SELECTION
Huan Liu and Hiroshi Motoda

CONSTRAINED CLUSTERING: Advances in Algorithms, Theory, and Applications
Sugato Basu, Ian Davidson, and Kiri L. Wagstaff

KNOWLEDGE DISCOVERY FOR COUNTERTERRORISM AND LAW ENFORCEMENT
David Skillicorn

MULTIMEDIA DATA MINING: A Systematic Introduction to Concepts and Theory
Zhongfei Zhang and Ruofei Zhang

NEXT GENERATION OF DATA MINING
Hillol Kargupta, Jiawei Han, Philip S. Yu, Rajeev Motwani, and Vipin Kumar

DATA MINING FOR DESIGN AND MARKETING
Yukio Ohsawa and Katsutoshi Yada

GEOGRAPHIC DATA MINING AND KNOWLEDGE DISCOVERY, Second Edition
Harvey J. Miller and Jiawei Han

THE TOP TEN ALGORITHMS IN DATA MINING
Xindong Wu and Vipin Kumar

Chapman & Hall/CRC
Data Mining and Knowledge Discovery Series

The Top Ten Algorithms in Data Mining

Edited by
Xindong Wu
Vipin Kumar

CRC Press
Taylor & Francis Group
Boca Raton London New York

CRC Press is an imprint of the
Taylor & Francis Group, an **informa** business
A CHAPMAN & HALL BOOK

Chapman & Hall/CRC
Taylor & Francis Group
6000 Broken Sound Parkway NW, Suite 300
Boca Raton, FL 33487-2742

International Standard Book Number-13: 978-1-4200-8964-6 (Hardcover)

Visit the Taylor & Francis Web site at
http://www.taylorandfrancis.com

and the CRC Press Web site at
http://www.crcpress.com

Contents

Preface

In an effort to identify some of the most influential algorithms that have been widely used in the data mining community, the IEEE International Conference on Data Mining (ICDM, http://www.cs.uvm.edu/~icdm/) identified the top 10 algorithms in data mining for presentation at ICDM '06 in Hong Kong. This book presents these top 10 data mining algorithms: C4.5, k-Means, SVM, Apriori, EM, PageRank, AdaBoost, kNN, Naïve Bayes, and CART.

As the first step in the identification process, in September 2006 we invited the ACM KDD Innovation Award and IEEE ICDM Research Contributions Award winners to each nominate up to 10 best-known algorithms in data mining. All except one in this distinguished set of award winners responded to our invitation. We asked each nomination to provide the following information: (a) the algorithm name, (b) a brief justification, and (c) a representative publication reference. We also advised that each nominated algorithm should have been widely cited and used by other researchers in the field, and the nominations from each nominator as a group should have a reasonable representation of the different areas in data mining.

After the nominations in step 1, we verified each nomination for its citations on Google Scholar in late October 2006, and removed those nominations that did not have at least 50 citations. All remaining (18) nominations were then organized in 10 topics: association analysis, classification, clustering, statistical learning, bagging and boosting, sequential patterns, integrated mining, rough sets, link mining, and graph mining. For some of these 18 algorithms, such as k-means, the representative publication was not necessarily the original paper that introduced the algorithm, but a recent paper that highlights the importance of the technique. These representative publications are available at the ICDM Web site (http://www.cs.uvm.edu/~icdm/algorithms/CandidateList.shtml).

In the third step of the identification process, we had a wider involvement of the research community. We invited the Program Committee members of KDD-06 (the 2006 ACM SIGKDD International Conference on Knowledge Discovery and Data Mining), ICDM '06 (the 2006 IEEE International Conference on Data Mining), and SDM '06 (the 2006 SIAM International Conference on Data Mining), as well as the ACM KDD Innovation Award and IEEE ICDM Research Contributions Award winners to each vote for up to 10 well-known algorithms from the 18-algorithm candidate list. The voting results of this step were presented at the ICDM '06 panel on Top 10 Algorithms in Data Mining.

At the ICDM '06 panel of December 21, 2006, we also took an open vote with all 145 attendees on the top 10 algorithms from the above 18-algorithm candidate list, and the top 10 algorithms from this open vote were the same as the voting results from the above third step. The three-hour panel was organized as the last session of the ICDM '06 conference, in parallel with seven paper presentation sessions of the Web Intelligence (WI '06) and Intelligent Agent Technology (IAT '06) conferences at the same location, and attracted 145 participants.

After ICDM '06, we invited the original authors and some of the panel presenters of these 10 algorithms to write a journal article to provide a description of each algorithm, discuss the impact of the algorithm, and review current and further research on the algorithm. The journal article was published in January 2008 in *Knowledge and Information Systems* [1]. This book expands upon this journal article, with a common structure for each chapter on each algorithm, in terms of algorithm description, available software, illustrative examples and applications, advanced topics, and exercises.

Each book chapter was reviewed by two independent reviewers and one of the two book editors. Some chapters went through a major revision based on this review before their final acceptance.

We hope the identification of the top 10 algorithms can promote data mining to wider real-world applications, and inspire more researchers in data mining to further explore these 10 algorithms, including their impact and new research issues. These 10 algorithms cover classification, clustering, statistical learning, association analysis, and link mining, which are all among the most important topics in data mining research and development, as well as for curriculum design for related data mining, machine learning, and artificial intelligence courses.

Acknowledgments

The initiative of identifying the top 10 data mining algorithms started in May 2006 out of a discussion between Dr. Jiannong Cao in the Department of Computing at the Hong Kong Polytechnic University (PolyU) and Dr. Xindong Wu, when Dr. Wu was giving a seminar on 10 Challenging Problems in Data Mining Research [2] at PolyU. Dr. Wu and Dr. Vipin Kumar continued this discussion at KDD-06 in August 2006 with various people, and received very enthusiastic support.

Naila Elliott in the Department of Computer Science and Engineering at the University of Minnesota collected and compiled the algorithm nominations and voting results in the three-step identification process. Yan Zhang in the Department of Computer Science at the University of Vermont converted the 10 section submissions in different formats into the same LaTeX format, which was a time-consuming process.

Xindong Wu and Vipin Kumar
September 15, 2008

References

[1] Xindong Wu, Vipin Kumar, J. Ross Quinlan, Joydeep Ghosh, Qiang Yang, Hiroshi Motoda, Geoffrey J. McLachlan, Angus Ng, Bing Liu, Philip S. Yu, Zhi-Hua Zhou, Michael Steinbach, David J. Hand, and Dan Steinberg, Top 10 algorithms in data mining, *Knowledge and Information Systems*, 14(2008), 1: 1–37.

[2] Qiang Yang and Xindong Wu (Contributors: Pedro Domingos, Charles Elkan, Johannes Gehrke, Jiawei Han, David Heckerman, Daniel Keim, Jiming Liu, David Madigan, Gregory Piatetsky-Shapiro, Vijay V. Raghavan, Rajeev Rastogi, Salvatore J. Stolfo, Alexander Tuzhilin, and Benjamin W. Wah), 10 challenging problems in data mining research, *International Journal of Information Technology & Decision Making*, 5, 4(2006), 597–604.

About the Authors

Xindong Wu is a professor and the chair of the Computer Science Department at the University of Vermont, United States. He holds a PhD in Artificial Intelligence from the University of Edinburgh, Britain. His research interests include data mining, knowledge-based systems, and Web information exploration. He has published over 170 referred papers in these areas in various journals and conferences, including IEEE TKDE, TPAMI, ACM TOIS, DMKD, KAIS, IJCAI, AAAI, ICML, KDD, ICDM, and WWW, as well as 18 books and conference proceedings. He won the IEEE ICTAI-2005 Best Paper Award and the IEEE ICDM-2007 Best Theory/Algorithms Paper Runner Up Award.

Dr. Wu is the editor-in-chief of the *IEEE Transactions on Knowledge and Data Engineering (TKDE*, by the IEEE Computer Society), the founder and current Steering Committee Chair of the *IEEE International Conference on Data Mining (ICDM)*, the founder and current honorary editor-in-chief of Knowledge and Information Systems (KAIS, by Springer), the founding chair (2002–2006) of the IEEE Computer Society Technical Committee on Intelligent Informatics (TCII), and a series editor of the Springer Book Series on Advanced Information and Knowledge Processing (AI&KP). He served as program committee chair for ICDM '03 (the 2003 IEEE International Conference on Data Mining) and program committee cochair for KDD-07 (the 13th ACM SIGKDD International Conference on Knowledge Discovery and Data Mining). He is the 2004 ACM SIGKDD Service Award winner, the 2006 IEEE ICDM Outstanding Service Award winner, and a 2005 chair professor in the Changjiang (or Yangtze River) Scholars Programme at the Hefei University of Technology sponsored by the Ministry of Education of China and the Li Ka Shing Foundation. He has been an invited/keynote speaker at numerous international conferences including NSF-NGDM'07, PAKDD-07, IEEE EDOC'06, IEEE ICTAI'04, IEEE/WIC/ACM WI'04/IAT'04, SEKE 2002, and PADD-97.

Vipin Kumar is currently William Norris professor and head of the Computer Science and Engineering Department at the University of Minnesota. He received BE degrees in electronics and communication engineering from Indian Institute of Technology, Roorkee (formerly, University of Roorkee), India, in 1977, ME degree in electronics engineering from Philips International Institute, Eindhoven, Netherlands, in 1979, and PhD in computer science from University of Maryland, College Park, in 1982. Kumar's current research interests include data mining, bioinformatics, and high-performance computing. His research has resulted in the development of the concept of isoefficiency metric for evaluating the scalability of parallel algorithms, as well as highly efficient parallel algorithms and software for sparse matrix factorization

(PSPASES) and graph partitioning (METIS, ParMetis, hMetis). He has authored over 200 research articles, and has coedited or coauthored 9 books, including widely used textbooks *Introduction to Parallel Computing* and *Introduction to Data Mining*, both published by Addison-Wesley. Kumar has served as chair/cochair for many conferences/workshops in the area of data mining and parallel computing, including *IEEE International Conference on Data Mining* (2002), *International Parallel and Distributed Processing Symposium* (2001), and *SIAM International Conference on Data Mining* (2001). Kumar serves as cochair of the steering committee of the *SIAM International Conference on Data Mining*, and is a member of the steering committee of the *IEEE International Conference on Data Mining* and the *IEEE International Conference on Bioinformatics and Biomedicine*. Kumar is a founding coeditor-in-chief of *Journal of Statistical Analysis and Data Mining*, editor-in-chief of *IEEE Intelligent Informatics Bulletin*, and editor of *Data Mining and Knowledge Discovery Book Series*, published by CRC Press/Chapman Hall. Kumar also serves or has served on the editorial boards of *Data Mining and Knowledge Discovery*, *Knowledge and Information Systems*, *IEEE Computational Intelligence Bulletin*, *Annual Review of Intelligent Informatics*, *Parallel Computing*, the *Journal of Parallel and Distributed Computing*, *IEEE Transactions of Data and Knowledge Engineering* (1993–1997), *IEEE Concurrency* (1997–2000), and *IEEE Parallel and Distributed Technology* (1995–1997). He is a fellow of the ACM, IEEE, and AAAS, and a member of SIAM. Kumar received the 2005 IEEE Computer Society's Technical Achievement award for contributions to the design and analysis of parallel algorithms, graph-partitioning, and data mining.

Contributors

Songcan Chen, *Nanjing University of Aeronautics and Astronautics, Nanjing, China*

Joydeep Ghosh, *University of Texas at Austin, Austin, TX*

David J. Hand, *Imperial College, London, UK*

Alexander Liu, *University of Texas at Austin, Austin, TX*

Bing Liu, *University of Illinois at Chicago, Chicago, IL*

Geoffrey J. McLachlan, *University of Queensland, Brisbane, Australia*

Hiroshi Motoda, *ISIR, Osaka University and AFOSR/AOARD, Air Force Research Laboratory, Japan*

Shu-Kay Ng, *Griffith University, Meadowbrook, Australia*

Kouzou Ohara, *ISIR, Osaka University, Japan*

Naren Ramakrishnan, *Virginia Tech, Blacksburg, VA*

Michael Steinbach, *University of Minnesota, Minneapolis, MN*

Dan Steinberg, *Salford Systems, San Diego, CA*

Pang-Ning Tan, *Michigan State University, East Lansing, MI*

Hui Xue, *Nanjing University of Aeronautics and Astronautics, Nanjing, China*

Qiang Yang, *Hong Kong University of Science and Technology, Clearwater Bay, Kowloon, Hong Kong*

Philip S. Yu, *University of Illinois at Chicago, Chicago, IL*

Yang Yu, *Nanjing University, Nanjing, China*

Zhi-Hua Zhou, *Nanjing University, Nanjing, China*

Chapter 1

C4.5

Naren Ramakrishnan

Contents

1.1 Introduction

C4.5 [30] is a suite of algorithms for classification problems in machine learning and data mining. It is targeted at supervised learning: Given an attribute-valued dataset where *instances* are described by collections of *attributes* and belong to one of a set of mutually exclusive *classes*, C4.5 learns a mapping from attribute values to classes that can be applied to classify new, unseen instances. For instance, see Figure 1.1 where rows denote specific days, attributes denote weather conditions on the given day, and the class denotes whether the conditions are conducive to playing golf. Thus, each row denotes an instance, described by values for attributes such as *Outlook* (a ternary-valued random variable) *Temperature* (continuous-valued), *Humidity*

Day	Outlook	Temperature	Humidity	Windy	Play Golf?
1	Sunny	85	85	False	No
2	Sunny	80	90	True	No
3	Overcast	83	78	False	Yes
4	Rainy	70	96	False	Yes
5	Rainy	68	80	False	Yes
6	Rainy	65	70	True	No
7	Overcast	64	65	True	Yes
8	Sunny	72	95	False	No
9	Sunny	69	70	False	Yes
10	Rainy	75	80	False	Yes
11	Sunny	75	70	True	Yes
12	Overcast	72	90	True	Yes
13	Overcast	81	75	False	Yes
14	Rainy	71	80	True	No

Figure 1.1 Example dataset input to C4.5.

(also continuous-valued), and *Windy* (binary), and the class is the Boolean *PlayGolf?* class variable. All of the data in Figure 1.1 constitutes "training data," so that the intent is to learn a mapping using this dataset and apply it on other, new instances that present values for only the attributes to predict the value for the class random variable.

C4.5, designed by J. Ross Quinlan, is so named because it is a descendant of the ID3 approach to inducing decision trees [25], which in turn is the third incarnation in a series of "iterative dichotomizers." A *decision tree* is a series of questions systematically arranged so that each question queries an attribute (e.g., *Outlook*) and branches based on the value of the attribute. At the leaves of the tree are placed predictions of the class variable (here, *PlayGolf?*). A decision tree is hence not unlike the series of troubleshooting questions you might find in your car's manual to help determine what could be wrong with the vehicle. In addition to inducing trees, C4.5 can also restate its trees in comprehensible rule form. Further, the rule postpruning operations supported by C4.5 typically result in classifiers that cannot quite be restated as a decision tree.

The historical lineage of C4.5 offers an interesting study into how different subcommunities converged on more or less like-minded solutions to classification. ID3 was developed independently of the original tree induction algorithm developed by Friedman [13], which later evolved into CART [4] with the participation of Breiman, Olshen, and Stone. But, from the numerous references to CART in [30], the design decisions underlying C4.5 appear to have been influenced by (to improve upon) how CART resolved similar issues, such as procedures for handling special types of attributes. (For this reason, due to the overlap in scope, we will aim to minimize with the material covered in the CART chapter, Chapter 10, and point out key differences at appropriate junctures.) In [25] and [36], Quinlan also acknowledged the influence of the CLS (Concept Learning System [16]) framework in the historical development of ID3 and C4.5. Today, C4.5 is superseded by the See5/C5.0 system, a commercial product offered by Rulequest Research, Inc.

The fact that two of the top 10 algorithms are tree-based algorithms attests to the widespread popularity of such methods in data mining. Original applications of decision trees were in domains with nominal valued or categorical data but today they span a multitude of domains with numeric, symbolic, and mixed-type attributes. Examples include clinical decision making, manufacturing, document analysis, bioinformatics, spatial data modeling (geographic information systems), and practically any domain where decision boundaries between classes can be captured in terms of tree-like decompositions or regions identified by rules.

1.2 Algorithm Description

C4.5 is not one algorithm but rather a suite of algorithms—C4.5, C4.5-no-pruning, and C4.5-rules—with many features. We present the basic C4.5 algorithm first and the special features later.

The generic description of how C4.5 works is shown in Algorithm 1.1. All tree induction methods begin with a root node that represents the entire, given dataset and recursively split the data into smaller subsets by testing for a given attribute at each node. The subtrees denote the partitions of the original dataset that satisfy specified attribute value tests. This process typically continues until the subsets are "pure," that is, all instances in the subset fall in the same class, at which time the tree growing is terminated.

Algorithm 1.1 C4.5(D)

Input: an attribute-valued dataset D

Tree = {}
if D is "pure" OR other stopping criteria met **then**
    terminate
end if
for all attribute $a \in D$ **do**
    Compute information-theoretic criteria if we split on a
end for
a_{best} = Best attribute according to above computed criteria
Tree = Create a decision node that tests a_{best} in the root
D_v = Induced sub-datasets from D based on a_{best}
for all D_v **do**
    $\text{Tree}_v = \text{C4.5}(D_v)$
    Attach Tree_v to the corresponding branch of Tree
end for
return Tree

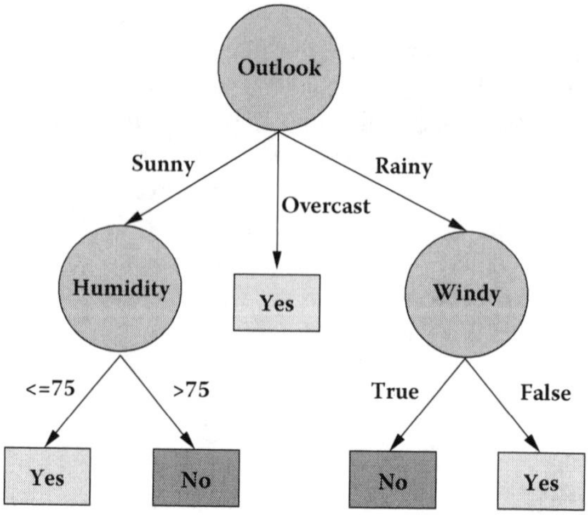

Figure 1.2 Decision tree induced by C4.5 for the dataset of Figure 1.1.

Figure 1.1 presents the classical "golf" dataset, which is bundled with the C4.5 installation. As stated earlier, the goal is to predict whether the weather conditions on a particular day are conducive to playing golf. Recall that some of the features are continuous-valued while others are categorical.

Figure 1.2 illustrates the tree induced by C4.5 using Figure 1.1 as training data (and the default options). Let us look at the various choices involved in inducing such trees from the data.

- **What types of tests are possible?** As Figure 1.2 shows, C4.5 is not restricted to considering binary tests, and allows tests with two or more outcomes. If the attribute is Boolean, the test induces two branches. If the attribute is categorical, the test is multivalued, but different values can be grouped into a smaller set of options with one class predicted for each option. If the attribute is numerical, then the tests are again binary-valued, and of the form $\{\leq \theta?, > \theta?\}$, where θ is a suitably determined threshold for that attribute.
- **How are tests chosen?** C4.5 uses information-theoretic criteria such as gain (reduction in entropy of the class distribution due to applying a test) and gain ratio (a way to correct for the tendency of gain to favor tests with many outcomes). The default criterion is gain ratio. At each point in the tree-growing, the test with the best criteria is greedily chosen.
- **How are test thresholds chosen?** As stated earlier, for Boolean and categorical attributes, the test values are simply the different possible instantiations of that attribute. For numerical attributes, the threshold is obtained by sorting on that attribute and choosing the split between successive values that maximize the criteria above. Fayyad and Irani [10] showed that not all successive values need to be considered. For two successive values v_i and v_{i+1} of a continuous-valued

attribute, if all instances involving v_i and all instances involving v_{i+1} belong to the same class, then splitting between them cannot possibly improve information gain (or gain ratio).

- **How is tree-growing terminated?** A branch from a node is declared to lead to a leaf if all instances that are covered by that branch are pure. Another way in which tree-growing is terminated is if the number of instances falls below a specified threshold.
- **How are class labels assigned to the leaves?** The majority class of the instances assigned to the leaf is taken to be the class prediction of that subbranch of the tree.

The above questions are faced by any classification approach modeled after trees and similar, or other reasonable, decisions are made by most tree induction algorithms. The practical utility of C4.5, however, comes from the next set of features that build upon the basic tree induction algorithm above. But before we present these features, it is instructive to instantiate Algorithm 1.1 for a simple dataset such as shown in Figure 1.1.

We will work out in some detail how the tree of Figure 1.2 is induced from Figure 1.1. Observe how the first attribute chosen for a decision test is the *Outlook* attribute. To see why, let us first estimate the entropy of the class random variable (*PlayGolf?*). This variable takes two values with probability 9/14 (for "Yes") and 5/14 (for "No"). The entropy of a class random variable that takes on c values with probabilities $p_1, p_2, \ldots, p_c$ is given by:

$$\sum_{i=1}^{c} -p_i \log_2 p_i$$

The entropy of *PlayGolf?* is thus

$$-(9/14)\log_2(9/14) - (5/14)\log_2(5/14)$$

or 0.940. This means that on average 0.940 bits must be transmitted to communicate information about the *PlayGolf?* random variable. The goal of C4.5 tree induction is to ask the right questions so that this entropy is reduced. We consider each attribute in turn to assess the improvement in entropy that it affords. For a given random variable, say *Outlook*, the improvement in entropy, represented as *Gain(Outlook)*, is calculated as:

$$\text{Entropy}(\textit{PlayGolf?} \text{ in } D) - \sum_{v} \frac{|D_v|}{|D|}\text{Entropy}(\textit{PlayGolf?} \text{ in } D_v)$$

where v is the set of possible values (in this case, three values for *Outlook*), D denotes the entire dataset, D_v is the subset of the dataset for which attribute *Outlook* has that value, and the notation $|\cdot|$ denotes the size of a dataset (in the number of instances).

This calculation will show that *Gain(Outlook)* is $0.940 - 0.694 = 0.246$. Similarly, we can calculate that *Gain(Windy)* is $0.940 - 0.892 = 0.048$. Working out the above calculations for the other attributes systematically will reveal that *Outlook* is indeed the best attribute to branch on. Observe that this is a greedy choice and does not take into account the effect of future decisions. As stated earlier, the tree-growing continues till termination criteria such as purity of subdatasets are met. In the above example, branching on the value "Overcast" for *Outlook* results in a pure dataset, that is, all instances having this value for *Outlook* have the value "Yes" for the class variable *PlayGolf?*; hence, the tree is not grown further in that direction. However, the other two values for *Outlook* still induce impure datasets. Therefore the algorithm recurses, but observe that *Outlook* cannot be chosen again (why?). For different branches, different test criteria and splits are chosen, although, in general, duplication of subtrees can possibly occur for other datasets.

We mentioned earlier that the default splitting criterion is actually the gain ratio, not the gain. To understand the difference, assume we treated the *Day* column in Figure 1.1 as if it were a "real" feature. Furthermore, assume that we treat it as a nominal valued attribute. Of course, each day is unique, so *Day* is really not a useful attribute to branch on. Nevertheless, because there are 14 distinct values for *Day* and each of them induces a "pure" dataset (a trivial dataset involving only one instance), *Day* would be unfairly selected as the best attribute to branch on. Because information gain favors attributes that contain a large number of values, Quinlan proposed the gain ratio as a correction to account for this effect. The gain ratio for an attribute a is defined as:

$$\text{GainRatio}(a) = \frac{\text{Gain}(a)}{\text{Entropy}(a)}$$

Observe that entropy(a) does not depend on the class information and simply takes into account the distribution of possible values for attribute a, whereas gain(a) does take into account the class information. (Also, recall that all calculations here are dependent on the dataset used, although we haven't made this explicit in the notation.) For instance, GainRatio(*Outlook*) $= 0.246/1.577 = 0.156$. Similarly, the gain ratio for the other attributes can be calculated. We leave it as an exercise to the reader to see if *Outlook* will again be chosen to form the root decision test.

At this point in the discussion, it should be mentioned that decision trees cannot model all decision boundaries between classes in a succinct manner. For instance, although they can model any Boolean function, the resulting tree might be needlessly complex. Consider, for instance, modeling an XOR over a large number of Boolean attributes. In this case every attribute would need to be tested along every path and the tree would be exponential in size. Another example of a difficult problem for decision trees are so-called "m-of-n" functions where the class is predicted by any m of n attributes, without being specific about which attributes should contribute to the decision. Solutions such as oblique decision trees, presented later, overcome such drawbacks. Besides this difficulty, a second problem with decision trees induced by C4.5 is the duplication of subtrees due to the greedy choice of attribute selection. Beyond an exhaustive search for the best attribute by fully growing the tree, this problem is not solvable in general.

1.3 C4.5 Features

1.3.1 Tree Pruning

Tree pruning is necessary to avoid overfitting the data. To drive this point, Quinlan gives a dramatic example in [30] of a dataset with 10 Boolean attributes, each of which assumes values 0 or 1 with equal accuracy. The class values were also binary: "yes" with probability 0.25 and "no" with probability 0.75. From a starting set of 1,000 instances, 500 were used for training and the remaining 500 were used for testing. Quinlan observes that C4.5 produces a tree involving 119 nodes (!) with an error rate of more than 35% when a simpler tree would have sufficed to achieve a greater accuracy. Tree pruning is hence critical to improve accuracy of the classifier on unseen instances. It is typically carried out after the tree is fully grown, and in a bottom-up manner.

The 1986 MIT AI lab memo authored by Quinlan [26] outlines the various choices available for tree pruning in the context of past research. The CART algorithm uses what is known as *cost-complexity pruning* where a series of trees are grown, each obtained from the previous by replacing one or more subtrees with a leaf. The last tree in the series comprises just a single leaf that predicts a specific class. The cost-complexity is a metric that decides which subtrees should be replaced by a leaf predicting the best class value. Each of the trees are then evaluated on a separate test dataset, and based on reliability measures derived from performance on the test dataset, a "best" tree is selected.

Reduced error pruning is a simplification of this approach. As before, it uses a separate test dataset but it directly uses the fully induced tree to classify instances in the test dataset. For every nonleaf subtree in the induced tree, this strategy evaluates whether it is beneficial to replace the subtree by the best possible leaf. If the pruned tree would indeed give an equal or smaller number of errors than the unpruned tree and the replaced subtree does not itself contain another subtree with the same property, then the subtree is replaced. This process is continued until further replacements actually increase the error over the test dataset.

Pessimistic pruning is an innovation in C4.5 that does not require a separate test set. Rather it *estimates* the error that might occur based on the amount of misclassifications in the training set. This approach recursively estimates the error rate associated with a node based on the estimated error rates of its branches. For a leaf with N instances and E errors (i.e., the number of instances that do not belong to the class predicted by that leaf), pessimistic pruning first determines the empirical error rate at the leaf as the ratio $(E + 0.5)/N$. For a subtree with L leaves and ΣE and ΣN corresponding errors and number of instances over these leaves, the error rate for the entire subtree is estimated to be $(\Sigma E + 0.5 * L)/\Sigma N$. Now, assume that the subtree is replaced by its best leaf and that J is the number of cases from the training set that it misclassifies. Pessimistic pruning replaces the subtree with this best leaf if $(J + 0.5)$ is within one standard deviation of $(\Sigma E + 0.5 * L)$.

This approach can be extended to prune based on desired confidence intervals (CIs). We can model the error rates e at the leaves as Bernoulli random variables and for

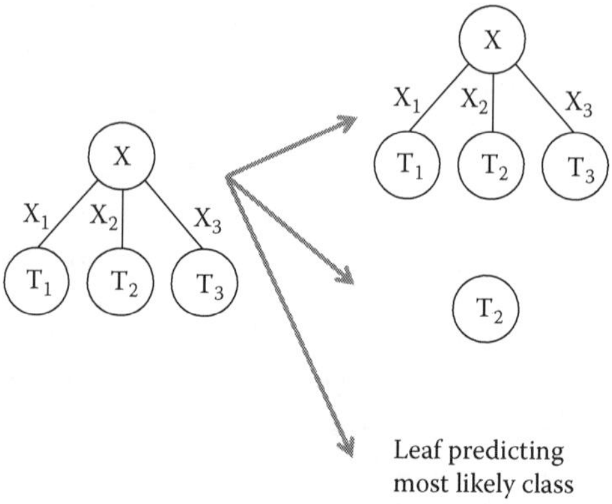

Figure 1.3 Different choices in pruning decision trees. The tree on the left can be retained as it is or replaced by just one of its subtrees or by a single leaf.

a given confidence threshold CI, an upper bound $e_{\max}$ can be determined such that $e < e_{\max}$ with probability $1 - CI$. (C4.5 uses a default CI of 0.25.) We can go even further and approximate e by the normal distribution (for large N), in which case C4.5 determines an upper bound on the expected error as:

$$\frac{e + \frac{z^2}{2N} + z\sqrt{\frac{e}{N} - \frac{e^2}{N} + \frac{z^2}{4N^2}}}{1 + \frac{z^2}{N}} \tag{1.1}$$

where z is chosen based on the desired confidence interval for the estimation, assuming a normal random variable with zero mean and unit variance, that is, $\mathcal{N}(0, 1)$).

What remains to be presented is the exact way in which the pruning is performed. A single bottom-up pass is performed. Consider Figure 1.3, which depicts the pruning process midway so that pruning has already been performed on subtrees T_1, T_2, and T_3. The error rates are estimated for three cases as shown in Figure 1.3 (right). The first case is to keep the tree as it is. The second case is to retain only the subtree corresponding to the most frequent outcome of X (in this case, the middle branch). The third case is to just have a leaf labeled with the most frequent class in the training dataset. These considerations are continued bottom-up till we reach the root of the tree.

1.3.2 Improved Use of Continuous Attributes

More sophisticated capabilities for handling continuous attributes are covered by Quinlan in [31]. These are motivated by the advantage shared by continuous-valued attributes over discrete ones, namely that they can branch on more decision criteria which might give them an unfair advantage over discrete attributes. One approach, of course, is to use the gain ratio in place of the gain as before. However, we run into a conundrum here because the gain ratio will also be influenced by the actual threshold used by the continuous-valued attribute. In particular, if the threshold apportions the instances nearly equally, then the gain ratio is minimal (since the entropy of the variable falls in the denominator). Therefore, Quinlan advocates going back to the regular information gain for choosing a threshold but continuing the use of the gain ratio for choosing the attribute in the first place. A second approach is based on Risannen's MDL (minimum description length) principle. By viewing trees as theories, Quinlan proposes trading off the complexity of a tree versus its performance. In particular, the complexity is calculated as both the cost of encoding the tree plus the exceptions to the tree (i.e., the training instances that are not supported by the tree). Empirical tests show that this approach does not unduly favor continuous-valued attributes.

1.3.3 Handling Missing Values

Missing attribute values require special accommodations both in the learning phase and in subsequent classification of new instances. Quinlan [28] offers a comprehensive overview of the variety of issues that must be considered. As stated therein, there are three main issues: (i) When comparing attributes to branch on, some of which have missing values for some instances, how should we choose an appropriate splitting attribute? (ii) After a splitting attribute for the decision test is selected, training instances with missing values cannot be associated with any outcome of the decision test. This association is necessary in order to continue the tree-growing procedure. Therefore, the second question is: How should such instances be treated when dividing the dataset into subdatasets? (iii) Finally, when the tree is used to classify a new instance, how do we proceed down a tree when the tree tests on an attribute whose value is missing for this new instance? Observe that the first two issues involve learning/inducing the tree whereas the third issue involves applying the learned tree on new instances. As can be expected, there are several possibilities for each of these questions. In [28], Quinlan presents a multitude of choices for each of the above three issues so that an integrated approach to handle missing values can be obtained by specific instantiations of solutions to each of the above issues. Quinlan presents a coding scheme in [28] to design a combinatorial strategy for handling missing values.

For the first issue of evaluating decision tree criteria based on an attribute a, we can: (I) ignore cases in the training data that have a missing value for a; (C) substitute the most common value (for binary and categorical attributes) or by the mean of the known values (for numeric attributes); (R) discount the gain/gain ratio for attribute a by the proportion of instances that have missing values for a; or (S) "fill in" the missing value in the training data. This can be done either by treating them as a distinct, new value, or by methods that attempt to determine the missing value based on the values of other known attributes [28]. The idea of surrogate splits in CART (see Chapter 10) can be viewed as one way to implement this last idea.

For the second issue of partitioning the training set while recursing to build the decision tree, if the tree is branching on a for which one or more training instances have missing values, we can: (I) ignore the instance; (C) act as if this instance had the most common value for the missing attribute; (F) assign the instance, fractionally, to each subdataset, in proportion to the number of instances with known values in each of the subdataset; (A) assign it to all subdatasets; (U) develop a separate branch of the tree for cases with missing values for a; or (S) determine the most likely value of a (as before, using methods referenced in [28]) and assign it to the corresponding subdataset. In [28], Quinlan offers a variation on (F) as well, where the instance is assigned to only one subdataset but again proportionally to the number of instances with known values in that subdataset.

Finally, when classifying instances with missing values for attribute a, the options are: (U) if there is a separate branch for unknown values for a, follow the branch; (C) branch on the most common value for a; (S) apply the test as before from [28] to determine the most likely value of a and branch on it; (F) explore all branchs simultaneously, combining their results to denote the relative probabilities of the different outcomes [27]; or (H) terminate and assign the instance to the most likely class.

As the reader might have guessed, some combinations are more natural, and other combinations do not make sense. For the proportional assignment options, as long as the weights add up to 1, there is a natural way to generalize the calculations of information gain and gain ratio.

1.3.4 Inducing Rulesets

A distinctive feature of C4.5 is its ability to prune based on rules derived from the induced tree. We can model a tree as a disjunctive combination of conjunctive rules, where each rule corresponds to a path in the tree from the root to a leaf. The antecedents in the rule are the decision conditions along the path and the consequent is the predicted class label. For each class in the dataset, C4.5 first forms rulesets from the (unpruned) tree. Then, for each rule, it performs a hill-climbing search to see if any of the antecedents can be removed. Since the removal of antecedents is akin to "knocking out" nodes in an induced decision tree, C4.5's pessimistic pruning methods are used here. A subset of the simplified rules is selected for each class. Here the minimum description length (MDL) principle is used to codify the cost of the theory involved in encoding the rules and to rank the potential rules. The number of resulting rules is typically much smaller than the number of leaves (paths) in the original tree. Also observe that because all antecedents are considered for removal, even nodes near the top of the tree might be pruned away and the resulting rules may not be compressible back into one compact tree. One disadvantage of C4.5 rulesets is that they are known to cause rapid increases in learning time with increases in the size of the dataset.

1.4 Discussion on Available Software Implementations

J. Ross Quinlan's original implementation of C4.5 is available at his personal site: http://www.rulequest.com/Personal/. However, this implementation is copyrighted software and thus may be commercialized only under a license from the author. Nevertheless, the permission granted to individuals to use the code for their personal use has helped make C4.5 a standard in the field. Many public domain implementations of C4.5 are available, for example, Ronny Kohavi's MLC++ library [17], which is now part of SGI's Mineset data mining suite, and the Weka [35] data mining suite from the University of Waikato, New Zealand (http://www.cs.waikato.ac.nz/ml/weka/). The (Java) implementation of C4.5 in Weka is referred to as J48. Commercial implementations of C4.5 include ODBCMINE from Intelligent Systems Research, LLC, which interfaces with ODBC databases and Rulequest's See5/C5.0, which improves upon C4.5 in many ways and which also comes with support for ODBC connectivity.

1.5 Two Illustrative Examples

1.5.1 Golf Dataset

We describe in detail the function of C4.5 on the golf dataset. When run with the default options, that is:

```
>c4.5 -f golf
```

C4.5 produces the following output:

```
C4.5 [release 8] decision tree generator   Wed Apr 16 09:33:21 2008
----------------------------------------

    Options:
        File stem <golf>

Read 14 cases (4 attributes) from golf.data

Decision Tree:

outlook = overcast: Play (4.0)
outlook = sunny:
|   humidity <= 75 : Play (2.0)
|   humidity > 75 : Don't Play (3.0)
outlook = rain:
|   windy = true: Don't Play (2.0)
|   windy = false: Play (3.0)

Tree saved

Evaluation on training data (14 items):

         Before Pruning            After Pruning
        ----------------   ---------------------------
        Size      Errors   Size      Errors   Estimate

           8   0( 0.0%)       8   0( 0.0%)    (38.5%)   <<
```

Referring back to the output from C4.5, observe the statistics presented toward the end of the run. They show the size of the tree (in terms of the number of nodes, where both internal nodes and leaves are counted) before and after pruning. The error over the training dataset is shown for both the unpruned and pruned trees as is the estimated error after pruning. In this case, as is observed, no pruning is performed.

The `-v` option for C4.5 increases the verbosity level and provides detailed, step-by-step information about the gain calculations. The `c4.5rules` software uses similar options but generates rules with possible postpruning, as described earlier. For the golf dataset, no pruning happens with the default options and hence four rules are output (corresponding to all but one of the paths of Figure 1.2) along with a default rule.

The induced trees and rules must then be applied on an unseen "test" dataset to assess its generalization performance. The `-u` option of C4.5 allows the provision of test data to evaluate the performance of the induced trees/rules.

1.5.2 Soybean Dataset

Michalski's Soybean dataset is a classical machine learning test dataset from the UCI Machine Learning Repository [3]. There are 307 instances with 35 attributes and many missing values. From the description in the UCI site:

> There are 19 classes, only the first 15 of which have been used in prior work. The folklore seems to be that the last four classes are unjustified by the data since they have so few examples. There are 35 categorical attributes, some nominal and some ordered. The value "dna" means does not apply. The values for attributes are encoded numerically, with the first value encoded as "0," the second as "1," and so forth. An unknown value is encoded as "?."

The goal of learning from this dataset is to aid soybean disease diagnosis based on observed morphological features.

The induced tree is too complex to be illustrated here; hence, we depict the evaluation of the tree size and performance before and after pruning:

```
 Before Pruning              After Pruning
----------------    ----------------------------
Size      Errors    Size        Errors   Estimate

 177   15( 2.2%)     105    26( 3.8%)     (15.5%)    <<
```

As can be seen here, the unpruned tree does not perfectly classify the training data and significant pruning has happened after the full tree is induced. Rigorous evaluation procedures such as cross-validation must be applied before arriving at a "final" classifier.

1.6 Advanced Topics

With the massive data emphasis of modern data mining, many interesting research issues in mining tree/rule-based classifiers have come to the forefront. Some are covered here and some are described in the exercises. Proceedings of conferences such as KDD, ICDM, ICML, and SDM showcase the latest in many of these areas.

1.6.1 Mining from Secondary Storage

Modern datasets studied in the KDD community do not fit into main memory and hence implementations of machine learning algorithms have to be completely rethought in order to be able to process data from secondary storage. In particular, algorithms are designed to minimize the number of passes necessary for inducing a classifer. The BOAT algorithm [14] is based on bootstrapping. Beginning from a small in-memory subset of the original dataset, it uses sampling to create many trees, which are then overlaid on top of each other to obtain a tree with "coarse" splitting criteria. This tree is then refined into the final classifier by conducting one complete scan over the dataset. The Rainforest framework [15] is an integrated approach to instantiate various choices of decision tree construction and apply them in a scalable manner to massive datasets. Other algorithms aimed at mining from secondary storage are SLIQ [21], SPRINT [34], and PUBLIC [33].

1.6.2 Oblique Decision Trees

An *oblique decision tree*, suitable for continuous-valued data, is so named because its decision boundaries can be arbitrarily positioned and angled with respect to the coordinate axes (see also Exercise 2 later). For instance, instead of a decision criterion such as $a_1 \leq 6$? on attribute a_1, we might utilize a criterion based on two attributes in a single node, such as $3a_1 - 2a_2 \leq 6$? A classic reference on decision trees that use linear combinations of attributes is the OC1 system described in Murthy, Kasif, and Salzberg [22], which acknowledges CART as an important basis for OC1. The basic idea is to begin with an axis-parallel split and then "perturb" it in order to arrive at a better split. This is done by first casting the axis-parallel split as a linear combination of attribute values and then iteratively adjusting the coefficients of the linear combination to arrive at a better decision criterion. Needless to say, issues such as error estimation, pruning, and handling missing values have to be revisited in this context. OC1 is a careful combination of hill climbing and randomization to tweaking the coefficients. Other approaches to inducing oblique decision trees are covered in, for instance, [5].

1.6.3 Feature Selection

Thus far, we have not highlighted the importance of feature selection as an important precursor to supervised learning using trees and/or rules. Some features could be irrelevant to predicting the given class and still other features could be redundant given other features. *Feature selection* is the idea of narrowing down on a smaller set of features for use in induction. Some feature selection methods work in concert with specific learning algorithms whereas methods such as described in Koller and Sahami [18] are learning algorithm-agnostic.

1.6.4 Ensemble Methods

Ensemble methods have become a mainstay in the machine learning and data mining literature. Bagging and boosting (see Chapter 7) are popular choices. Bagging is based on random resampling, with replacement, from the training data, and inducing one tree from each sample. The predictions of the trees are then combined into one output, for example, by voting. In boosting [12], as studied in Chapter 7, we generate a series of classifiers, where the training data for one is dependent on the classifier from the previous step. In particular, instances incorrectly predicted by the classifier in a given step are weighted more in the next step. The final prediction is again derived from an aggregate of the predictions of the individual classifiers. The C5.0 system supports a variant of boosting, where an ensemble of classifiers is constructed and which then vote to yield the final classification. Opitz and Maclin [23] present a comparison of ensemble methods for decision trees as well as neural networks. Dietterich [8] presents a comparison of these methods with each other and with "randomization," where the internal decisions made by the learning algorithm are themselves randomized. The alternating decision tree algorithm [11] couples tree-growing and boosting in a tighter manner: In addition to the nodes that test for conditions, an alternating decision tree introduces "prediction nodes" that add to a score that is computed alongside the path from the root to a leaf. Experimental results show that it is as robust as boosted decision trees.

1.6.5 Classification Rules

There are two distinct threads of research that aim to identify rules for classification similar in spirit to C4.5 rules. They can loosely be classified based on their origins: as predictive versus descriptive classifiers, but recent research has blurred the boundaries.

The predictive line of research includes algorithms such as CN2 [6] and RIPPER [7]. These algorithms can be organized as either bottom-up or top-down approaches and are typically organized as "sequential discovery" paradigms where a rule is mined, instances covered by the rule are removed from the training set, a new rule is induced, and so on. In a bottom-up approach, a rule is induced by concatenating the attribute and class values of a single instance. The attributes forming the conjunction of the rule are then systematically removed to see if the predictive accuracy of the rule is improved. Typically a local, beam search is conducted as opposed to a global search. After this rule is added to the theory, examples covered by the rule are removed, and a new rule is induced from the remaining data. Analogously, a top-down approach starts with a rule that has an empty antecedent predicting a class value and systematically adds attribute-tests to identify a suitable rule.

The descriptive line of research originates from association rules, a popular technique in the KDD community [1, 2] (see Chapter 4). Traditionally, associations are between two sets, X and Y, of items, denoted by $X \rightarrow Y$, and evaluated by measures such as support (the fraction of instances in the dataset that have both X and Y) and confidence (the fraction of instances with X that also have Y). The goal of association rule mining is to find *all* associations satisfying given support and confidence thresholds. CBA (Classification based on Association Rules) [20] is an adaptation of association rules to classification, where the goal is to determine all association rules that have a certain class label in the consequent. These rules are then used to build a classifier. Pruning is done similarly to error estimation methods in C4.5. The key difference between CBA and C4.5 is the exhaustive search for all possible rules and efficient algorithms adapted from association rule mining to mine rules. This thread of research is now an active one in the KDD community with new variants and applications.

1.6.6 Redescriptions

Redescriptions are a generalization of rules to equivalences, introduced in [32]. As the name indicates, to *redescribe* something is to describe anew or to express the same concept in a different vocabulary. Given a vocabulary of descriptors, the goal of redescription mining is to construct two expressions from the vocabulary that induce the same subset of objects. The underlying premise is that sets that can indeed be defined in (at least) two ways are likely to exhibit concerted behavior and are, hence, interesting. The CARTwheels algorithm for mining redescriptions grows two C4.5-like trees in opposite directions such that they are matched at the leaves. Essentially, one tree exposes a partition of objects via its choice of subsets and the other tree tries to grow to match this partition using a different choice of subsets. If partition correspondence is established, then paths that join can be read off as redescriptions. CARTwheels explores the space of possible tree matchings via an alternation process whereby trees are repeatedly regrown to match the partitions exposed by the other tree. Redescription mining has since been generalized in many directions [19, 24, 37].

1.7 Exercises

1. Carefully quantify the big-Oh time complexity of decision tree induction with C4.5. Describe the complexity in terms of the number of attributes and the number of training instances. First, bound the depth of the tree and then cast the time required to build the tree in terms of this bound. Assess the cost of pruning as well.
2. Design a dataset with continuous-valued attributes where the decision boundary between classes is not isothetic, that is, it is not parallel to any of the coordinate

axes. Apply C4.5 on this dataset and comment on the quality of the induced trees. Take factors such as accuracy, size of the tree, and comprehensibility into account.

3. An alternative way to avoid overfitting is to restrict the growth of the tree rather than pruning back a fully grown tree down to a reduced size. Explain why such prepruning may not be a good idea.
4. Prove that the impurity measure used by C45 (i.e., entropy) is concave. Why is it important that it be concave?
5. Derive Equation (1.1). As stated in the text, use the normal approximation to the Bernoulli random variable modeling the error rate.
6. Instead of using information gain, study how decision tree induction would be affected if we directly selected the attribute with the highest prediction accuracy. Furthermore, what if we induced rules with only one antecedent? *Hint:* You are retracing the experiments of Robert Holte as described in R. Holte, Very Simple Classification Rules Perform Well on Most Commonly Used Datasets, *Machine Learning*, vol. 11, pp. 63–91, 1993.
7. In some machine learning applications, attributes are set-valued, for example, an object can have multiple colors and to classify the object it might be important to model color as a set-valued attribute rather than as an instance-valued attribute. Identify decision tests that can be performed on set-valued attributes and explain which can be readily incorporated into the C4.5 system for growing decision trees.
8. Instead of classifying an instance into a single class, assume our goal is to obtain a ranking of classes according to the (posterior) probability of membership of the instance in various classes. Read F. Provost and P. Domingos, Tree Induction for Probability Based Ranking, *Machine Learning*, vol. 52, no. 3, pp. 199–215, 2003, who explain why the trees induced by C4.5 are not suited to providing reliable probability estimates; they also suggest some ways to fix this problem using probability smoothing methods. Do these same objections and solution strategy apply to C4.5 rules as well? Experiment with datasets from the UCI repository.
9. (Adapted from S. Nijssen and E. Fromont, Mining Optimal Decision Trees from Itemset Lattices, *Proceedings of the 13th ACM SIGKDD International Conference on Knowledge Discovery and Data Mining*, pp. 530–539, 2007.) The trees induced by C4.5 are driven by heuristic choices but assume that our goal is to identify an optimal tree. Optimality can be posed in terms of various considerations; two such considerations are the most accurate tree up to a certain maximum depth and the smallest tree in which each leaf covers at least k instances and the expected accuracy is maximized over unseen examples. Describe an efficient algorithm to induce such optimal trees.
10. First-order logic is a more expressive notation than the attribute-value representation considered in this chapter. Given a collection of first-order relations, describe how the basic algorithmic approach of C4.5 can be generalized to use

first-order features. Your solution must allow the induction of trees or rules of the form:

```
grandparent(X,Z) :- parent(X,Y), parent(Y,Z).
```

that is, `X` is a grandparent of `Z` if there exists `Y` such that `Y` is the parent of `X` and `Z` is the parent of `Y`. Several new issues result from the choice of first-order logic as the representational language. First, unlike the attribute value situation, first-order features (such as `parent(X,Y)`) are not readily given and must be generalized from the specific instances. Second, it is possible to obtain nonsensical trees or rules if the variables participate in the head of a rule but not the body, for example:

```
grandparent(X,Y) :- parent(X,Z).
```

Describe how you can place checks and balances into the induction process so that a complete first-order theory can be induced from data. *Hint:* You are exploring the field of inductive logic programming [9], specifically, algorithms such as FOIL [29].

References

[1] R. Agrawal, T. Imielinski, and A. N. Swami. Mining association rules between sets of items in large databases. In *Proceedings of the ACM SIGMOD International Conference on Management of Data (SIGMOD'93)*, pp. 207–216, May 1993.

[2] R. Agrawal and R. Srikant. Fast algorithms for mining association rules in large databases. In *Proceedings of the 20th International Conference on Very Large Databases (VLDB'94)*, pp. 487–499, Sep. 1994.

[3] A. Asuncion and D. J. Newman. UCI Machine Learning Repository, 2007. http://www.ics.uci.edu/~mlearn/MLRepository.html. University of California, Irvine, School of Information and Computer Sciences.

[4] L. Breiman, J. Friedman, C. J. Stone, and R. A. Olshen. *Classification and Regression Trees*. Chapman & Hall/CRC, Jan. 1984.

[5] C. E. Brodely and P. E. Utgoff. Multivariate Decision Trees. *Machine Learning*, 19:45–77, 1995.

[6] P. Clark and T. Niblett. The CN2 Induction Algorithm. *Machine Learning*, 3(4):261–283, 1999.

[7] W. Cohen. Fast Efficient Rule Induction. In *Proceedings of the Twelfth International Conference on Machine Learning*, pp. 115–123, 1995.

[8] T. G. Dietterich. An Experimental Comparison of Three Methods for Constructing Ensembles of Decision Trees: Bagging, Boosting, and Randomization. *Machine Learning*, 40(2):139–157, 2000.

[9] S. Dzeroski and N. Lavrac, eds. *Relational Data Mining*. Springer, Berlin, 2001.

[10] U. M. Fayyad and K. B. Irani. On the Handling of Continuous-Valued Attributes in Decision Tree Generation. *Machine Learning*, 8(1):87–102, Jan. 1992.

[11] Y. Freund and L. Mason. The Alternating Decision Tree Learning Algorithm. In *Proceedings of the Sixteenth International Conference on Machine Learning (ICML 1999)*, pp. 124–133, 1999.

[12] Y. Freund and R. E. Schapire. A Short Introduction to Boosting. *Journal of the Japanese Society for Artificial Intelligence*, 14(5):771–780, Sep. 1999.

[13] J. H. Friedman. A Recursive Partitioning Decision Rule for Nonparametric Classification. *IEEE Transactions on Computers*, 26(4):404–408, Apr. 1977.

[14] J. Gehrke, V. Ganti, R. Ramakrishnan, and W.-H. Loh. BOAT: Optimistic Decision Tree Construction. In *Proceedings of the ACM SIGMOD International Conference on Management of Data (SIGMOD'99)*, pp. 169–180, 1999.

[15] J. Gehrke, R. Ramakrishnan, and V. Ganti. RainForest: A Framework for Fast Decision Tree Construction of Large Datasets. *Data Mining and Knowledge Discovery*, 4(2/3):127–162, 2000.

[16] E. B. Hunt, J. Marin, and P. J. Stone. *Experiments in Induction*. Academic Press, New York, 1966.

[17] R. Kohavi, D. Sommerfield, and J. Dougherty. Data Mining Using MLC++: A Machine Learning Library in C++. In *Proceedings of the Eighth International Conference on Tools with Artificial Intelligence (ICTAI '96)*, pp. 234–245, 1996.

[18] D. Koller and M. Sahami. Toward Optimal Feature Selection. In *Proceedings of the Thirteenth International Conference on Machine Learning (ICML'96)*, pp. 284–292, 1996.

[19] D. Kumar, N. Ramakrishnan, R. F. Helm, and M. Potts. Algorithms for Storytelling. In *Proceedings of the Twelfth ACM SIGKDD International Conference on Knowledge Discovery and Data Mining (KDD'06)*, pp. 604–610, Aug. 2006.

[20] B. Liu, W. Hsu, and Y. Ma. Integrating Classification and Association Rule Mining. In *Proceedings of the Fourth International Conference on Knowledge Discovery and Data Mining (KDD'98)*, pp. 80–86, Aug. 1998.

[21] M. Mehta, R. Agrawal, and J. Rissanen. SLIQ: A Fast Scalable Classifier for Data Mining. In *Proceedings of the 5th International Conference on Extending Database Technology (EDBT'96)*, pp. 18–32, Mar. 1996.

[22] S. K. Murthy, S. Kasif, and S. Salzberg. A System for Induction of Oblique Decision Trees. *Journal of Artificial Intelligence Research*, 2:1–32, 1994.

[23] D.W. Opitz and R. Maclin. Popular Ensemble Methods: An Empirical Study. *Journal of Artificial Intelligence Research*, 11:169–198, 1999.

[24] L. Parida and N. Ramakrishnan. Redescription Mining: Structure Theory and Algorithms. In *Proceedings of the Twentieth National Conference on Artificial Intelligence (AAAI'05)*, pp. 837–844, July 2005.

[25] J. R. Quinlan. Induction of Decision Trees. *Machine Learning*, 1(1):81–106, 1986.

[26] J. R. Quinlan. Simplifying Decision Trees. Technical Report 930, MIT AI Lab Memo, Dec. 1986.

[27] J. R. Quinlan. Decision Trees as Probabilistic Classifiers. In P. Langley, ed., *Proceedings of the Fourth International Workshop on Machine Learning*. Morgan Kaufmann, CA, 1987.

[28] J. R. Quinlan. Unknown Attribute Values in Induction. Technical report, Basser Department of Computer Science, University of Sydney, 1989.

[29] J. R. Quinlan. Learning Logical Definitions from Relations. *Machine Learning*, 5:239–266, 1990.

[30] J. R. Quinlan. *C4.5: Programs for Machine Learning*. Morgan Kaufmann, 1993.

[31] J. R. Quinlan. Improved Use of Continuous Attributes in C4.5. *Journal of Artificial Intelligence Research*, 4:77–90, 1996.

[32] N. Ramakrishnan, D. Kumar, B. Mishra, M. Potts, and R. F. Helm. Turning CARTwheels: An Alternating Algorithm for Mining Redescriptions. In *Proceedings of the Tenth ACM SIGKDD International Conference on Knowledge Discovery and Data Mining (KDD'04)*, pp. 266–275, Aug. 2004.

[33] R. Rastogi and K. Shim. PUBLIC: A Decision Tree Classifier that Integrates Building and Pruning. In *Proceedings of the 24th International Conference on Very Large Data Bases (VLDB'98)*, pp. 404–415, Aug. 1998.

[34] J. C. Shafer, R. Agrawal, and M. Mehta. SPRINT: A Scalable Parallel Classifier for Data Mining. In *Proceedings of the 22th International Conference on Very Large Data Bases (VLDB'96)*, pp. 544–555, Sep. 1996.

[35] I. H. Witten and E. Frank. *Data Mining: Practical Machine Learning Tools and Techniques*. Morgan Kaufmann, 2005.

[36] X. Wu, V. Kumar, J. R. Quinlan, J. Ghosh, Q. Yang, H. Motoda, G. J. McLachlan, A. Ng, B. Liu, P. S. Yu, Z.-H. Zhou, M. Steinbach, D. J. Hand, and D. Steinberg. Top 10 Algorithms in Data Mining. *Knowledge and Information Systems*, 14:1–37, 2008.

[37] L. Zhao, M. Zaki, and N. Ramakrishnan. BLOSOM: A Framework for Mining Arbitrary Boolean Expressions over Attribute Sets. In *Proceedings of the Twelfth ACM SIGKDD International Conference on Knowledge Discovery and Data Mining (KDD'06)*, pp. 827–832, Aug. 2006.

Chapter 2

K-Means

Joydeep Ghosh and Alexander Liu

Contents

2.1 Introduction

In this chapter, we describe the `k-means` algorithm, a straightforward and widely used clustering algorithm. Given a set of objects (records), the goal of clustering or segmentation is to divide these objects into groups or "clusters" such that objects within a group tend to be more similar to one another as compared to objects belonging to different groups. In other words, clustering algorithms place similar points in the same cluster while placing dissimilar points in different clusters. Note that, in contrast to *supervised* tasks such as regression or classification where there is a notion of a target value or class label, the objects that form the inputs to a clustering procedure do not come with an associated target. Therefore, *clustering* is often referred to as unsupervised learning. Because there is no need for labeled data, unsupervised algorithms are suitable for many applications where labeled data is difficult to obtain. Unsupervised tasks such as clustering are also often used to explore and characterize the dataset before running a supervised learning task. Since clustering makes no use of class labels, some notion of similarity must be defined based on the attributes of the objects. The definition of similarity and the method in which points are clustered differ based on the clustering algorithm being applied. Thus, different clustering algorithms are suited to different types of datasets and different purposes. The "best" clustering algorithm to use therefore depends on the application. It is not uncommon to try several different algorithms and choose depending on which is the most useful.

The k-means algorithm is a simple iterative clustering algorithm that partitions a given dataset into a user-specified number of clusters, k. The algorithm is simple to implement and run, relatively fast, easy to adapt, and common in practice. It is historically one of the most important algorithms in data mining.

Historically, k-means in its essential form has been discovered by several researchers across different disciplines, most notably by Lloyd (1957, 1982)[16],[1] Forgey (1965) [9], Friedman and Rubin (1967) [10], and McQueen (1967) [17]. A detailed history of k-means along with descriptions of several variations are given in Jain and Dubes [13]. Gray and Neuhoff [11] provide a nice historical background for k-means placed in the larger context of hill-climbing algorithms.

In the rest of this chapter, we will describe how k-means works, discuss the limitations of k-means, give some examples of k-means on artificial and real datasets, and briefly discuss some extensions to the k-means algorithm. We should note that our list of extensions to k-means is far from exhaustive, and the reader is encouraged to continue their own research on the aspect of k-means of most interest to them.

2.2 The k-means Algorithm

The k-means algorithm applies to objects that are represented by points in a d-dimensional vector space. Thus, it clusters a set of d-dimensional vectors, $D = \{\mathbf{x_i} | i = 1, \ldots, N\}$, where $\mathbf{x_i} \in \Re^d$ denotes the ith object or "data point." As discussed in the introduction, k-means is a clustering algorithm that partitions D into k clusters of points. That is, the k-means algorithm clusters all of the data points in D such that each point $\mathbf{x_i}$ falls in one and only one of the k partitions. One can keep track of which point is in which cluster by assigning each point a cluster ID. Points with the same cluster ID are in the same cluster, while points with different cluster IDs are in different clusters. One can denote this with a cluster membership vector $\mathbf{m}$ of length N, where m_i is the cluster ID of $\mathbf{x_i}$.

The value of k is an input to the base algorithm. Typically, the value for k is based on criteria such as prior knowledge of how many clusters actually appear in D, how many clusters are desired for the current application, or the types of clusters found by exploring/experimenting with different values of k. How k is chosen is not necessary for understanding how k-means partitions the dataset D, and we will discuss how to choose k when it is not prespecified in a later section.

In k-means, each of the k clusters is represented by a single point in $\Re^d$. Let us denote this set of cluster representatives as the set $C = \{\mathbf{c_j} | j = 1, \ldots, k\}$. These k cluster representatives are also called the *cluster means* or *cluster centroids*; we will discuss the reason for this after describing the k-means objective function.

---

[1] Lloyd first described the algorithm in a 1957 Bell Labs technical report, which was finally published in 1982.

In clustering algorithms, points are grouped by some notion of "closeness" or "similarity." In `k-means`, the default measure of closeness is the Euclidean distance. In particular, one can readily show that `k-means` attempts to minimize the following nonnegative cost function:

$$Cost = \sum_{i=1}^{N} (argmin_j ||\mathbf{x_i} - \mathbf{c_j}||_2^2) \tag{2.1}$$

In other words, `k-means` attempts to minimize the total squared Euclidean distance between each point $\mathbf{x_i}$ and its closest cluster representative $\mathbf{c_j}$. Equation 2.1 is often referred to as the `k-means` objective function.

The `k-means` algorithm, depicted in Algorithm 2.1, clusters D in an iterative fashion, alternating between two steps: (1) reassigning the cluster ID of all points in D and (2) updating the cluster representatives based on the data points in each cluster. The algorithm works as follows. First, the cluster representatives are initialized by picking k points in $\Re^d$. Techniques for selecting these initial seeds include sampling at random from the dataset, setting them as the solution of clustering a small subset of the data, or perturbing the global mean of the data k times. In Algorithm 2.1, we initialize by randomly picking k points. The algorithm then iterates between two steps until convergence.

Step 1: Data assignment. Each data point is assigned to its *closest* centroid, with ties broken arbitrarily. This results in a partitioning of the data.

Step 2: Relocation of "means." Each cluster representative is relocated to the center (i.e., arithmetic mean) of all data points assigned to it. The rationale of this step is based on the observation that, given a set of points, the single best representative for this set (in the sense of minimizing the sum of the squared Euclidean distances between each point and the representative) is nothing but the mean of the data points. This is also why the cluster representative is often interchangeably referred to as the *cluster mean* or *cluster centroid*, and where the algorithm gets its name from.

The algorithm converges when the assignments (and hence the $\mathbf{c_j}$ values) no longer change. One can show that the `k-means` objective function defined in Equation 2.1 will decrease whenever there is a change in the assignment or the relocation steps, and convergence is guaranteed in a finite number of iterations.

Note that each iteration needs $N \times k$ comparisons, which determines the time complexity of one iteration. The number of iterations required for convergence varies and may depend on N, but as a first cut, `k-means` can be considered linear in the dataset size. Moreover, since the comparison operation is linear in d, the algorithm is also linear in the dimensionality of the data.

Limitations. The greedy-descent nature of `k-means` on a nonconvex cost implies that the convergence is only to a local optimum, and indeed the algorithm is typically quite sensitive to the initial centroid locations. In other words,

Algorithm 2.1 The `k-means` algorithm

Input: Dataset D, number clusters k
Output: Set of cluster representatives C, cluster membership vector $\mathbf{m}$
  /* Initialize cluster representatives C */
  Randomly choose k data points from D
  Use these k points as initial set of cluster representatives C
  repeat
    /* Data Assignment */
    Reassign points in D to closest cluster mean
    Update $\mathbf{m}$ such that m_i is cluster ID of ith point in D
    /* Relocation of means */
    Update C such that c_j is mean of points in jth cluster
  until convergence of objective function $\sum_{i=1}^{N}(argmin_j||\mathbf{x_i} - \mathbf{c_j}||_2^2)$

initializing the set of cluster representatives C differently can lead to very different clusters, even on the same dataset D. A poor initialization can lead to very poor clusters. We will see an example of this in the next section when we look at examples of `k-means` applied to artificial and real data. The local minima problem can be countered to some extent by running the algorithm multiple times with different initial centroids and then selecting the best result, or by doing limited local search about the converged solution. Other approaches include methods such as those described in [14] that attempt to keep `k-means` from converging to local minima. [8] also contains a list of different methods of initialization, as well as a discussion of other limitations of `k-means`.

As mentioned, choosing the optimal value of k may be difficult. If one has knowledge about the dataset, such as the number of partitions that naturally comprise the dataset, then that knowledge can be used to choose k. Otherwise, one must use some other criteria to choose k, thus solving the *model selection* problem. One naive solution is to try several different values of k and choose the clustering which minimizes the `k-means` objective function (Equation 2.1). Unfortunately, the value of the objective function is not as informative as one would hope in this case. For example, the cost of the optimal solution decreases with increasing k till it hits zero when the number of clusters equals the number of distinct data points. This makes it more difficult to use the objective function to (a) directly compare solutions with different numbers of clusters and (b) find the optimum value of k. Thus, if the desired k is not known in advance, one will typically run `k-means` with different values of k, and then use some other, more suitable criterion to select one of the results. For example, SAS uses the cube-clustering criterion, while X-means adds a complexity term (which increases with k) to the original cost function (Equation 2.1) and then identifies the k which minimizes this adjusted cost [20]. Alternatively, one can progressively increase the number of clusters, in conjunction with a suitable stopping criterion. Bisecting `k-means` [21] achieves this by first putting all the data into a single cluster, and then recursively splitting the least compact cluster into two clusters using 2-means. The celebrated LBG algorithm [11] used for vector quantization doubles the number of clusters till a suitable code-book size is obtained. Both these approaches thus alleviate the need to know k beforehand. Many other researchers have studied this problem, such as [18] and [12].

In addition to the above limitations, `k-means` suffers from several other problems that can be understood by first noting that the problem of fitting data using a mixture of k Gaussians with identical, isotropic covariance matrices ($\Sigma = \sigma^2\mathbf{I}$), where $\mathbf{I}$ is the identity matrix, results in a "soft" version of `k-means`. More precisely, if the soft assignments of data points to the mixture components of such a model are instead hardened so that each data point is solely allocated to the most likely component [3], then one obtains the `k-means` algorithm. From this connection it is evident that `k-means` inherently assumes that the dataset is composed of a mixture of k balls or hyperspheres of data, and each of the k clusters corresponds to one of the mixture components. Because of this implicit assumption, `k-means` will falter whenever the data is not well described by a superposition of reasonably separated spherical Gaussian distributions. For example, `k-means` will have trouble if there are nonconvex-shaped clusters in the data. This problem may be alleviated by rescaling the data to "whiten" it before clustering, or by using a different distance measure that is more appropriate for the dataset. For example, information-theoretic clustering uses the KL-divergence to measure the distance between two data points representing two discrete probability distributions. It has been recently shown that if one measures distance by selecting any member of a very large class of divergences called *Bregman divergences* during the assignment step and makes no other changes, the essential properties of `k-means`, including guaranteed convergence, linear separation boundaries, and scalability, are retained [1]. This result makes `k-means` effective for a much larger class of datasets so long as an appropriate divergence is used.

Another method of dealing with nonconvex clusters is by pairing `k-means` with another algorithm. For example, one can first cluster the data into a large number of groups using `k-means`. These groups are then agglomerated into larger clusters using single link hierarchical clustering, which can detect complex shapes. This approach also makes the solution less sensitive to initialization, and since the hierarchical method provides results at multiple resolutions, one does not need to worry about choosing an exact value for k either; instead, one can simply use a large value for k when creating the initial clusters.

The algorithm is also sensitive to the presence of outliers, since "mean" is not a robust statistic. A preprocessing step to remove outliers can be helpful. Postprocessing the results, for example, to eliminate small clusters, or to merge close clusters into a large cluster, is also desirable. Ball and Hall's ISODATA algorithm from 1967 effectively used both pre- and postprocessing on `k-means`.

Another potential issue is the problem of "empty" clusters [4]. When running `k-means`, particularly with large values of k and/or when data resides in very high dimensional space, it is possible that at some point of execution, there exists a cluster representative c_j such that all points x_i in D are closer to some other cluster representative that is not c_j. When points in D are assigned to their closest cluster, the jth cluster will have zero points assigned to it. That is, cluster j is now an empty cluster.

The standard algorithm does not guard against empty clusters, but simple extensions (such as reinitializing the cluster representative of the empty cluster or "stealing" some points from the largest cluster) are possible.

2.3 Available Software

Because of the `k-means` algorithm's simplicity, effectiveness, and historical importance, software to run the k-means algorithm is readily available in several forms. It is a standard feature in many popular data mining software packages. For example, it can be found in Weka or in SAS under the FASTCLUS procedure. It is also commonly included as add-ons to existing software. For example, several implementations of `k-means` are available as parts of various toolboxes in MATLAB®. `k-means` is also available in Microsoft Excel after adding XLMiner. Finally, several stand-alone versions of `k-means` exist and can be easily found on the Internet.

The algorithm is also straightforward to code, and the reader is encouraged to create their own implementation of `k-means` as an exercise.

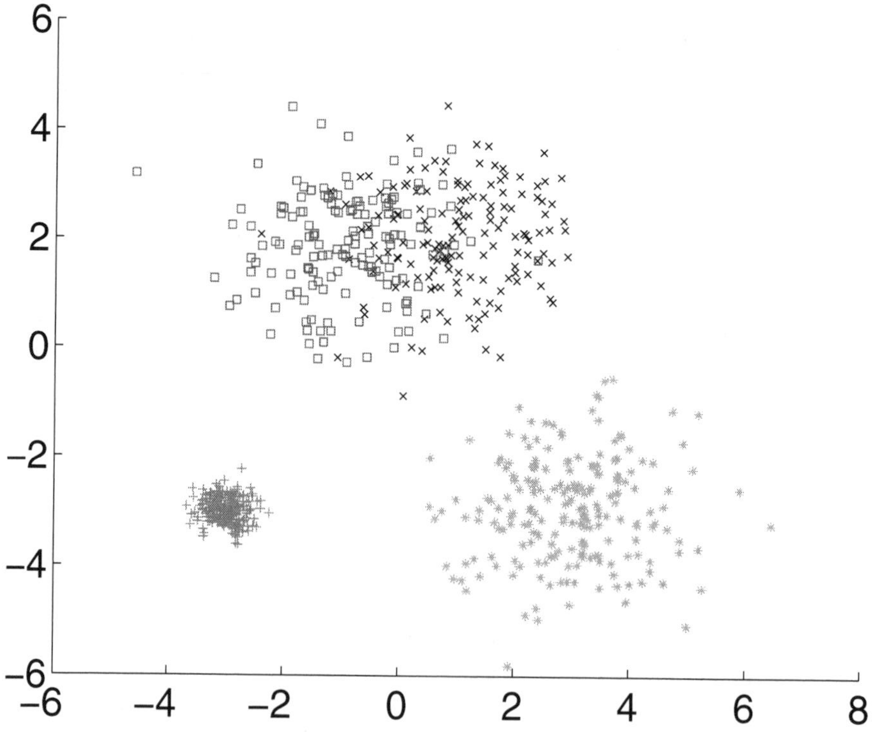

Figure 2.1 The artificial dataset used in our example; the data is drawn from a mixture of four Gaussians.

2.4 Examples

Let us first show an example of `k-means` on an artificial dataset to illustrate how `k-means` works. We will use artificial data drawn from four 2-D Gaussians and use a value of $k = 4$; the dataset is illustrated in Figure 2.1. Data drawn from a particular Gaussian is plotted in the same color in Figure 2.1. The blue data consists of 200 points drawn from a Gaussian with mean at $(-3, -3)$ and covariance matrix $.0625 \times \mathbf{I}$, where $\mathbf{I}$ is the identity matrix. The green data consists of 200 points drawn from a Gaussian with mean at $(3, -3)$ and covariance matrix $\mathbf{I}$. Finally, we have overlapping yellow and red data drawn from two nearby Gaussians. The yellow data consists of 150 points drawn from a Gaussian with mean $(-1, 2)$ and covariance matrix $\mathbf{I}$, while the red data consists of 150 points drawn from a Gaussian with mean (1,2) and covariance matrix $\mathbf{I}$. Despite the overlap between the red and yellow points, one would expect `k-means` to do well since we do have the right value of k and the data is generated by a mixture of spherical Gaussians, thus matching nicely with the underlying assumptions of the algorithm.

The first step in `k-means` is to initialize the cluster representatives. This is illustrated in Figure 2.2a, where k points in the dataset have been picked randomly. In this figure and the following figures, the cluster means C will be represented by a large colored circle with a black outline. The color corresponds to the cluster ID of that particular cluster, and all points assigned to that cluster are represented as points of the same color. These colors have no definite connection with the colors in Figure 2.1 (see Exercise 7). Since points have not been assigned cluster IDs in Figure 2.2a, they are plotted in black.

The next step is to assign all points to their closest cluster representative; this is illustrated in Figure 2.2b, where each point has been plotted to match the color of its closest cluster representative. The third step in `k-means` is to update the k cluster representatives to correspond to the mean of all points currently assigned to that cluster. This step is illustrated in Figure 2.2c. In particular, we have plotted the old cluster representatives with a black "X" symbol and the new, updated cluster representatives as a large colored circle with a black outline. There is also a line connecting the old cluster mean with the new, updated cluster mean. One can observe that the cluster representatives have moved to reflect the current centroids of each cluster.

The `k-means` algorithm now iterates between two steps until convergence: reassigning points in D to their closest cluster representative and updating the k cluster representatives. We have illustrated the first four iterations of `k-means` in Figures 2.2 and 2.3. The final clusters after convergence are shown in Figure 2.3d. Note that this example took eight iterations to converge. Visually, however, there is little change in the diagrams between iterations 4 and 8, and these pictures are omitted for space reasons. As one can see by comparing Figure 2.3d with Figure 2.1, the clusters found by `k-means` match well with the true, underlying distribution.

In the previous section, we mentioned that `k-means` is sensitive to the initial points picked as clusters. In Figure 2.4, we show what happens when the k representatives are

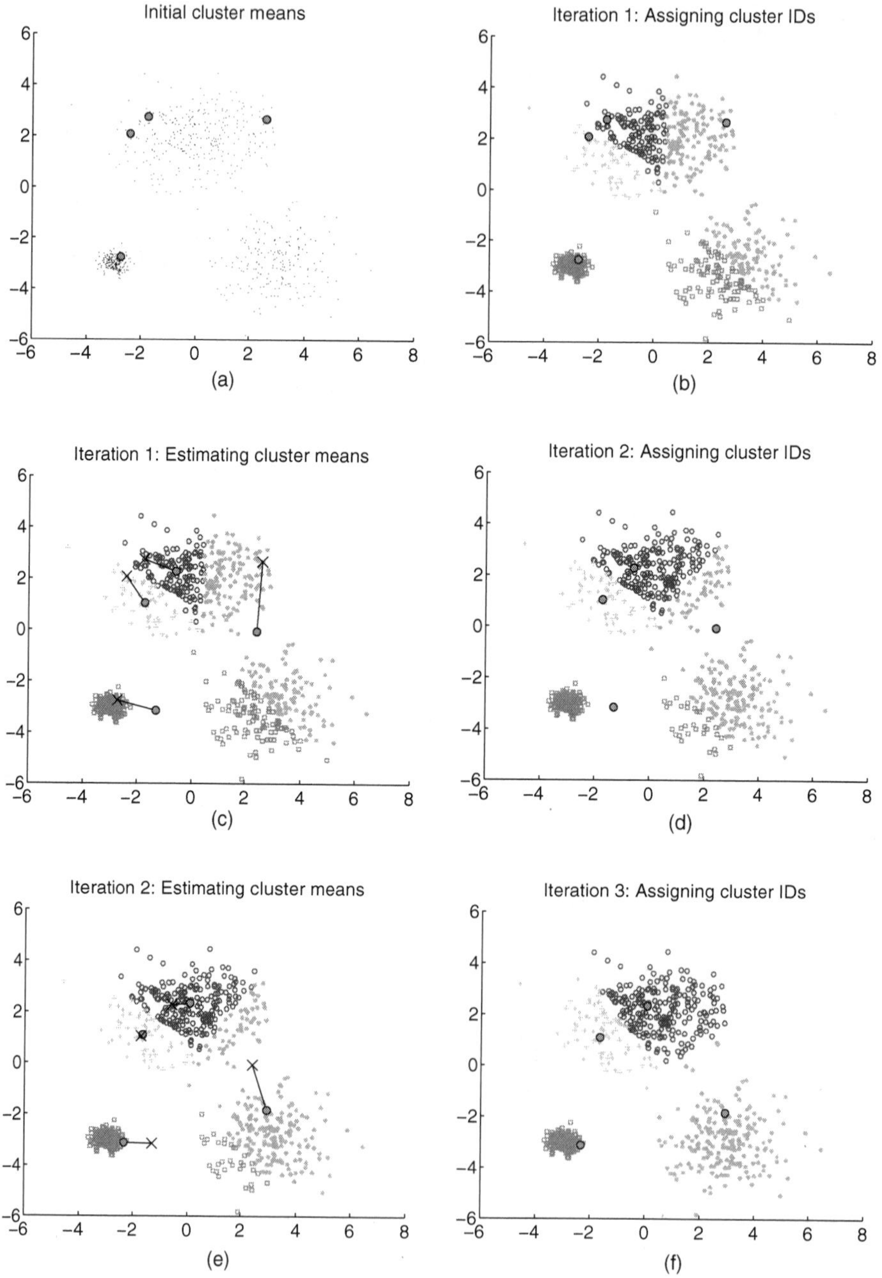

Figure 2.2 k-means on artificial data.

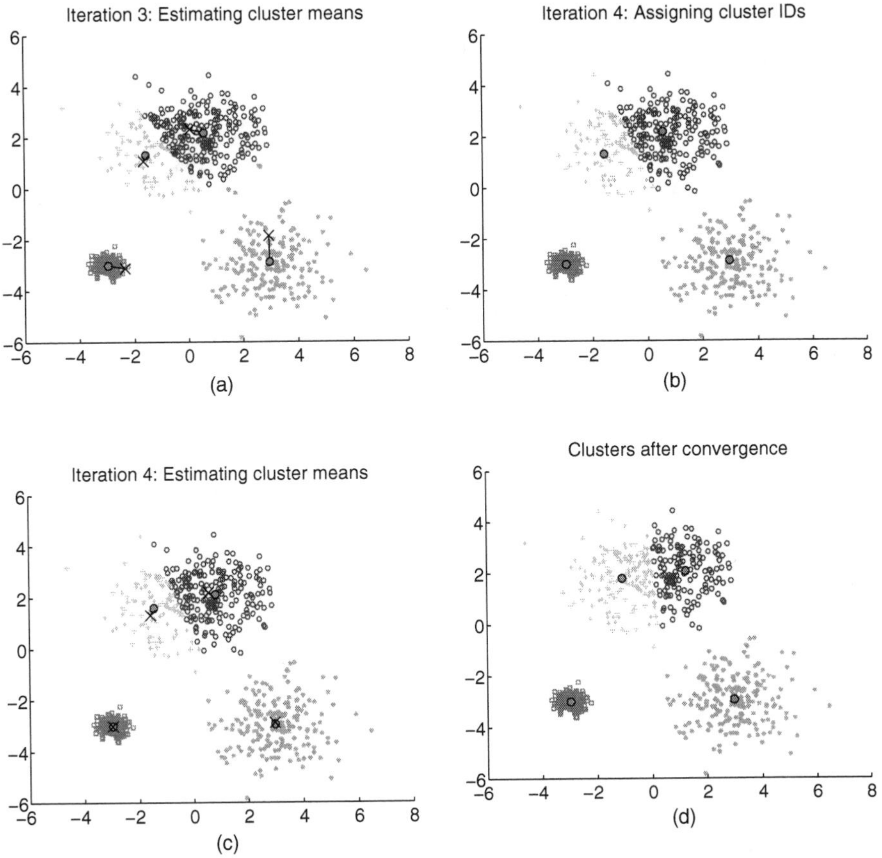

Figure 2.3 `k-means` on artificial data. (Continued from Figure 2.2.)

initialized poorly on the same artificial dataset used in Figures 2.2 and 2.3. Figures 2.4a and c show two initializations that lead to poor clusters in Figures 2.4b and d. These results are considered poor since they do not correspond well to the true underlying distribution.

Finally, let us examine the performance of `k-means` on a simple, classic benchmark dataset. In our example, we use the Iris dataset (available from the UCI data mining repository), which contains 150 data points from three classes. Each class represents a different species of the Iris flower, and there are 50 points from each class. While there are four dimensions (representing sepal width, sepal length, petal width, and petal length), only two dimensions (petal width and petal length) are necessary to discriminate the three classes. The Iris dataset is plotted in Figure 2.5a along the dimensions of petal width and petal length.

In Figure 2.5b, we show an example of the `k-means` algorithm run on the Iris dataset with $k = 3$, using only the attributes of petal width and petal length. The

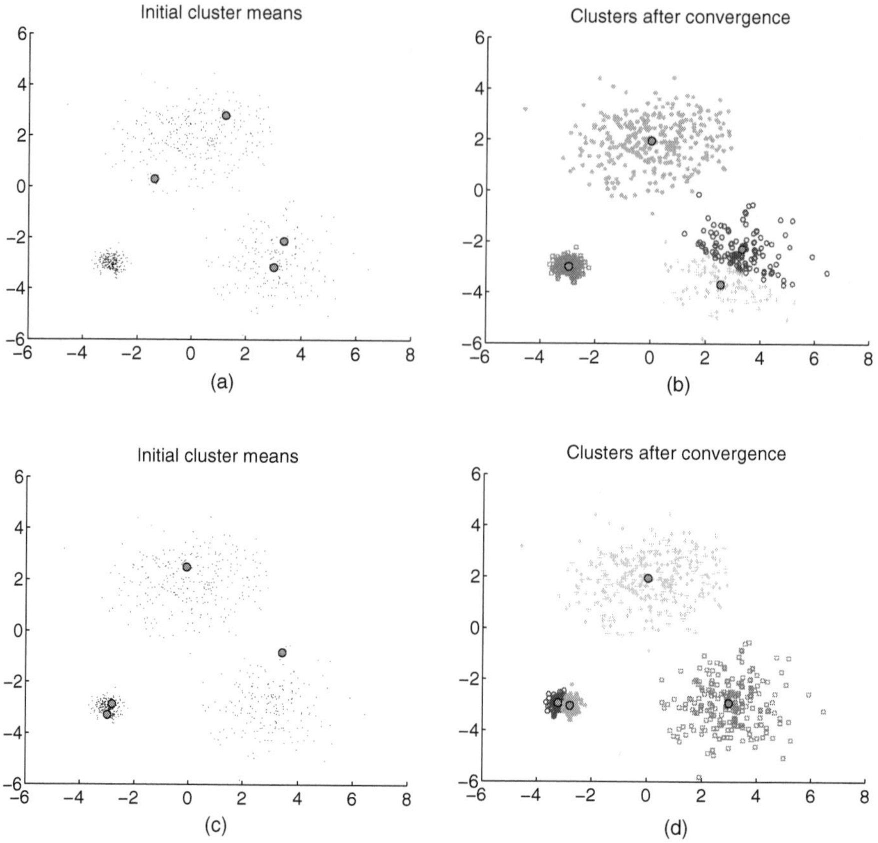

Figure 2.4 Examples of poor clustering after poor initialization; these resultant clusters are considered "poor" in the sense that they do not match well with the true, underlying distribution.

`k-means` algorithm is able to cluster the data points such that each cluster is composed mostly of flowers from the same species.

2.5 Advanced Topics

In this section, we discuss some generalizations, connections, and extensions that have been made to the `k-means` algorithm. However, we should note that this section is far from exhaustive. Research on `k-means` has been extensive and is still active. Instead, the goal of this section is to complement some of the previously discussed issues regarding `k-means`.

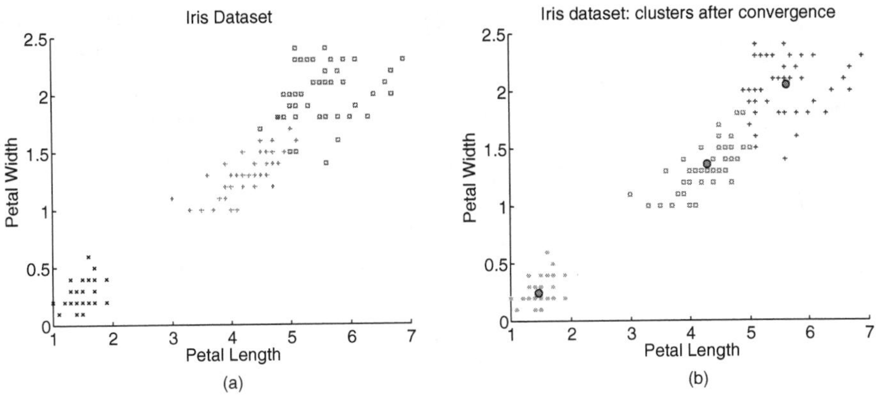

Figure 2.5 (a) Iris dataset; each color is a different species of Iris; (b) Result of `k-means` on Iris dataset; each color is a different cluster; note that there is not necessarily a correspondence between colors in (a) and (b) (see Exercise 7).

As mentioned earlier, `k-means` is closely related to fitting a mixture of k isotropic Gaussians to the data. Moreover, the generalization of the distance measure to all Bregman divergences is related to fitting the data with a mixture of k components from the exponential family of distributions. Another broad generalization is to view the "means" as probabilistic models instead of points in R^d. Here, in the assignment step, each data point is assigned to the model most likely to have generated it. In the "relocation" step, the model parameters are updated to best fit the assigned datasets. Such *model-based* `k-means` [23] allow one to cater to more complex data, for example, sequences described by Hidden Markov models.

One can also "kernelize" `k-means` [5]. Though boundaries between clusters are still linear in the implicit high-dimensional space, they can become nonlinear when projected back to the original space, thus allowing kernel `k-means` to deal with more complex clusters. Dhillon et al. [5] have shown a close connection between kernel `k-means` and spectral clustering. The *K-medoid* [15] algorithm is similar to `k-means`, except that the centroids have to belong to the dataset being clustered. Fuzzy c-means [6] is also similar, except that it computes fuzzy membership functions for each cluster rather than a hard one.

To deal with very large datasets, substantial effort has also gone into further speeding up `k-means`, most notably by using kd-trees [19] or exploiting the triangular inequality [7] to avoid comparing each data point with all the centroids during the assignment step.

Finally, we discuss two straightforward extensions of `k-means`. The first is a variant of `k-means` called `soft k-means`. In the standard `k-means` algorithm, each point x_i belongs to one and only one cluster. In `soft k-means`, this constraint is relaxed, and each point x_i can belong to each cluster with some unknown probability. In `soft k-means`, for each point x_i, one maintains a set of k probabilities or weights that describe the likelihood that x_i belongs to each cluster. These weights are based on the distance of x_i to each of the cluster representatives C, where the probability that x_i is from cluster j is proportional to the similarity between x_i and c_j. The cluster representatives in this case are found by taking the expected value of the cluster mean over all points in the dataset D.

The second extension of `k-means` deals with semisupervised learning. In the introduction, we made a distinction between supervised learning and unsupervised learning. In brief, supervised learning makes use of class labels while unsupervised learning does not. The `k-means` algorithm is a purely unsupervised algorithm. There also exists a category of learning algorithms called *semisupervised algorithms*. Semisupervised learning algorithms are capable of making use of both labeled and unlabeled data. Semisupervised learning is a useful compromise between purely supervised methods and purely unsupervised methods. Supervised learning methods typically require very large amounts of labeled data; semisupervised methods are useful when very few labeled examples are available. Unsupervised learning methods, which do not look at class labels, may learn models inappropriate for the application at hand. When running `k-means`, one has no control over the final clusters that are discovered; these clusters may or may not correspond well to some underlying concept that one is interested in. For example, in Figure 2.5b, a poor initialization may have resulted in clusters which do not correspond well to the Iris species in the dataset. Semisupervised methods, which can take guidance in the form of labeled points, are more likely to create clusters which correspond to a given set of class labels.

Research into semisupervised variants of `k-means` include [22] and [2]. One of the algorithms from [2] called `seeded k-means` is a simple extension to `k-means` that uses labeled data to help initialize the value of k and the cluster representatives C. In this approach, k is chosen to be the same as the number of classes in the labeled data, while c_j is initialized as the mean of all labeled points in the jth class. Note that, unlike unsupervised `k-means`, there is now a known correspondence between the jth cluster and the jth class. After initialization, `seeded k-means` iterates over the same two steps as `k-means` (updating cluster memberships and updating cluster means) until convergence.

2.6 Summary

The `k-means` algorithm is a simple iterative clustering algorithm that partitions a dataset into k clusters. At its core, the algorithm works by iterating over two steps: (1) clustering all points in the dataset based on the distance between each point and its closest cluster representative and (2) reestimating the cluster representatives. Limitations of the `k-means` algorithm include the sensitivity of `k-means` to initialization and determining the value of k.

Despite its drawbacks, `k-means` remains the most widely used partitional clustering algorithm in practice. The algorithm is simple, easily understandable, and reasonably scalable, and can be easily modified to deal with different scenarios such as semisupervised learning or streaming data. Continual improvements and generalizations of the basic algorithm have ensured its continued relevance and gradually increased its effectiveness as well.

2.7 Exercises

1. Using the standard benchmark Iris dataset (available online from the UCI dataset repository), run `k-means` to obtain results similar to Figure 2.5b. It is sufficient to look at only the attributes of "petal width" and "petal length."

   What happens when one uses a value for k other than three? How do different cluster initializations affect the final clusters? Why are these results potentially different than the results given in Figure 2.5b?
2. Prove that the value of the `k-means` objective function converges when `k-means` is run.
3. Describe three advantages and three disadvantages of `k-means` compared to other clustering methods (e.g., agglomerative clustering).
4. Describe or plot a two-dimensional example where `k-means` would be unsuitable for finding clusters.
5. In `k-means`, after the cluster means have converged, what is the shape of the cluster boundaries? How is this related to Voronoi tesselations?
6. Does `k-means` guarantee that points within the same cluster are more similar than points from different clusters? That is, prove or disprove that, after `k-means` has converged, the squared Euclidean distance between two points in the same cluster is always less than the squared Euclidean distance between two points from different clusters.
7. Assume one is given a hypothetical dataset D consisting of 10 points. `k-means` is run twice on this dataset. Let us denote the cluster IDs of the 10 points in D as a vector $\mathbf{m}$, where m_i, the ith entry in the vector, is the cluster ID of the ith point in D.

   The cluster IDs of the 10 points from the first time `k-means` is run are $\mathbf{m}^1 = [1, 1, 1, 2, 2, 2, 3, 3, 3, 3]$, while the cluster IDs obtained from the second run of `k-means` are $\mathbf{m}^2 = [3, 3, 3, 1, 1, 1, 2, 2, 2, 2]$.

   What is the difference between the two sets of cluster IDs? Do the actual cluster IDs of the points in D mean anything? What does this imply when comparing the results of different clustering algorithms? What does this imply when comparing the results of clustering algorithms with known class labels?
8. Create your own implementation of `k-means` and a method of creating artificial data drawn from k Gaussian distributions. Test your code on the artificial data and keep track of how many iterations it takes for `k-means` to converge.

9. Using the code generated in the previous exercise, plot the average distance of each point from its cluster mean versus the number of clusters k. Is the average distance of a point from its cluster mean a good method of automatically determining the number of clusters k? Why or why not? What can potentially happen when the number of clusters k is equal to the number of points in the dataset?

10. Research and describe an extension to the standard `k-means` algorithm. Depending on individual interests, this could include recent work on making `k-means` more computationally efficient, work on extending `k-means` to semisupervised learning, work on adapting other distance metrics into `k-means`, or many other possibilities.

References

[1] A. Banerjee, S. Merugu, I. Dhillon, and J. Ghosh. "Clustering with Bregman divergences," *Journal of Machine Learning Research (JMLR)*, vol. 6, pp. 1705–1749, 2005.

[2] S. Basu, A. Banerjee, and R. Mooney. "Semi-supervised clustering by seeding," *International Conference on Machine Learning 2002*, pp. 27–34, 2002.

[3] C. M. Bishop. *Pattern Recognition and Machine Learning (Information Science and Statistics)*. 2006.

[4] P. S. Bradley, K. P. Bennett, and A. Demiriz. "Constrained k-means clustering," *Technical Report MSR-TR-2000-65*, 2000.

[5] I. S. Dhillon, Y. Guan, and B. Kulis. "Kernel k-means: Spectral clustering and normalized cuts," *KDD 2004*, pp. 551–556, 2004.

[6] J. C. Dunn. "A fuzzy relative of the ISODATA process and its use in detecting compact well-separated clusters," *Journal of Cybernetics*, vol. 3, pp. 32–57, 1974.

[7] C. Elkan. "Using the triangle inequality to accelerate k-means," *International Conference on Machine Learning 2003*, pp. 147–153, 2003.

[8] C. Elkan. "Clustering with k-means: Faster, smarter, cheaper," *Keynote talk at Workshop on Clustering High-Dimensional Data, SIAM International Conference on Data Mining*, 2004.

[9] E. Forgey. "Cluster analysis of multivariate data: Efficiency vs. interpretability of classification," *Biometrics*, 21, pp. 768, 1965.

[10] H. P. Friedman and J. Rubin. "On some invariant criteria for grouping data," *Journal of American Statistical Association*, 62, pp. 1159–1178, 1967.

[11] R. M. Gray and D. L. Neuhoff. "Quantization," *IEEE Transactions on Information Theory,* vol. 44, no. 6, pp. 2325–2384, 1998.

[12] G. Hamerly and C. Elkan. "Learning the k in k-means," *Neural Information Processing Systems*, 2003.

[13] A. K. Jain and R. C. Dubes. *Algorithms for Clustering Data*, Prentice Hall, 1988.

[14] T. Kanungo, D. M. Mount, N. Netanyahu, C. Piatko, R. Silverman, and A. Y. Wu. "A local search approximation algorithm for k-means clustering," *Computational Geometry: Theory and Applications*, 28 (2004), pp. 89–112, 2004.

[15] L. Kaufman and P. J. Rousseeuw. *Finding Groups in Data: An Introduction to Cluster Analysis*, 1990.

[16] S. P. Lloyd. "Least squares quantization in PCM," unpublished Bell Lab. Tech. Note, portions presented at the Institute of Mathematical Statistics Meet., Atlantic City, NJ, Sept. 1957. Also, *IEEE Trans. Inform. Theory* (Special Issue on Quantization), vol. IT-28, pp. 129–137, Mar. 1982.

[17] J. McQueen. "Some methods for classification and analysis of mutivariate observations," *Proc. 5th Berkeley Symp. Math., Statistics and Probability*, 1, pp. 281–296, 1967.

[18] G. W. Milligan. "Clustering validation: Results and implications for applied analyses," *Clustering and Classification*, P. Arabie, L. J. Hubery, and G. De Soete, ed., pp. 341–375, 1996.

[19] D. Pelleg and A. Moore. "Accelerating exact k-means algorithms with geometric reasoning," *KDD 1999*, pp. 227–281, 1999.

[20] D. Pelleg and A. Moore. "X-means: Extending k-means with efficient estimation of the number of clusters," *International Conference on Machine Learning 2000*, pp. 727–734, 2000.

[21] M. Steinbach, G. Karypis, and V. Kumar. "A comparison of document clustering techniques," *Proc. KDD Workshop on Text Mining*, 2000.

[22] K. Wagstaff, C. Cardie, S. Rogers, S. Schrödl. "Constrained k-means clustering with background knowledge," *International Conference on Machine Learning 2001*, pp. 577–584, 2001.

[23] S. Zhong and J. Ghosh. "A unified framework for model-based clustering," *Journal of Machine Learning Research* (*JMLR*), vol. 4, pp. 1001–1037, 2003.

Chapter 3

SVM: Support Vector Machines

Hui Xue, Qiang Yang, and Songcan Chen

Contents

Support vector machines (SVMs), including support vector classifier (SVC) and support vector regressor (SVR), are among the most robust and accurate methods in all well-known data mining algorithms. SVMs, which were originally developed by Vapnik in the 1990s [1–11], have a sound theoretical foundation rooted in statistical learning theory, require only as few as a dozen examples for training, and are often insensitive to the number of dimensions. In the past decade, SVMs have been developed at a fast pace both in theory and practice.

3.1 Support Vector Classifier

For a two-class linearly separable learning task, the aim of SVC is to find a hyperplane that can separate two classes of given samples with a maximal margin which has been proved able to offer the best generalization ability. *Generalization ability* refers to the fact that a classifier not only has good classification performance (e.g., accuracy) on the training data, but also guarantees high predictive accuracy for the future data from the same distribution as the training data.

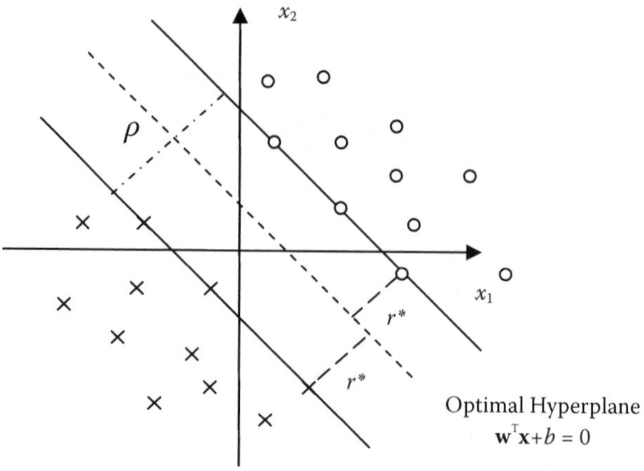

Figure 3.1 Illustration of the optimal hyperplane in SVC for a linearly separable case.

Intuitively, a *margin* can be defined as the amount of space, or separation, between the two classes as defined by a hyperplane. Geometrically, the margin corresponds to the shortest distance between the closest data points to any point on the hyperplane. Figure 3.1 illustrates a geometric construction of the corresponding optimal hyperplane under the above conditions for a two-dimensional input space.

Let $\mathbf{w}$ and b denote the weight vector and bias in the optimal hyperplane, respectively. The corresponding hyperplane can be defined as

$$\mathbf{w}^T\mathbf{x} + b = 0 \tag{3.1}$$

The desired directionally geometrical distance from the sample $\mathbf{x}$ to the optimal hyperplane [12,13] is

$$r = \frac{g(\mathbf{x})}{\|\mathbf{w}\|} \tag{3.2}$$

where $g(\mathbf{x}) = \mathbf{w}^T\mathbf{x} + b$ is the discriminant function [7] as defined by the hyperplane and also called $\mathbf{x}$'s functional margin given $\mathbf{w}$ and b.

Consequently, SVC aims to find the parameters $\mathbf{w}$ and b for an optimal hyperplane in order to maximize the margin of separation [ρ in Equation (3.5)] that is determined by the shortest geometrical distances r^* from the two classes, respectively, thus SVC is also called *maximal margin classifier*. Now without loss of generality, we fix the functional margin [7] to be equal to 1; that is, given a training set $\{\mathbf{x}_i, y_i\}_{i=1}^n \in \mathbf{R}^m \times \{\pm 1\}$, we have

$$\begin{aligned} \mathbf{w}^T\mathbf{x}_i + b &\geq 1 \quad \textit{for} \quad y_i = +1 \\ \mathbf{w}^T\mathbf{x}_i + b &\leq -1 \quad \textit{for} \quad y_i = -1 \end{aligned} \tag{3.3}$$

The particular data points $(\mathbf{x}_i, y_i)$ for which the equalities of the first or second parts in Equation (3.3) are satisfied are called *support vectors*, which are exactly the closest data points to the optimal hyperplane [13]. Then, the corresponding geometrical distance from the support vector $\mathbf{x}^*$ to the optimal hyperplane is

$$r^* = \frac{g(\mathbf{x}^*)}{\|\mathbf{w}\|} = \begin{cases} \dfrac{1}{\|\mathbf{w}\|} & if \quad y^* = +1 \\ -\dfrac{1}{\|\mathbf{w}\|} & if \quad y^* = -1 \end{cases} \tag{3.4}$$

From Figure 3.1, clearly the margin of separation ρ is

$$\rho = 2r^* = \frac{2}{\|\mathbf{w}\|} \tag{3.5}$$

To ensure that the maximum margin hyperplane can be found, SVC attempts to maximize ρ with respect to $\mathbf{w}$ and b:

$$\begin{aligned} &\max_{\mathbf{w},b} \frac{2}{\|\mathbf{w}\|} \\ &s.t.\ y_i\left(\mathbf{w}^T\mathbf{x}_i + b\right) \geq 1, \quad i = 1, \ldots, n \end{aligned} \tag{3.6}$$

Equivalently,

$$\begin{aligned} &\min_{\mathbf{w},b} \frac{1}{2}\|\mathbf{w}\|^2 \\ &s.t.\ y_i(\mathbf{w}^T\mathbf{x}_i + b) \geq 1, \quad i = 1, \ldots, n \end{aligned} \tag{3.7}$$

Here, we often use $\|\mathbf{w}\|^2$ instead of $\|\mathbf{w}\|$ for the convenience of carrying out the subsequent optimization steps.

Generally, we solve the constrained optimization problem in Equation (3.7), known as the *primal problem*, by using the method of Lagrange multipliers. We construct the following Lagrange function:

$$L(\mathbf{w}, b, \alpha) = \frac{1}{2}\mathbf{w}^T\mathbf{w} - \sum_{i=1}^{n} \alpha_i \left[y_i\left(\mathbf{w}^T\mathbf{x}_i + b\right) - 1\right] \tag{3.8}$$

where α_i is the Lagrange multiplier with respect to the ith inequality.

Differentiating $L(\mathbf{w}, b, \alpha)$ with respect to $\mathbf{w}$ and b, and setting the results equal to zero, we get the following two conditions of optimality:

$$\begin{cases} \dfrac{\partial L(\mathbf{w}, b, \alpha)}{\partial \mathbf{w}} = 0 \\ \dfrac{\partial L(\mathbf{w}, b, \alpha)}{\partial b} = 0 \end{cases} \tag{3.9}$$

Then we obtain

$$\begin{cases} \mathbf{w} = \sum_{i=1}^{n} \alpha_i y_i \mathbf{x}_i \\ \sum_{i=1}^{n} \alpha_i y_i = 0 \end{cases} \tag{3.10}$$

Substituting Equation (3.10) into the Lagrange function Equation (3.8), we can get the corresponding *dual problem*:

$$\begin{aligned} \max_{\alpha} W(\alpha) &= \sum_{i=1}^{n} \alpha_i - \frac{1}{2} \sum_{i=1}^{n} \sum_{j=1}^{n} \alpha_i \alpha_j y_i y_j \mathbf{x}_i^T \mathbf{x}_j \\ s.t. & \sum_{i=1}^{n} \alpha_i y_i = 0 \\ & \alpha_i \geq 0, \quad i = 1, \ldots, n \end{aligned} \tag{3.11}$$

And at the same time, the Karush-Kuhn-Tucker complementary condition is

$$\alpha_i \left[y_i \left(\mathbf{w}^T \mathbf{x}_i + b \right) - 1 \right] = 0, \quad i = 1, \ldots, n \tag{3.12}$$

Consequently, only the support vectors $(\mathbf{x}_i, y_i)$ that are the closest data points to the optimal hyperplane and determine the maximal margin, correspond to the nonzero α_is. All the other α_is equal zero.

The *dual* problem in Equation (3.11) is a typical *convex quadratic programming optimization* problem. In many cases, it can efficiently converge to the global optimum by adopting some appropriate optimization techniques, such as the sequential minimal optimization (SMO) algorithm [7].

After determining the optimal Lagrange multipliers α_i^*, we can compute the optimal weight vector $\mathbf{w}^*$ by Equation (3.10):

$$\mathbf{w}^* = \sum_{i=1}^{n} \alpha_i^* y_i \mathbf{x}_i \tag{3.13}$$

Then, taking advantage of a positive support vector $\mathbf{x}_s$, the corresponding optimal bias b^* can be written as [13]:

$$b^* = 1 - \mathbf{w}^{*T} \mathbf{x}_s \quad for\ y_s = +1 \tag{3.14}$$

3.2 SVC with Soft Margin and Optimization

Maximal margin SVC, including the following SVR, represents the original starting point of the SVM algorithms. However, in many real-world problems, it may be too rigid to require that all points are linearly separable, especially in many complex nonlinear classification cases. When the samples cannot be completely linearly separated, the margins may be negative. In these cases, the feasible region of the primal problem is empty, and thus the corresponding dual problem is an unbounded objective function. This makes it impossible to solve the optimization problem [7].

To solve these inseparable problems, we generally adopt two approaches. The first one is to relax the rigid inequalities in Equation (3.7) and thus lead to so-called soft margin optimization. Another method is to apply the kernel trick to linearize those nonlinear problems. In this section, we first introduce soft margin optimization. Consequently, relative to the soft margin SVC, we usually name SVC derived from the optimization problem [Equation (3.7)] the hard margin SVC.

Imagine the cases where there are a few points of the opposite classes mixed together in the data. These points represent the training error that exists even for the maximum margin hyperplane. The "soft margin" idea aims to extend the SVC algorithm so that the hyperplane allows a few of such noisy data to exist. In particular, a slack variable ξ_i is introduced to account for the amount of a violation of classification by the classifier:

$$\min_{\mathbf{w},b} \frac{1}{2}\|\mathbf{w}\|^2 + C\sum_{i=1}^{n}\xi_i$$

$$s.t. \quad y_i\left(\mathbf{w}^T\mathbf{x}_i + b\right) \geq 1 - \xi_i, \quad \xi_i \geq 0, \quad i = 1, \ldots, n \tag{3.15}$$

where the parameter C controls the trade-off between complexity of the machine and the number of inseparable points. It may be viewed as a "regularization" parameter and selected by the user either experimentally or analytically.

The slack variable ξ_i has a direct geometric explanation through the distance from a misclassified data instance to the hyperplane. This distance measures the deviation of a sample from the ideal condition of pattern separability. Using the same method of Lagrange multipliers that are introduced in the above section, we can formulate the *dual* problem of the soft margin as:

$$\max_{\alpha} W(\alpha) = \sum_{i=1}^{n}\alpha_i - \frac{1}{2}\sum_{i=1}^{n}\sum_{j=1}^{n}\alpha_i\alpha_j y_i y_j \mathbf{x}_i^T\mathbf{x}_j$$

$$s.t. \quad \sum_{i=1}^{n}\alpha_i y_i = 0$$

$$0 \leq \alpha_i \leq C, \quad i = 1, \ldots, n \tag{3.16}$$

Comparing Equation (3.11) with Equation (3.16), it is noteworthy that the slack variables ξ_is do not appear in the dual problem. The major difference between the linearly inseparable and separable cases is that the constraint $\alpha_i \geq 0$ is replaced with the more stringent constraint $0 \leq \alpha_i \leq C$. Otherwise, the two cases are similar, including the computations of the optimal values of the weight vector $\mathbf{w}$ and bias b, especially the definition of the support vectors [7,13].

The Karush-Kuhn-Tucker complementary condition in the inseparable case is

$$\alpha_i \left[y_i \left(\mathbf{w}^T \mathbf{x}_i + b \right) - 1 + \xi_i \right] = 0, \quad i = 1, \ldots, n \tag{3.17}$$

and

$$\gamma_i \xi_i = 0, \quad i = 1, \ldots, n \tag{3.18}$$

where γ_is are the Lagrange multipliers corresponding to ξ_i that have been introduced to enforce the nonnegativity of ξ_i [13]. At the saddle point at which the derivative of the Lagrange function for the primal problem with respect to ξ_i is zero, the evaluation of the derivative yields

$$\alpha_i + \gamma_i = C \tag{3.19}$$

Combining Equations (3.18) and (3.19), we have

$$\xi_i = 0 \quad \textit{if} \quad \alpha_i < C \tag{3.20}$$

Consequently, we have the optimal weight $\mathbf{w}^*$ as follows:

$$\mathbf{w}^* = \sum_{i=1}^{n} \alpha_i^* y_i \mathbf{x}_i \tag{3.21}$$

The optimal bias b^* can be obtained by taking any data point $(\mathbf{x}_i, y_i)$ in the training set for which we have $0 < \alpha_i^* < C$ and the corresponding $\xi_i = 0$, and using the data point in Equation (3.17) [13].

3.3 Kernel Trick

The kernel trick is another commonly used technique to solve linearly inseparable problems. The issue is to define an appropriate kernel function based on the *inner product* between the given data, as a nonlinear transformation of data from the input space to a feature space with higher (even infinite) dimension in order to make the problems linearly separable. The underlying justification can be found in *Cover's theorem* on the separability of patterns; that is, a complex pattern classification problem cast in a high-dimensional space nonlinearly is *more likely* to be linearly separable than in a low-dimensional space [13].

Let $\mathbf{\Phi} : \mathbf{X} \rightarrow \mathbf{H}$ denote a nonlinear transformation from the input space $\mathbf{X} \subset \mathbf{R}^m$ to the feature space $\mathbf{H}$ where the problem can be linearly separable. We may define the corresponding optimal hyperplane as follows:

$$\mathbf{w}^{\mathbf{\Phi}T}\mathbf{\Phi}(\mathbf{x}) + b = 0 \tag{3.22}$$

Without loss of generality, we set the bias $b = 0$, and simplify Equation (3.22) as:

$$\mathbf{w}^{\mathbf{\Phi}T}\mathbf{\Phi}(\mathbf{x}) = 0 \tag{3.23}$$

Similar to the linear separable cases, we seek the optimal weight vector $\mathbf{w}^{\mathbf{\Phi}*}$ in the feature space in virtue of the similar Lagrange multiplier method, and obtain:

$$\mathbf{w}^{\mathbf{\Phi}*} = \sum_{i=1}^{n} \alpha_i^* y_i \mathbf{\Phi}(\mathbf{x}_i) \tag{3.24}$$

Thus, the optimal hyperplane computed in the feature space is:

$$\sum_{i=1}^{n} \alpha_i^* y_i \mathbf{\Phi}^T(\mathbf{x}_i)\mathbf{\Phi}(\mathbf{x}) = 0 \tag{3.25}$$

The term $\mathbf{\Phi}^T(\mathbf{x}_i)\mathbf{\Phi}(\mathbf{x})$ represents the inner product of two vectors, $\mathbf{\Phi}(\mathbf{x})$ and $\mathbf{\Phi}(\mathbf{x}_i)$. Hence, here we deduce the inner product kernel function:

Definition 3.3.1 (Inner Product Kernel) [7]. Kernel is a function $\mathbf{K}(\mathbf{x}, \mathbf{x}')$, for all $\mathbf{x}, \mathbf{x}' \in \mathbf{X} \subset \mathbf{R}^m$, satisfied:

$$\mathbf{K}(\mathbf{x}, \mathbf{x}') = \mathbf{\Phi}^T(\mathbf{x})\mathbf{\Phi}(\mathbf{x}') \tag{3.26}$$

where $\mathbf{\Phi}$ is a transformation from the input space $\mathbf{X}$ to the feature space $\mathbf{H}$.

The significance of the kernel is that we may use it to construct the optimal hyperplane in the feature space *without having to consider the concrete form of the transformation* $\mathbf{\Phi}$, which usually need not be explicitly formulated in the higher dimension (even infinite) feature space. As a result, the application of the kernel can make the algorithm insensitive to the dimension, so as to train a linear classifier in a space with higher dimension to solve linearly inseparable problems efficiently. This is done by using $\mathbf{K}(\mathbf{x}_i, \mathbf{x})$ in Equation (3.25) to substitute $\mathbf{\Phi}^T(\mathbf{x}_i)\mathbf{\Phi}(\mathbf{x})$; then the optimal hyperplane is:

$$\sum_{i=1}^{n} \alpha_i^* y_i \mathbf{K}(\mathbf{x}_i, \mathbf{x}) = 0 \tag{3.27}$$

As indicated, the kernel trick is an appealing method for simplifying the computation, by which we can avoid computing the complex feature space directly not only in the computation of the inner products but also in the design of the classifier.

However, before implementing the kernel trick, we should consider how to construct a kernel function, that is, a kernel function should satisfy which characteristics. To answer this question, we first introduce Mercer's theorem, which characterizes the property of a function $\mathbf{K}(\mathbf{x}, \mathbf{x}')$ for when it is considered a true kernel function:

Theorem 3.3.2 ***Mercer's Theorem*** [13] *Let* $\mathbf{K}(\mathbf{x}, \mathbf{x}')$ *be a continuous symmetric kernel that is defined in the closed interval* $\mathbf{a} \le \mathbf{x} \le \mathbf{b}$ *and likewise for* $\mathbf{x}'$. *The kernel* $\mathbf{K}(\mathbf{x}, \mathbf{x}')$ *can be expanded in the series*

$$\mathbf{K}(\mathbf{x}, \mathbf{x}') = \sum_{i=1}^{\infty} \lambda_i \varphi_i(\mathbf{x}) \varphi_i(\mathbf{x}') \tag{3.28}$$

with positive coefficients, $\lambda_i > 0$ *for all* i. *For this expansion to be valid and for it to converge, it is necessary and sufficient that the condition*

$$\int_{\mathbf{b}}^{\mathbf{a}} \int_{\mathbf{b}}^{\mathbf{a}} \mathbf{K}(\mathbf{x}, \mathbf{x}') \psi(\mathbf{x}) \psi(\mathbf{x}') \, d\mathbf{x} \, d\mathbf{x}' \ge 0 \tag{3.29}$$

holds for all $\psi(\cdot)$ *for which*

$$\int_{\mathbf{b}}^{\mathbf{a}} \psi^2(\mathbf{x}) \, d\mathbf{x} < \infty \tag{3.30}$$

In light of the theorem, we can summarize the most useful characteristic in the construction of the kernel, which is termed Mercer kernel. That is, for any random limited subsets belonging to the input space $\mathbf{X}$, the corresponding matrix constructed by the kernel function $\mathbf{K}(\mathbf{x}, \mathbf{x}')$

$$\mathbf{K} = \left(\mathbf{K}\left(\mathbf{x}_i, \mathbf{x}_j'\right)\right)_{i,j=1}^{n} \tag{3.31}$$

is a symmetric and semidefinite matrix, which is called a Gram matrix [7].

Under this requirement, there is still some freedom in how to choose a kernel function in practice. For example, besides linear kernel functions, we can also define polynomial or radial basis kernel functions. More studies in recent years have gone into the research of different kernels for SVC classification and for many other statistical tests. We will mention these in the following section.

In Section 3.2, we introduced the soft margin SVC to solve linearly inseparable problems. Compared with the kernel trick, it is obvious that the two approaches actually solve the problems in different manners. The soft margin slackens the constraints in the original input space and allows some errors to exist. However, when the problem is heavily linearly inseparable and the misclassified error is too high, the soft margin is unworkable. The kernel trick maps the data to a high-dimension feature space implicitly by the kernel function in order to make the inseparable problems separable. However, in fact the kernel trick cannot always guarantee the problems to be absolutely linearly separable due to the complexity of the problems. Therefore, in practice we often integrate them to exert the different advantages of the two techniques and solve the linearly inseparable problems more efficiently. As a result, the corresponding dual form for the constrained optimization problem in the kernel soft margin SVC is as follows:

$$\max_{\alpha} W(\alpha) = \sum_{i=1}^{n} \alpha_i - \frac{1}{2} \sum_{i=1}^{n} \sum_{j=1}^{n} \alpha_i \alpha_j y_i y_j \mathbf{K}(\mathbf{x}_i, \mathbf{x}_j)$$

$$s.t. \quad \sum_{i=1}^{n} \alpha_i y_i = 0$$

$$0 \leq \alpha_i \leq C, \quad i = 1, \ldots, n \tag{3.32}$$

Following the similar Lagrange multipliers method, we can obtain the optimal classifier:

$$f(\mathbf{x}) = \sum_{i=1}^{n} \alpha_i^* y_i \mathbf{K}(\mathbf{x}_i, \mathbf{x}) + b^* \tag{3.33}$$

where $b^* = 1 - \sum_{i=1}^{n} \alpha_i^* y_i \mathbf{K}(\mathbf{x}_i, \mathbf{x}_s)$, for a positive support vector $y_s = +1$.

Example 3.3.3 **(Illustrative Example)** The XOR problem is a typical extremely linearly inseparabe problem in classification. Here we use it to illustrate the significance of the soft margin SVC combined with kernel trick in the complex classification problems. A two-dimensional XOR dataset can be randomly generated under four different Gaussian distributions, where "*" and "•" denote the samples in the two classes, respectively.

As shown in Figure 3.2*a*, the hard margin SVC in the linear kernel completely fails in the XOR problem. A linear boundary cannot discriminate the two classes and can be seen to divide all the samples into two parts. This clearly cannot achieve the classification objective for the problem. Consequently, we use the soft margin SVC combined with a radial basis kernel to solve the problem

$$\mathbf{K}(\mathbf{x}_i, \mathbf{x}) = \exp\left(-\frac{\|\mathbf{x} - \mathbf{x}_i\|^2}{\sigma^2}\right)$$

We fix the regularization parameter $C = 1$ and the kernel parameter or bandwidth $\sigma = 1$. The corresponding discriminant boundary is presented in Figure 3.2*b*. By using the kernel trick, the boundary is no longer linear, for it now encloses only one class. By judging the samples inside or outside the boundary, the classifier can be seen to classify the samples accurately.

Example 3.3.4 **Real Application Example** SVC algorithm has been widely applied in many important scientific fields, such as bioinformatics, physics, chemistry, iatrology, astronomy, and so on. Here we carefully select five datasets in the iatrology area from the UCI Machine Learning Repository (http://ida.first.fraunhofer.de/projects/bench/benchmarks.htm) to illustrate real applications of SVC. The five

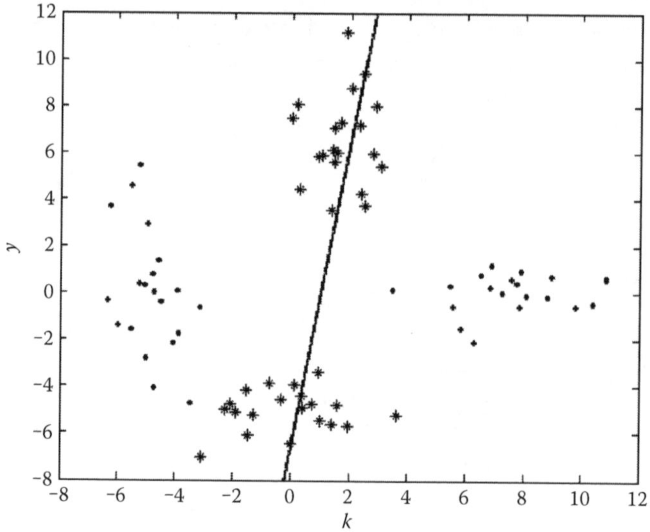

(a)

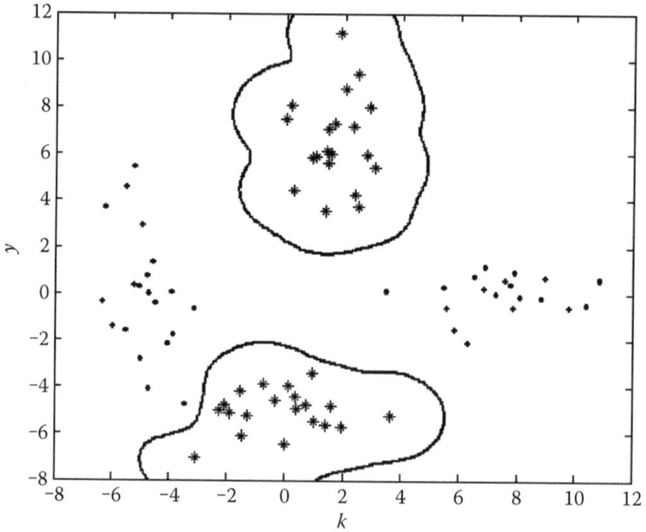

(b)

Figure 3.2 The discriminant boundaries of SVC in the XOR problem. (a) The hard margin SVC in the linear kernel. (b) The soft margin SVC in the radial basis kernel.

TABLE 3.1 Results of the SVC Algorithm for the Five Datasets

Dataset	Dimension	Training	Testing	C	σ	SV	Accuracy
B.-cancer	9	200	77	1.519e+01	5.000e+01	138.80	0.7396±4.74
Diabetes	8	468	300	1.500e+01	2.000e+01	308.60	0.7647±1.73
Heart	13	170	100	3.162e+00	1.200e+02	86.00	0.8405±3.26
Thyroid	5	140	75	1.000e+01	3.000e+00	45.80	0.9520±2.19
Splice	60	1000	2175	1.000e+03	7.000e+01	762.40	0.8912±0.66

datasets, respectively, are B.-cancer (breast cancer Wisconsin data), diabetes (Pima Indians diabetes data), heart (heart data), thyroid (thyroid disease data), and splice (splice-junction gene sequences data).

The two to four columns of Table 3.1 summarize some characteristics about the datasets, where Dimension denotes the dimension of the samples, and Training and Testing denote the numbers of the training and testing samples in each dataset. We perform independently repeated 100 runs and 20 runs, respectively, for the first four datasets and splice dataset, which have been offered by the database. Then the average experimental results of the SVC algorithm have been reported in the five to eight columns of Table 3.1. C and σ are the optimal regularization and kernel parameters selected by the cross-validation. SV is the average number of support vectors. Accuracy denotes the corresponding classification accuracies and variances.

As shown in Table 3.1, the values of SV are typically less than the numbers of training samples, which validates the good sparsity of the algorithm. Furthermore, the high accuracies show the good classification performance; meanwhile, the relatively low variances show the good stability of SVC in the real applications.

3.4 Theoretical Foundations

In the above sections, we have described the SVC algorithm both in the linearly separable and inseparable cases. The introduction of the kernel trick further improves the expression performance of the classifier, which can keep the inherent linear property in a high-dimensional feature space and avoid the possible *curse of dimension*. In this section, we will discuss the theoretical foundation of the SVC. By the Vapnik-Chervonenkis (VC) theory [4,5], we will first present a general error bound of a linear classifier which can guide globally how to control the classifier complexity. We will then deduce a concrete generalization bound of the SVC to explain the significance of the maximum margin in the SVC to guarantee the good generalization capacity of the algorithm.

The VC theory generalizes the probably approximately correct (PAC) learning model in statistical learning and directly leads to the proposal of the SVMs. It provides an analytical generalization bound that can be used for estimating generalization error by defining a new measure of complexity, known as the *VC dimension* [14,15].

Concretely, assume that training and testing data are generated according to a fixed but unknown probability distribution $\mathbf{D}$, we define the error $err_{\mathbf{D}}(h)$ of a classification function h on the $\mathbf{D}$ as

$$err_{\mathbf{D}}(h) = \mathbf{D}\{(\mathbf{x}, y) : h(\mathbf{x}) \neq y\} \tag{3.34}$$

which measures the expected error [7].

PAC models bound the distribution of the generalization error random variable $err_{\mathbf{D}}(h_s)$ and the corresponding PAC bound has the form $\varepsilon = \varepsilon(n, H, \delta)$; that is, a PAC model considers that in the hypothesis h_s, the probability of the error in the training data S satisfies [7]:

$$\mathbf{D}^n\{S : err_{\mathbf{D}}(h_s) > \varepsilon(n, H, \delta)\} < \delta \tag{3.35}$$

If there are $|H|$ hypotheses having large errors in the set S, then the PAC bound is

$$\varepsilon = \varepsilon(n, H, \delta) = \frac{1}{n} \ln \frac{|H|}{\delta} \tag{3.36}$$

PAC bound presents that the function class H can directly influence the error bound. VC theory further generalizes the PAC bound to the unlimited function class and introduces the concept of the VC dimension d. The VC dimension d measures the maximum number of training data where the function class can still be used to learn perfectly, by obtaining zero error rates on the training data, for any assignment of class labels to these points. Then the generalized PAC bound of a linear classifier can be described as follows:

Theorem 3.4.1 ***Vapnik and Chervonenkis*** [7] *Let H denote a hypothesis space whose VC dimension is d. For random probability distribution $\mathbf{D}$ on $\mathbf{X} \times \{-1, 1\}$, with probability $1 - \delta$, the generalization error of random hypothesis $h \in H$ on the training set S is no more than*

$$err_{\mathbf{D}}(h) \leq \varepsilon(n, H, \delta) = \frac{2}{n}\left(\log \frac{2}{\delta} + d \log \frac{2en}{d}\right) \tag{3.37}$$

under the condition that $d \leq n$, $n > 2/\varepsilon$.

In light of the theorem, the first term of Equation (3.37) is the training error, and the second term is proportional to the VC dimension d. Thus, the theorem shows that if we can minimize d, we can minimize the future error, as long as the hypothesis h controls the empirical risk error in a small degree.

Theorem 3.4.1 provides a general error bound of a linear classifier and gives the global guidance on how to control the classifier complexity. In the following, we will generalize the bound for the SVC algorithm and deduce the corresponding generalization error bound of SVC.

We first give a formal definition of the margin:

Definition 3.4.2 (Margin) [7]. Consider using a real value function class F to classify in the input space $\mathbf{X}$, and the threshold value is 0. We define the margin of the example $(\mathbf{x}_i, y_i) \in \mathbf{X} \times \{-1, 1\}$ to the function or hyperplane $f \in F$ as:

$$\gamma_i = y_i f(\mathbf{x}_i) \tag{3.38}$$

Note that $\gamma_i > 0$ denotes that the example $(\mathbf{x}_i, y_i)$ is correctly classified. The marginal distribution of f corresponding to the training set S is the marginal distribution of the examples in S. The minimum of the marginal distribution is called the *margin* $m_S(f)$ of f corresponding to the training set S.

Although the VC dimension d is theoretically meaningful, in practice d is sometimes infinite and thus the generalization bound is inapplicable to many real problems. Consequently, we introduce a similar measure related to the margin in SVC instead of the traditional VC dimension:

Definition 3.4.3 (Cover of Function Class) [7]. Let F be a real value function class in $\mathbf{X}$. For a series of input data

$$S = \{\mathbf{x}_1, \mathbf{x}_2, \ldots, \mathbf{x}_n\}$$

The γ-cover of F is the limited function set B, such that for all $f \in F$, existing $g \in B$, there is $\max_{1 \le i \le n}(|f(\mathbf{x}_i) - g(\mathbf{x}_i)|) < \gamma$. $N(F, S, \gamma)$ denotes the minimal size of the cover. The number of data that Fcovers is

$$N(F, n, \gamma) = \max_{S \in X^n} N(F, S, \gamma) \tag{3.39}$$

Then we use $N(F, n, \gamma)$ to reformulate Theorem 3.4.1 for the case that the hypothesis f is such that $m_S(f) = \gamma$ on the training set S.

Theorem 3.4.4 ***VC Theorem with Margin*** [7] *Consider a bounded real value function space F and fix $\gamma \in \mathbf{R}^+$. For any probability distribution $\mathbf{D}$ on $\mathbf{X} \times \{-1, 1\}$, with probability $1 - \delta$, the generalization error of a hypothesis $f \in F$ on the training set S, which has a margin $m_S(f) \ge \gamma$, satisfies*

$$err_{\mathbf{D}}(f) \le \varepsilon(n, F, \delta, \gamma) = \frac{2}{n}\left(\log\frac{2}{\delta} + \log N(F, 2n, \gamma/2)\right) \tag{3.40}$$

under the condition that $n > 2/\varepsilon$.

Theorem 3.4.4 shows how to use $m_S(f)$ to bound the generalization error which can be obtained by the training data. $N(F, 2n, \gamma/2)$ may be viewed as another form of the VC dimension, where a larger γ corresponds to a smaller $N(F, 2n, \gamma/2)$. As a result, we may draw a conclusion that large margin can ensure good generalization performance of the classifier for small size samples.

Although Theorem 3.4.4 is a generalization of Theorem 3.4.1, the value $N(F, 2n, \gamma/2)$ cannot be efficiently quantified in the real-world problems. Consequently, we further deduce a more concrete error bound for the specific SVC algorithm:

Theorem 3.4.5 ***Generalization Bound of SVC*** [7] *Assume that the input space* $\mathbf{X}$ *is a hyperball in the inner product space* $\mathbf{H}$ *whose radius is* R, $\mathbf{X} = \{\mathbf{x} \in \mathbf{H} : \|\mathbf{x}\|_{\mathbf{H}} \leq R\}$. *Consider the function class* Ψ:

$$\Psi = \left\{\mathbf{x} \mapsto \mathbf{w}^T\mathbf{x} : \|\mathbf{w}\|_{\mathbf{H}} \leq 1, \mathbf{x} \in \mathbf{X}\right\}$$

Fix $\gamma \in \mathbf{R}^+$. *For a probability distribution* $\mathbf{D}$ *on* $\mathbf{X} \times \{-1, 1\}$, *with probability* $1 - \delta$, *the generalization error of a hypothesis* $f \in \Psi$ *on the training set* S, *which has the margin* $m_S(f) \geq \gamma$, *is no more than*

$$err_{\mathbf{D}}(f) \leq \varepsilon(n, \Psi, \delta, \gamma) = \frac{2}{n}\left(\log\frac{4}{\delta} + \frac{64R^2}{\gamma^2}\log\frac{en\gamma}{4R}\log\frac{128nR^2}{\gamma^2}\right) \tag{3.41}$$

under the condition that $n > 2/\varepsilon$, $64R^2/\gamma^2 < n$.

It is noteworthy that the dimension of the input space does not appear in the bound. Hence the bound can be used in the infinite dimension space, which denotes that the bound may overcome the curse of dimension. Furthermore, when the samples distribute well, the bound may guarantee in a high probability that there is a small error for random testing samples. In that case, the margin γ can be viewed as a measure about the quality of the sample distribution, and thus may further measure the generalization performance of the SVC algorithm [7].

3.5 Support Vector Regressor

Up to this point, we have focused on the SVC method for classification tasks. In this section, we will consider using SVM to solve nonlinear *regression* problems, thus called SVR. Similar to the classification algorithm, we also expect to explore the main characteristics of the maximum margin method by exploiting nonlinear functions, which can be obtained using linear learning methods and the kernel trick. In addition, the corresponding algorithms must be efficient under high dimensions [7].

However, for regression problems, the traditional least-squares estimator may not be quite feasible in the presence of outliers, resulting in the regressor to perform poorly when the underlying distribution of the additive noise has a long tail [13]. Thus we need to develop a robust estimator insensitive to small changes in the model; that is, we seek a so-called ε-insensitive loss function.

Definition 3.5.1 (**ε-Insensitive Loss Function**) [7]
Let f be a real valued function in $\mathbf{X}$. The ε-insensitive loss function $L^{\varepsilon}(\mathbf{x}, y, f)$ is defined as:

$$L^{\varepsilon}(\mathbf{x}, y, f) = |y - f(\mathbf{x})|_{\varepsilon} = \max(0, |y - f(\mathbf{x})| - \varepsilon) \tag{3.42}$$

Note that $L^{\varepsilon}(\mathbf{x}, y, f) = 0$ if the absolute value of the deviation about the estimator output $f(\mathbf{x})$ from the desired response y is less than ε or equal to zero. It is equal to the absolute value of the deviation minus ε otherwise.

Now consider a nonlinear regression model

$$y = g(\mathbf{x}) + v \tag{3.43}$$

where the additive noise term v is statistically independent of the input vector $\mathbf{x}$. The function $g(\cdot)$ and the statistics of noise v are unknown. All that we have available is a set of training data

$$S = \{(\mathbf{x}_1, y_1), \ldots, (\mathbf{x}_n, y_n)\}$$

and a function class

$$F = \{f(\mathbf{x}) = \mathbf{w}^T\mathbf{x} + b, \mathbf{w} \in \mathbf{R}^m, b \in \mathbf{R}\}$$

The objective is to select appropriate parameters $\mathbf{w}$ and b, so as to make $f(\mathbf{x})$ approximate the unknown target function $g(\mathbf{x})$. The primal problem can be represented as follows:

$$\begin{aligned} &\min_{\mathbf{w},b} \frac{1}{2}\|\mathbf{w}\|^2 + C\sum_{i=1}^{n}(\xi_i + \hat{\xi}_i) \\ s.t.\ &\left(\mathbf{w}^T\mathbf{x}_i + b\right) - y_i \le \varepsilon + \xi_i, \quad i = 1, \ldots, n \\ &y_i - \left(\mathbf{w}^T\mathbf{x}_i + b\right) \le \varepsilon + \hat{\xi}_i, \quad i = 1, \ldots, n \\ &\xi_i, \hat{\xi}_i \ge 0 \quad i = 1, \ldots, n \end{aligned} \tag{3.44}$$

Using the similar method of Lagrange multipliers, the dual problem is:

$$\begin{aligned} \max_{\alpha,\hat{\alpha}} W(\alpha, \hat{\alpha}) &= \sum_{i=1}^{n} y_i(\hat{\alpha}_i - \alpha_i) - \varepsilon\sum_{i=1}^{n}(\hat{\alpha}_i + \alpha_i) - \frac{1}{2}\sum_{i=1}^{n}\sum_{j=1}^{n}(\hat{\alpha}_i - \alpha_i)(\hat{\alpha}_j - \alpha_j)\mathbf{x}_i^T\mathbf{x}_j \\ s.t.\ &\sum_{i=1}^{n}(\hat{\alpha}_i - \alpha_i) = 0 \\ 0 \le \alpha_i, \hat{\alpha}_i \le C, &\quad i = 1, \ldots, n \end{aligned} \tag{3.45}$$

We can further introduce the inner product kernel in the optimization problem Equation (3.45), and extend the regression algorithm to a feature space so as to make the nonlinear functions able to be obtained by means of the linear learning machines in the kernel space.

Compared with SVC, SVR has an additional free parameter ε. The two free parameters ε and C control the VC dimension of the approximating function

$$f(x) = \mathbf{w}^T\mathbf{x} = \sum_{i=1}^{n}(\hat{\alpha}_i - \alpha_i)\mathbf{K}(\mathbf{x}_i, \mathbf{x}) \tag{3.46}$$

when we set the bias $b = 0$. ε and C should be selected by the user and directly influence the complexity control for regression. How to select ε and C simultaneously to get a better approximation function is an open research problem.

3.6 Software Implementations

LibSVM [16] and SVMlight [17] are two of the most famous software about the implementation of SVM algorithms.

LibSVM provides not only compiler languages used in the Windows system, but also C++ and Java source codes which are easy to improve, revise, and apply in other operating systems. Specially, LibSVM has relatively fewer tunable parameters involved in SVM algorithms than other software and provides lots of default parameters to solve real application problems effectively.

SVMlight is another implementation in C language. It adopts an efficient set selection technique based on steepest feasible descent, and two effective computational policies "Shrinking" and "Caching" of kernel evaluations. SVMlight mainly includes two C programs: SVM_learn, used for learning training samples and training the corresponding classifier, and SVM_classifiy, used for classifying testing samples. The software also provides two efficient estimation methods for assessing the generalization performance: XiAlpha-estimates, computed at essentially no computational expense but conservatively biased, and Leave-one-out testing, almost unbiased.

Furthermore, there are lots of complete machine learning toolboxes, including SVM algorithms, such as Torch (in C++), Spider (in MATLAB), and Weka (in Java), which are all available at http://www.kernel-machines.org.

3.7 Current and Future Research

In the past decade, SVMs have been developed at a fast pace both in theory and in practice. Many future works remain. In this section, we enumerate a few of the major research directions where major progress is being made and many research problems are still open.

3.7.1 Computational Efficiency

One of the initial drawbacks of the SVMs is its costly computational complexity in the training phase, which leads to inapplicable algorithms in the large datasets. However, this problem is being solved with great success. One approach is to break a large optimization problem into a series of smaller problems, where each problem only involves a couple of carefully chosen variables so that the optimization can be done efficiently. The process iterates until all the decomposed optimization problems are solved successfully.

A more recent approach is to consider the problem of learning SVMs as that of finding an approximate minimum enclosing ball of a set of instances [18–21]. These instances, when mapped to an N-dimensional space, represent a core set that can be used to construct an approximation to the minimum enclosing ball. Solving the SVMs' learning problems on these core sets can produce good approximation solutions in very fast speed. For example, the core vector machine [18] and the further ball vector machine [21] can learn SVMs for millions of data in seconds.

3.7.2 Kernel Selection

In the kernel SVMs, the selection of the kernel function is generally required to satisfy the Mercer's theorem. Hence, the common kernel functions involve three types, that is, sigmoid, polynomial, and radial basis functions, which may sometimes limit the applicability of the kernel trick. Recently, Pekalska et al. provided a novel view to design a kernel function based on a general proximity relation mapping [22]. The new kernel function needs neither be satisfied by the Mercer's conditions nor be limited to only one feature space, and shows better classification performance than the common Mercer kernels experimentally. However, the theoretical foundation of the new generalized kernel needs further research.

Furthermore, another popular approach is multiple kernel learning which considers more than one kernel; through the combinations one can achieve better results [23–29]. This is similar to using an ensemble of kernels. By setting the proper objective functions, better selection of the kernel parameters can be done to allow mixture kernels.

3.7.3 Generalization Analysis

We are accustomed to using the VC dimension to estimate the generalization error bound of the kernel machines. However, the bound involves a fixed complexity penalty which does not depend on the training data, which as a result, cannot be made universally effective [30]. To solve this problem, Rademacher's complexity is introduced as an alternative to evaluate the complexity of a classifier instead of the classical VC dimension [31–34], which is based on the intuition that we can measure the capacity (or complexity) of a classifier by its ability to fit random data. It is defined as follows:

Definition 3.7.1 (Rademacher Complexity) [35]. For the sample $S = \{\mathbf{x}_1, \ldots, \mathbf{x}_n\}$ generated by a distribution D on a set $\mathbf{X}$ and a real value function class F with domain $\mathbf{X}$, the empirical Rademacher complexity of F is the random variable

$$\hat{R}_n(\mathbf{F}) = E_{\boldsymbol{\sigma}}\left[\sup_{f \in F}\left|\frac{2}{n}\sum_{i=1}^{n}\sigma_i f(\mathbf{x}_i)\right| \,\middle|\, \mathbf{x}_1, \ldots, \mathbf{x}_n\right] \tag{3.47}$$

where $\boldsymbol{\sigma} = \{\sigma_1, \ldots, \sigma_n\}$ are independent uniform $\{\pm 1\}$-valued (Rademacher) random variables. The Rademacher complexity of F is

$$R_n(\mathbf{F}) = E_S[\hat{R}_n(\mathbf{F})] = E_{S\boldsymbol{\sigma}}\left[\sup_{f \in F}\left|\frac{2}{n}\sum_{i=1}^{n}\sigma_i f(\mathbf{x}_i)\right|\right] \tag{3.48}$$

The sup part inside the expectation formula measures the best correlation that can be found between a function of the class and the random labels. Furthermore, in the kernel machines, we can obtain an upper bound to the Rademacher complexity:

Theorem 3.7.2 ***Complexity Analysis*** [35]. *If $k : \mathbf{X} \times \mathbf{X} \to \mathbf{R}$ is a kernel, and $S = \{\mathbf{x}_1, \ldots, \mathbf{x}_n\}$ is a sample of points from $\mathbf{X}$, then the empirical Rademacher complexity of the classifier F_B satisfies*

$$\hat{R}_n(\mathbf{F}_B) \leq \frac{2B}{n}\sqrt{\sum_{i=1}^{n} k(\mathbf{x}_i, \mathbf{x}_i)} = \frac{2B}{n}\sqrt{tr(\mathbf{K})} \tag{3.49}$$

where B is the bound of the weights $\mathbf{w}$ in the classifier.

It is noteworthy that the bound of the Rademacher complexity only involves the trace of the corresponding kernel matrix, which is determined by the concrete training data. It is more feasible to use than the traditional VC dimension to control the complexity of a classifier as well as estimate the generalization performance.

3.7.4 Structural SVM Learning

Margin maximization is the initial motivation of the SVM algorithms [36]. Consequently, SVM (SVC) usually places more focus on the separability between the classes of samples but does not sufficiently use the prior data distribution information within classes. The well-known "No Free Lunch" theorem [12] indicates that there does not exist a pattern classification method that is inherently superior to any other, or even to random guessing without using additional information. It is the type of problem, prior information, and the amount of training samples that determine the form of classifier to apply. In fact, corresponding to different real-world problems, different classes may have different underlying data structures. A classifier should adjust the discriminant boundaries to fit the structures which are vital for classification, especially for the generalization capacity of the classifier. However, the traditional SVM does not differentiate the structures, and the derived decision hyperplane lies unbiasedly right in the middle of the support vectors [36,37], which may lead to a nonoptimal classifier in the real-world problems.

Recently, some algorithms have been developed to give more concern to the structural information than the traditional SVM. They provide a novel view to design a classifier, where the classifier can be sensitive to the structure of the data distribution. These algorithms are mainly divided into two approaches. The first approach is through manifold learning. It assumes that the data actually live on a submanifold in the input space, and the most typical algorithm involves Laplacian support vector machines (LapSVM) [38,39]. We can construct LapSVM first through a Laplacian graph in each class. Then we introduce a manifold structure of the data within the corresponding Laplacian matrices into the traditional framework of SVM as an additional term.

The second approach is by exploiting clustering algorithms [40] by assuming that the data contain several clusters that hold the prior distribution information. This assumption seems more general than the manifold assumption, which has in fact led to several popular large margin machines. A recent approach is known as *structured large margin machine* (SLMM) [37]. SLMM applies clustering techniques to capture the structural information in the different classes first. It then uses the Mahalanobis distance as a distance measure from the samples to the decision hyperplanes, instead of the traditional Euclidean distance, to introduce the involved structure information into the constraints. Some popular large margin machines, such as support vector machine minimax probability machine (MPM) [41], and maxi-min margin machine (M^4) [36], can all be viewed as the special cases of SLMM. Experimentally, SLMM has shown better classification performance. However, since the optimization problem of SLMM is formulated as sequential second order cone programming (SOCP) rather than the QP in SVM, SLMM has much higher computational cost in training time as compared to traditional SVM. Furthermore, it is not easy to be generalized to large-scale or multiclass problems. Consequently, a novel structural support vector machine (SSVM) was developed in [42] to exploit the classical framework of SVM rather than as constraints in SLMM. As a result, the corresponding optimization problem can still be solved by the QP as in SVM, and keep the solution not only sparsity but also scalability. Furthermore, SSVM has been shown to be theoretically and empirically better in generalization than SVM and SLMM.

3.8 Exercises

1. Consider a simple binary classification problem:

$$c_1 : (1, 1)^T \quad (-1, 3)^T \quad (2, 6)^T$$

$$c_2 : (-1, -2)^T \quad (1, -3)^T \quad (-5, -7)^T$$

   (a) Compute the optimal hyperplane and geometrical margin.
   (b) Point out the support vectors.
   (c) Using the method of Lagrange multipliers, compute the solution in the dual space.

2. Consider another binary classification problem:

$$c_1 : (1, 1)^T \quad (3, 7)^T \quad (5, 9)^T$$

$$c_2 : (-1, -2)^T \quad (1, 6)^T \quad (2, -1)^T$$

   Use a soft margin SVC to construct the optimal hyperplane and compute the corresponding solution in the dual space.

3. Construct a simple XOR problem similar to Example 3.3.3, and discuss how the selection of the kernel parameter in the radial basis kernel can influence the classification performance.

4. Let $\mathbf{K}_1$ and $\mathbf{K}_2$ be the kernels in $\mathbf{X} \times \mathbf{X}, \mathbf{X} \subseteq \mathbf{R}^n$, $a \in \mathbf{R}^+$, $f(\cdot)$ be a real value function in $\mathbf{X}$:

$$\phi : \mathbf{X} \to \mathbf{R}^m$$

where $\mathbf{K}_3$ is a kernel in $\mathbf{R}^m \times \mathbf{R}^m$, and $\mathbf{B}$ is an $n \times n$ symmetrical semidefinite matrix. Prove the following functions are kernel functions:

   (a) $\mathbf{K}(\mathbf{x}, \mathbf{z}) = \mathbf{K}_1(\mathbf{x}, \mathbf{z}) + \mathbf{K}_2(\mathbf{x}, \mathbf{z})$
   (b) $\mathbf{K}(\mathbf{x}, \mathbf{z}) = \mathbf{a}\mathbf{K}_1(\mathbf{x}, \mathbf{z})$
   (c) $\mathbf{K}_1(\mathbf{x}, \mathbf{z})\mathbf{K}_2(\mathbf{x}, \mathbf{z})$
   (d) $\mathbf{K}(\mathbf{x}, \mathbf{z}) = f(\mathbf{x})f(\mathbf{z})$
   (e) $\mathbf{K}(\mathbf{x}, \mathbf{z}) = \mathbf{K}_3(\phi(\mathbf{x}), \phi(\mathbf{z}))$
   (f) $\mathbf{K}(\mathbf{x}, \mathbf{z}) = \mathbf{x}^T\mathbf{B}\mathbf{z}$

5. Discuss the generalization bounds of SVR derived from the VC theorem.
6. We have discussed the use of SVC for binary classification problems. Discuss how to extend SVC to solve multiclass classification problems.
7. Discuss the robustness properties of SVM algorithms.
8. Discuss the cases that SVC does not sufficiently use the prior data distribution information within classes, where the resulting discriminant hyperplane lies right in the middle of the support vectors.

References

[1] V. Vapnik. *The Nature of Statistical Learning Theory*, Springer Verlag, 1995.

[2] V. Vapnik. *Statistical Learning Theory*, Wiley, 1998.

[3] B. Schölkopf, C.J.C. Burges, and A.J. Smola. *Advances in Kernel Methods—Support Vector Learning*, MIT Press, 1999.

[4] O. Chapelle, P. Haffner, and V. Vapnik. Support vector machines for histogram-based image classification. *IEEE Trans. on Neural Networks*, vol. 10(3.5), 1055–1064, 1999.

[5] C. Cortes and V. Vapnik. Support vector networks. *Machine Learning*, vol. 20, 273–297, 1995.

[6] N. Cristianini, C. Campbell, and J. Shawe-Taylor. A multiplicative updating algorithm for training support vector machine. In *Proceedings of the 6th European Symposium on Artificial Neural Networks (ESANN)*, 1999.

[7] N. Cristianini and J. Shawe-Taylor. *An Introduction to Support Vector Machines and Other Kernel-based Learning Methods*, Cambridge University Press, 2000.

[8] M.S. Kearns, S.A. Solla, and D.A. Cohn. *Advances in Neural Information Processing Systems*, MIT Press, 1999.

[9] U.M. Fayyad, G. Piatetsky-Shapiro, P. Smythand, and R. Uthurusamy. *Advances in Knowledge Discovery and Data Mining*, MIT Press, 1996.

[10] A.J. Smola, P. Bartlett, B. Schölkopf, and C. Schuurmans. *Advances in Large Margin Classifiers*, MIT Press, 1999.

[11] B. Schölkopf. *Support Vector Learning*, R. Oldenbourg Verlag, 1997.

[12] R.O. Duda, P.E. Hart, and D.G. Stork. *Pattern Classification*, Wiley, 2001.

[13] S. Haykin. *Neural Networks: A Comprehensive Foundation*, Tsinghua University Press, 2001.

[14] V. Cherkassky, X. Shao, F. Mulier, and V. Vapnik. Model complexity control for regression using VC generalization bounds. *IEEE Transactions on Neural Networks*, vol. 10, 1075–1089, 1999.

[15] V. Cherkassky and F. Mulier. *Learning From Data: Concepts, Theory and Methods,* Wiley, 1998.

[16] C.-C. Chang and C.-J. Lin. LibSVM: A library for support vector machines. Software available at http://www.csie.ntu.edu.tw/~cjlin/libsvm, 2001.

[17] T. Joachims. Making Large-scale SVM learning practical. *Advances in Kernel Methods—Support Vector Learning*, B. Schölkopf, C. Burges, and A. Smola (eds.), MIT Press, 1999.

[18] I. W. Tsang, J.T. Kwok, and P.-M. Cheung. Core vector machines: Fast SVM training on very large data sets. *Journal of Machine Learning Research*, vol. 6, 363–392, 2005.

[19] I.W. Tsang, J.T. Kwok, and K.T. Lai. Core vector regression for very large regression problems. *ICML*, 913–920, 2005.

[20] I.W. Tsang and J.T. Kwok. Large-scale sparsified manifold regularization. *NIPS*, Vancouver, Canada, 2006.

[21] I.W. Tsang, A. Kocsor, and J.T. Kwok. Simpler core vector machines with enclosing balls. *ICML*, 2007.

[22] E. Pekalska, P. Paclik, and R.P.W. Duin. A generalized kernel approach to dissimilarity-based classification. *Journal of Machine Learning Research*, vol. 2, 175–211, 2001.

[23] J. Bi, T. Zhang, and K. Bennett. Column-generation boosting methods for mixture of kernels. *KDD*, 521–526, 2004.

[24] I.M. de Diego, J.M. Moguerza, and A. Munoz. Combining kernel information for support vector classification. Multiple Classifier Systems, 102–111, 2004.

[25] Y. Grandvalet and S. Canu. Adaptive scaling for feature selection in SVMs. *Neural Information Processing Systems*, 2002.

[26] G.R.G. Lanckriet, T.D. Bie, N. Cristianini, M.I. Jordan, and W.S. Noble. A statistical framework for genomic data fusion. *Bioinformatics*, vol. 20(3.16), 2626–2635, 2004.

[27] G.R.G. Lanckriet, N. Cristianini, P. Bartlett, L.E. Ghaoui, and M.I. Jordan. Learning the kernel matrix with semidefinite programming. *JMLR*, vol. 5, 27–72, 2004.

[28] C.S. Ong, A.J. Smola, and R.C. Williamson. Learning the kernel with hyperkernels. *JMLR*, vol. 6, 1043–1071, 2005.

[29] Z. Wang, S. Chen, and T. Sun. MultiK-MHKS: A novel multiple kernel learning algorithm. *IEEE Transactions on Pattern Analysis and Machine Intelligence*, vol. 30(3.2), 348–353, 2008.

[30] P.L. Bartlett and S. Mendelson. Rademacher and Gaussian complexities: Risk bounds and structural results. *Journal of Machine Learning Research*, vol. 3, 463–482, 2002.

[31] P.L. Bartlett. The sample complexity of pattern classification with neural networks: The size of the weights is more important than the size of the network. *IEEE Transactions on Information Theory*, vol. 44(3.2), 525–536, 1998.

[32] V. Koltchinskii. Rademacher penalties and structural risk minimization. *IEEE Transactions Information Theory*, vol. 47(3.5), 1902–1914, 2001.

[33] V. Koltchinskii and D. Panchenko. Empirical margin distributions and bounding the generalization error of combined classifiers. Technical Report, Department of Mathematics and Statistics, University of New Mexico, 2000a.

[34] V. Koltchinskii and D. Panchenko. Rademacher processes and bounding the risk of function learning. In E. Gine, D. Mason, and J. Wellner (ed.), *High Dimensional Probability II*, 443–459, 2000b.

[35] J. Shawe-Taylor and N. Cristianini. *Kernel Methods for Pattern Analysis*. Cambridge University Press, 2004.

[36] K. Huang, H. Yang, I. King, and M.R. Lyu. Learning large margin classifiers locally and globally. *ICML*, 2004.

[37] D.S. Yeung, D. Wang, W.W.Y. Ng, E.C.C. Tsang, and X. Zhao. Structured large margin machines: Sensitive to data distributions. *Machine Learning*, vol. 68, 171–200, 2007.

[38] M. Belkin, P. Niyogi, and V. Sindhwani. Manifold regularization: A geometric framework for learning from examples. Department of Computer Science, University of Chicago, Tech. Rep, TR-2004-06, 2004.

[39] M. Belkin, P. Niyogi, and V. Sindhwani. On manifold regularization. In *Proceedings of International Workshop on Artificial Intelligence and Statistics*, 2005.

[40] P. Rigollet. Generalization error bounds in semi-supervised classification under the cluster assumption. *Journal of Machine Learning Research*, vol. 8, 1369–1392, 2007.

[41] G.R.G. Lanckriet, L.E. Ghaoui, C. Bhattacharyya, and M.I. Jordan. A robust minimax approach to classification. *Journal of Machine Learning Research*, vol. 3, 555–582, 2002.

[42] H. Xue, S. Chen, and Q. Yang. Structural support vector machine. *The Fifth International Symposium on Neural Networks*, Part I, LNCS5263, 2008.

Chapter 4

Apriori

Hiroshi Motoda and Kouzou Ohara

Contents

4.1 Introduction

Many of the pattern finding algorithms such as those for decision tree building, classification rule induction, and data clustering that are frequently used in data mining have been developed in the machine learning research community. Frequent pattern and association rule mining is one of the few exceptions to this tradition. Its introduction boosted data mining research and its impact is tremendous. The basic algorithms are simple and easy to implement. In this chapter the most fundamental algorithms of frequent pattern and association rule mining, known as Apriori and AprioriTid [3, 4], and Apriori's extension to sequential pattern mining, known as AprioriAll [6, 5], are explained based on the original papers with working examples, and performance analysis of Apriori is shown using a freely available implementation [1] for a dataset in UCI repository [8]. Since Apriori is so fundamental and the form of database is limited to market transaction, there have been many works for improving computational efficiency, finding more compact representation, and extending the types of data that can be handled. Some of the important works are also briefly described as advanced topics.

4.2 Algorithm Description

4.2.1 Mining Frequent Patterns and Association Rules

One of the most popular data mining approaches is to find frequent itemsets from a transaction dataset and derive association rules. The problem is formally stated as follows. Let $\mathcal{I} = \{i_1, i_2, \ldots, i_m\}$ be a set of items. Let $\mathcal{D}$ be a set of transactions, where each transaction t is a set of items such that $t \subseteq \mathcal{I}$. Each transaction has a unique identifier, called its *TID*. A transaction t contains X, a set of some items in $\mathcal{I}$, if $X \subseteq t$. An association rule is an implication of the form $X \Rightarrow Y$, where $X \subset \mathcal{I}$, $Y \subset \mathcal{I}$, and $X \cap Y = \emptyset$. The rule $X \Rightarrow Y$ holds in $\mathcal{D}$ with confidence c $(0 \leq c \leq 1)$ if the fraction of transactions that also contain Y in those which contain X in $\mathcal{D}$ is c. The rule $X \Rightarrow Y$ (and equivalently $X \cup Y$) has support[1] s $(0 \leq s \leq 1)$ in $\mathcal{D}$ if the fraction of transactions in $\mathcal{D}$ that contain $X \cup Y$ is s. Given a set of transactions $\mathcal{D}$, the problem of mining association rules is to generate all association rules that have support and confidence no less than the user-specified minimum support (called *minsup*) and minimum confidence (called *minconf*), respectively.

Finding frequent[2] itemsets (itemsets with support no less than *minsup*) is not trivial because of the computational complexity due to combinatorial explosion. Once

[1] An alternative support definition is the absolute count of frequency. In this chapter the latter definition is also used where appropriate.

[2] The Apriori paper [3] uses "large" to mean "frequent," but large is often associated with the number of items in the itemset. Thus, we prefer to use "frequent."

frequent itemsets are obtained, it is straightforward to generate association rules with confidence no less than *minconf*. Apriori and AprioriTid, proposed by R. Agrawal and R. Srikant, are seminal algorithms that are designed to work for a large transaction dataset [3].

4.2.1.1 Apriori

Apriori is an algorithm to find all sets of items (itemsets) that have support no less than *minsup*. The support for an itemset is the ratio of the number of transactions that contain the itemset to the total number of transactions. Itemsets that satisfy minimum support constraint are called *frequent itemsets*. Apriori is characterized as a level-wise complete search (breadth first search) algorithm using anti-monotonicity property of itemsets: "If an itemset is not frequent, any of its superset is never frequent," which is also called the *downward closure property*. The algorithm makes multiple passes over the data. In the first pass, the support of individual items is counted and frequent items are determined. In each subsequent pass, a seed set of itemsets found to be frequent in the previous pass is used for generating new potentially frequent itemsets, called *candidate itemsets*, and their actual support is counted during the pass over the data. At the end of the pass, those satisfying minimum support constraint are collected, that is, frequent itemsets are determined, and they become the seed for the next pass. This process is repeated until no new frequent itemsets are found.

By convention, Apriori assumes that items within a transaction or itemset are sorted in lexicographic order. The number of items in an itemset is called its *size* and an itemset of size k is called a k-itemset. Let the set of frequent itemsets of size k be F_k and their candidates be C_k. Both F_k and C_k maintain a field, support count.

Apriori algorithm is given in Algorithm 4.1. The first pass simply counts item occurrences to determine the frequent 1-itemsets. A subsequent pass consists of two phases. First, the frequent itemsets F_{k-1} found in the $(k-1)$-th pass are used to generate the candidate itemsets C_k using the apriori-gen function. Next, the database is scanned and the support of candidates in C_k is counted. The subset function is used for this counting.

The apriori-gen function takes as argument F_{k-1}, the set of all frequent $(k-1)$-itemsets, and returns a superset of the set of all frequent k-itemsets. First, in the join steps, F_{k-1} is joined with F_{k-1}.

insert into C_k
select $p.\text{fitemset}_1, p.\text{fitemset}_2, \ldots, p.\text{fitemset}_{k-1}, q.\text{fitemset}_{k-1}$
from $F_{k-1}p, F_{k-1}q$
where $p.\text{fitemset}_1 = q.\text{fitemset}_1, \ldots, p.\text{fitemset}_{k-2} = q.\text{fitemset}_{k-2}$,
$p.\text{fitemset}_{k-1} < q.\text{fitemset}_{k-1}$

Here, $F_k p$ means that the itemset p is a frequent k-itemset, and $p.\text{fitemset}_k$ is the k-th item of the frequent itemset p.

Then, in the prune step, all the itemsets $c \in C_k$ for which some $(k-1)$-subset is not in F_{k-1} are deleted.

Algorithm 4.1 Apriori Algorithm

$F_1 = \{\text{frequent 1-itemsets}\}$;
for $(k = 2; F_{k-1} \neq \emptyset; k++)$ **do begin**
  C_k = apriori-gen(F_{k-1}); //New candidates
  foreach transaction $t \in \mathcal{D}$ **do begin**
    C_t = subset(C_k, t); //Candidates contained in t
    foreach candidate $c \in C_t$ **do**
      $c.count++$;
  end
  $F_k = \{c \in C_k \quad | c.count \geq minsup\}$;
end
Answer $= \cup_k F_k$;

The subset function takes as arguments C_k and a transaction t, and returns all the candidate itemsets contained in the transaction t. For fast counting, Apriori adopts a hash-tree to store the candidate itemsets C_k. Itemsets are stored in leaves. Every node is initially a leaf node, and the depth of the root node is defined to be 1. When the number of itemsets in a leaf node exceeds a specified threshold, the leaf node is converted to an interior node. An interior node at depth d points to nodes at depth $d + 1$. Which branch to follow is decided by applying a hash function to the d-th item of the itemset. Thus, each leaf node is ensured to contain at most a certain number of itemsets (to be precise, this is true only when creating an interior node takes place at depth d smaller than k), and an itemset in the leaf node can be reached by successively hashing each item in the itemset in sequence from the root. Once the hash-tree is constructed, the subset function finds all the candidates contained in a transaction t, starting from the root node. At the root node, every item in t is hashed, and each branch determined is followed one depth down. If a leaf node is reached, itemsets in the leaf that are in the transaction t are searched and those found are made reference to the answer set. If an interior node is reached by hashing the item i, items that come after i in t are hashed recursively until a leaf node is reached. It is evident that itemsets in the leaves that are never reached are not contained in t.

Clearly, any subset of a frequent itemset satisfies the minimum support constraint. The join operation is equivalent to extending F_{k-1} with each item in the database and then deleting those itemsets for which the $(k-1)$-itemset obtained by deleting the $(k-1)$-th item is not in F_{k-1}. The condition $p.\text{fitemset}_{k-1} < q.\text{fitemset}_{k-1}$ ensures that no duplication is made. The prune step where all the itemsets whose $(k-1)$-subsets are not in F_{k-1} are deleted from C_k does not delete any itemset that could be in F_k. Thus, $C_k \supseteq F_k$, and Apriori algorithm is correct.

The remaining task is to generate the desired association rules from the frequent itemsets. A straightforward algorithm for this task is as follows. To generate rules, all nonempty subsets of every frequent itemset f are enumerated and for every such subset a, a rule of the form $a \Rightarrow (f - a)$ is generated if the ratio of support(f) to support(a) is at least *minconf*. Here, note that the confidence of the rule $\hat{a} \Rightarrow (f - \hat{a})$ cannot be larger than the confidence of $a \Rightarrow (f - a)$ for any $\hat{a} \subset a$. This in turn means that for a rule $(f - a) \Rightarrow a$ to hold, all rules of the form $(f - \hat{a}) \Rightarrow \hat{a}$ must hold. Using this property, the algorithm to generate association rules is given in Algorithm 4.2.

Algorithm 4.2 Association Rule Generation Algorithm

```
H_1 = ∅ //Initialize
foreach; frequent k-itemset f_k, k ≥ 2 do begin
  A = (k − 1)-itemsets a_{k−1} such that a_{k−1} ⊂ f_k;
  foreach a_{k−1} ∈ A do begin
    conf = support(f_k)/support(a_{k−1});
    if (conf ≥ minconf) then begin
      output the rule a_{k−1} ⇒ (f_k − a_{k−1})
                with confidence = conf and support = support(f_k);
      add (f_k − a_{k−1}) to H_1;
    end
  end
  call ap-genrules(f_k, H_1);
end

Procedure ap-genrules(f_k: frequent k-itemset, H_m: set of m-item
                                    consequents)
if (k > m + 1) then begin
  H_{m+1} = apriori-gen(H_m);
  foreach h_{m+1} ∈ H_{m+1} do begin
    conf = support(f_k)/support(f_k − h_{m+1});
    if (conf ≥ minconf) then
      output the rule f_k − h_{m+1} ⇒ h_{m+1}
                with confidence = conf and support = support(f_k);
    else
      delete h_{m+1} from H_{m+1};
  end
  call ap-genrules(f_k, H_{m+1});
end
```

Apriori achieves good performance by reducing the size of candidate sets. However, in situations with very many frequent itemsets or very low minimum support, it still suffers from the cost of generating a huge number of candidate sets and scanning the database repeatedly to check a large set of candidate itemsets.

4.2.1.2 AprioriTid

AprioriTid is a variation of Apriori. It does not reduce the number of candidates but it does not use the database $\mathcal{D}$ for counting support after the first pass. It uses a new dataset $\overline{C}_k$. Each member of the set $\overline{C}_k$ is of the form $< TID, \{ID\} >$, where each ID is the identifier of a potentially frequent k-itemset present in the transaction with identifier TID except $k = 1$. For $k = 1$, $\overline{C}_1$ corresponds to the database $\mathcal{D}$, although conceptually each item i is replaced by the itemset $\{i\}$. The member of $\overline{C}_k$ corresponding to a transaction t is $< t.TID, \{c \in C_k | c \text{ contained in } t\} >$.

The intuition for using $\overline{C}_k$ is that it will be smaller than the database $\mathcal{D}$ for large values of k because some transactions may not contain any candidate k-itemset, in which case $\overline{C}_k$ does not have an entry for this transaction, or because very few candidates may be contained in the transaction and each entry may be smaller than the number of items in the corresponding transaction. AprioriTid algorithm is given in Algorithm 4.3. Here, $c[i]$ represents the i-th item in k-itemset c.

Algorithm 4.3 AprioriTid Algorithm

$F_1 = \{\text{frequent 1-itemsets}\}$;
$\overline{C}_1 = \text{database } \mathcal{D}$;
for $(k = 2; F_{k-1} \neq \emptyset; k++)$ **do begin**
  $C_k = \text{apriori-gen}(F_{k-1})$; //New candidates
  $\overline{C}_k = \emptyset$;
  foreach entry $t \in \overline{C}_{k-1}$ **do begin**
    // determine candidate itemsets in C_k contained
    // in the transaction with identifier t.TID
    $C_t = \{c \in C_k | (c - c[k]) \in t.\text{set-of-itemsets} \wedge$
        $(c - c[k-1]) \in t.\text{set-of-itemsets}\}$;
    foreach candidate $c \in C_t$ **do**
      $c.count++$;
    if $(C_t \neq \emptyset)$ **then** $\overline{C}_k += \langle t.\text{TID}, C_t \rangle$;
  end
  $F_k = \{c \in C_k \ | c.count \geq minsup \}$;
end
Answer $= \bigcup_k F_k$;

Each $\overline{C}_k$ is stored in a sequential structure. A candidate k-itemset c_k in C_k maintains two additional fields; generator and extensions, in addition to the field, support count. The generator field stores the *ID*s of the two frequent $(k-1)$-itemsets whose join generated c_k. The extension field stores the *ID*s of all the $(k+1)$-candidates that are extensions of c_k. When a candidate c_k is generated by joining f^1_{k-1} and f^2_{k-1}, their *ID*s are saved in the generator field of c_k and the *ID* of c_k is added to the extension field of f^1_{k-1}. The t.set-of-itemsets field of an entry t in $\overline{C}_{k-1}$ gives the *ID*s of all

$(k-1)$-candidates contained in *t.TID*. For each such candidate c_{k-1} the extension field gives T_k, the set of *ID*s of all the candidate k-itemsets that are extensions of c_{k-1}. For each c_k in T_k, the generator field gives the *ID*s of the two itemsets that generated c_k. If these itemsets are present in the entry for t.set-of-itemsets, it is concluded that c_k is present in transaction *t.TID*, and c_k is added to $\overline{C}_t$.

AprioriTid has an overhead to calculate $\overline{C}_k$ but an advantage that $\overline{C}_k$ can be stored in memory when k is large. It is thus expected that Apriori beats AprioriTid in earlier passes (small k) and AprioriTid beats Apriori in later passes (large k). Since both Apriori and AprioriTid use the same candidate generation procedure and therefore count the same itemsets, it is possible to make a combined use of these two algorithms in sequence. AprioriHybrid uses Apriori in the initial passes and switches to AprioriTid when it expects that the set $\overline{C}_k$ at the end of the pass will fit in memory.

4.2.2 Mining Sequential Patterns

Agrawal and Srikant extended Apriori algorithm to the problem of sequential pattern mining [6]. In Apriori there is no notion of sequence, and thus, the problem of finding which items appear together can be viewed as finding intratransaction patterns. Here, sequence matters and the problem of finding sequential patterns can be viewed as intertransaction patterns.

Each transaction consists of sequence-id, transaction-time, and a set of items. The same sequence-id has no more than one transaction with the same transaction-time. A *sequence* is an ordered list of itemsets. Thus, a sequence consists of a list of sets of characters (items), rather than being simply a list of characters. The length of a sequence is the number of itemsets in the sequence. A sequence of length k is called a k-sequence. Without loss of generality, the set of items is assumed to be mapped to a set of contiguous integers, and an itemset i is denoted by $(i_1 i_2 \ldots i_m)$ where i_j is an item. A sequence s is denoted by $\langle s_1 s_2 \ldots s_n \rangle$. A sequence $\langle a_1 a_2 \ldots a_n \rangle$ is contained in another sequence $\langle b_1 b_2 \ldots b_m \rangle$ $(n \leq m)$ if there exist integers $i_1 < i_2 < \cdots < i_n$ such that $a_1 \subseteq b_{i_1}, a_2 \subseteq b_{i_2}, \ldots, a_n \subseteq b_{i_n}$. All the transactions with the same sequence-id which are sorted by transaction-time together form a sequence (transaction sequence). A sequence-id supports a sequence s if s is contained in its transaction sequence. The support for a sequence is defined as the fraction of total number of sequence-ids that support this sequence. Likewise, the support for an itemset i is defined as the fraction of sequence-ids that have items in i in any one of their transactions. Note that this definition is different from that used in Apriori. Thus the itemset i and the 1-sequence $\langle i \rangle$ have the same support.

Given a transaction database $\mathcal{D}$, the problem of mining sequential patterns is to find the maximal[3] sequences among all sequences that satisfy a certain user-specified minimum support constraint. Each such maximal sequence represents a sequential pattern. A sequence satisfying the minimum support constraint is called a *frequent sequence* (not necessarily maximal), and an itemset satisfying the minimum support

[3]Later R. Agrawal and R. Srikant removed this constraint in their generalized sequential patterns (GSP) [32].

constraint is called a frequent itemset, or fitemset for short. Any frequent sequence must be a list of fitemsets.

The algorithm consists of five phases: (1) sort phase, (2) fitemset phase, (3) transformation phase, (4) sequence phase, and (5) maximal phase. The first three are preprocessing phases and the last one is a postprocessing phase.

In the sort phase, the database $\mathcal{D}$ is sorted with sequence-id as the major key and transaction-time as the minor key. In the fitemset phase, the set of all fitemsets is obtained using Apriori algorithm with the corresponding modification of counting a support, and is mapped to a set of contiguous integers. This makes comparing two fitemsets for equality in a constant time. Note that the set of all frequent 1-sequences are simultaneously found in this phase. In the transformation phase, each transaction is replaced by the set of all fitemsets that are in that transaction. If a transaction does not contain any fitemset, it is not retained in the transformed sequence. If a transaction sequence does not contain any fitemset, this sequence is removed from the transformed database, but it is still used in counting the total number of sequence-ids. After the transformation, a transaction sequence is represented by a list of sets of fitemsets. Each set of fitemsets is represented by $\{f_1, f_2, \ldots, f_n\}$, where f_i is an fitemset. This transformation is designed for efficiently testing which given frequent sequences are contained in a transaction sequence. The transformed database is denoted as $\mathcal{D}_T$.

The sequence phase is the main part where the frequent sequences are to be enumerated. Two families of algorithms are proposed: count-all and count-some. They differ in the way the frequent sequences are counted. Count-all algorithm counts all the frequent sequences, including nonmaximal sequences that must be pruned later, whereas count-some algorithm avoids counting sequences which are contained in a longer sequence because the final goal is to obtain only maximal sequences. Agrawal and Srikant developed one count-all algorithm called AprioriAll and two count-some algorithms called AprioriSome and DynamicSome. Here, only AprioriAll is explained due to the space limitation.

In the last maximal phase, maximal sequences are extracted from the set of all frequent sequences. The hash-tree (similar to the one used in the subset function in Apriori) is used to quickly find all subsequences of a given sequence.

4.2.2.1 AprioriAll

The algorithm is given in Algorithm 4.4. In each pass the frequent sequences from the previous pass are used to generate the candidate sequences and then their support is measured by making a pass over the database. At the end of the pass, the support of the candidates is used to determine the frequent sequences.

The apriori-gen-2 function takes as argument F_{k-1}, the set of all frequent $(k-1)$-sequences. First, join operation is performed as

insert into C_k

select p.fitemset$_1$, p.fitemset$_2$, ... , p.fitemset$_{k-1}$, q.fitemset$_{k-1}$

from $F_{k-1}p$, $F_{k-1}q$

where p.fitemset$_1$ = q.fitemset$_1$, ... , p.fitemset$_{k-2}$ = q.fitemset$_{k-2}$,

Algorithm 4.4 AprioriAll Algorithm

$F_1 = \{$frequent 1-sequences$\}$; // Result of fitemset phase
for ($k = 2$; $F_{k-1} \neq \emptyset$; $k{+}{+}$) **do begin**
  $C_k =$ apriori-gen-2(F_{k-1}); //New candidate sequences
  foreach transaction sequence $t \in \mathcal{D}_T$ **do begin**
    $C_t =$ subseq(C_k, t); //Candidate sequences contained in t
    foreach candidate $c \in C_t$ **do**
      $c.count{+}{+}$;
  end
  $F_k = \{c \in C_k \mid c.count \geq minsup\}$;
end
Answer = maximal sequences in $\cup_k F_k$;

then, all the sequences $c \in C_k$ for which some $(k-1)$-subsequence is not in F_{k-1} are deleted. The subseq function is similar to the subset function in Apriori. As in Apriori, the candidate sequences C_k are stored in a hash-tree to quickly find all candidates contained in a transaction sequence. Note that the transformed transaction sequence is a list of sets of fitemsets and all the fitemsets in a set have the same transaction-time, and no more than one transaction with the same transaction-time is allowed for the same sequence-id. This constraint has to be imposed in the subseq function.

4.2.3 Discussion

Both Apriori and AprioriTid need *minsup* and *minconf* to be specified in advance. The algorithms have to be rerun each time these values are changed, throwing everything away that was obtained in previous runs. If no appropriate values for these thresholds are known in advance and we want to know how the results change with these values without rerunning the algorithms, the best we can do is to generate and count only those itemsets that appear at least once in the database without duplication and store them all in an efficient way. Note that Apriori generates candidates that do not exist in the database.

Apriori and AprioriTid use a hash-tree to store the candidate itemsets. Another data structure that is often used is a trie-structure [35, 9]. Each node in the depth k of the trie corresponds to a candidate k-itemset and stores the k-th item and the support of the itemset. As two frequent k-itemsets that share the first $(k-1)$-itemsets are siblings below their parent node at the depth $k-1$ in the trie, the candidate generation is simply to join the two siblings, and extend the tree to one more depth below the first frequent k-itemset after pruning. In order to find the candidate k-itemsets that are contained in a transaction t, each item in the transaction is fed from the root node and the branch is followed according to the succeeding item until a k-th item is reached. Many practical implementations of Apriori use this trie-structure to store not only candidates but also transactions [10, 9].

If we go a step further, we can get rid of generating candidate itemsets at all. Further, it is not necessary to enumerate all the frequent itemsets. These topics are discussed in Section 4.5.

Apriori and almost all other association rule minings use two-phase strategy: first mine frequent patterns and then generate association rules. This is not the sole way. Webb's MagnumOpus uses another strategy that immediately generates a large subset of all association rules [38].

There are direct extensions of the original Apriori family. Use of taxonomy and incorporating temporal constraint are two examples. Generalized association rules [30] employ a set of user-specified taxonomies, which makes it possible to extract frequent itemsets that are expressed by higher concepts even when use of the base level concepts produces only infrequent itemsets. The basic algorithm is to add all ancestors of each item in a transaction to the transaction and then run Apriori algorithm. Several optimizations can be added to improve efficiency, one example being that the support for an itemset X that contains both an item x and its ancestor $\hat{x}$ is the same as the support of the itemset $X - \hat{x}$, and thus need not be counted. Generalized sequential patterns [32] place, in addition to the introduction of taxonomies, time constraints that specify a minimum and/or maximum time period between adjacent elements (itemsets) in a pattern and relax the restrictions that items in an element of a sequential pattern must come from the same transaction by allowing the items to be present in a set of transactions of the same sequence-id whose transaction-times are within a user-specified time window. It also finds all frequent sequential patterns (not limited to maximal sequential patterns). GSP algorithm runs about 20 times faster than AprioriAll, one reason being that GSP counts fewer candidates than AprioriAll.

4.3 Discussion on Available Software Implementations

There are many available implementations of Apriori ranging from free software to commercial products. Here, we will present only three well-known implementations which are freely downloadable via Internet.

The first one is an implementation embedded in the most famous open-source machine learning and data mining toolkit, Weka, provided by the University of Waikato [40]. Apriori in Weka can be used through Weka's common graphical user interface together with many other algorithms that are available in Weka. The implementation includes Weka's own extensions. For example, *minsup* is iteratively decreased from an upper bound U_{minsup} to a lower bound L_{minsup} with an interval δ_{minsup}. Further, in addition to confidence the metrics lift, leverage, and conviction are available to evaluate association rules. Lift and leverage are discussed in Section 4.5. Conviction [11] is a metric that was proposed to measure the departure from independence of an association rule taking implication into account. When using one of these metrics, its minimal value has to be given as a threshold.

The second implementation is the one by Christian Borgelt [1], which is distributed under the terms of the GNU Lesser (Library) General Public License. This implementation is basically a command line application, and some graphical user interfaces are separately available. It essentially follows the flow of the original Apriori, but has its own extensions, too, to make it faster and to reduce its memory use. It employs a trie called the prefix tree to store both transactions and itemsets for efficient support counting [10]. The prefix tree is slightly different from the trie explained in Subsection 4.2.3. Optionally, the user can choose to use a simple list instead of a prefix tree to store transactions. Furthermore, this implementation can find not only frequent itemsets and association rules, but also closed itemsets, and maximal itemsets. Closed and maximal itemsets are discussed in Section 4.5. In addition, several metrics other than confidence, such as information gain, are also available in this implementation to evaluate and select association rules.

The third implementation is the one by Fence Bodon, which is freely distributed for research purposes [2]. This implementation is also trie-based, similar to Borgelt's, but adopts a trie with a simpler structure, and computes only frequent itemsets and association rules. It works as a command line application, and accepts four arguments. The first three are mandatory: an input file, including transactions, an output file, and *minsup*. The fourth is *minconf*, which is optional. If *minconf* is given, association rules are mined, as well as frequent itemsets; otherwise, it outputs only frequent itemsets. This implementation is written in C++ to provide object-oriented components which can be easily reused to develop other Apriori-based algorithms.

4.4 Two Illustrative Examples

4.4.1 Working Examples

We will illustrate the detailed behavior of the aforementioned algorithms using a small database shown in Table 4.1, where SID and TT mean the sequence-id and transaction-time, respectively. We use this database in both association rule (frequent itemset) mining and maximal sequential pattern mining. In the former case SID and TT are ignored.

4.4.1.1 Frequent Itemset and Association Rule Mining

Suppose that we want to find frequent itemsets under $minsup = 0.2$ and association rules with $minconf = 0.6$.

Apriori (Algorithm 4.1)
Apriori first scans the whole database and derives a set of frequent 1-itemsets appearing in at least three transactions, $F_1 = \{a, c, d, f, g\}$. From this F_1, the apriori-gen function derives a set of candidate frequent 2-itemsets $C_2 = \{ac, ad, af, ag, cd, cf, cg, df, dg, fg\}$. C_2 consists of all possible pairs of elements of F_1 since no pruning is made at this stage.

TABLE 4.1 A Transaction Database of the Working Example

TID	SID	TT	Items
001	1	May 03	*c*, *d*
002	1	May 05	*f*
003	4	May 05	*a*, *c*
004	3	May 05	*c*, *d*, *f*
005	2	May 05	*b*, *c*, *f*
006	3	May 06	*d*, *f*, *g*
007	4	May 06	*a*
008	4	May 07	*a*, *c*, *d*
009	3	May 08	*c*, *d*, *f*, *g*
010	1	May 08	*d*, *e*
011	2	May 08	*b*, *d*
012	3	May 09	*d*, *g*
013	1	May 09	*e*, *f*
014	3	May 10	*c*, *d*, *f*

Next, Apriori computes their support by scanning the database using the subset function, which utilizes a hash-tree. Figure 4.1 briefly illustrates how a hash-tree is constructed and used. Suppose that the elements of C_2 are added into the hash-tree in lexicographic order, and the maximum number of itemsets allowed to be in a leaf node is 4. Thus, the number of itemsets in the root (leaf) node exceeds the threshold when the fifth itemset *cd* is to be added. Then, the node is converted into an interior

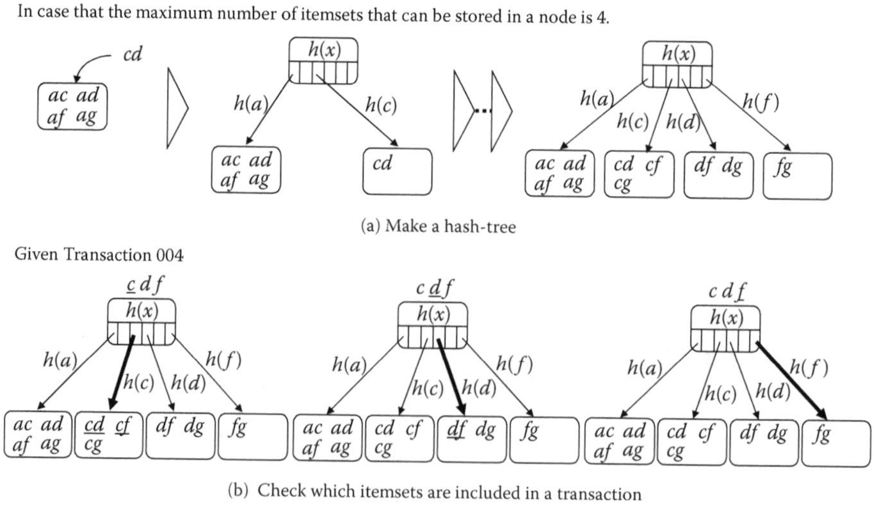

Figure 4.1 Example of hash-tree.

one, and each itemset branches into the corresponding new leaf node according to the hash value given by the function $h(x)$, where x is an item, the first item in each itemset in this case. We assume that $h(x)$ is given in advance and is common for all nodes. Since the first four itemsets share the same first item a, they fall into the same leaf node, while cd falls into a different one. When checking which of the candidates are included in a transaction, for example, Transaction 004, each item in the transaction is hashed at the root node. For example, by hashing c in cdf, it reaches the second left leaf node, and two itemsets cd and cf are found to be subsets of cdf as shown in the left tree of Figure 4.1(b). Next, by hashing d, df is found in the third left leaf node (the middle tree), but by hashing f, no subset of cdf is found in the rightmost leaf node (the right tree). As a result, the support counts of these itemsets found, cd, cf, and df, are increased by 1. Note that, after all the transactions have been processed, the frequencies of the candidates af and ag are found to be 0. This means that Apriori may generate candidates that do not exist in a given database.

After this support counting, $F_2 = \{cd, cf, df, dg\}$ is derived. These frequent 2-itemsets in F_2 are used as the seeds of frequent 3-itemsets. The itemsets cd and cf in F_2 sharing the first item c are joined and yield a new candidate cdf by apriori-gen because df is also included in F_2. The itemsets df and dg are also joined as well, but the resulting condidate is pruned because its subset fg is not included in F_2. Consequently, C_3, a set of candidate frequent 3-itemsets, consists of cdf only. Then, Apriori counts its support by scanning the database again, and derives $F_3 = \{cdf\}$. No candidate frequent 4-itemsets can be generated from this F_3 because it contains only one itemset. Thus, Apriori terminates.

AprioriTid (Algorithm 4.3)

Apriori has to scan the whole database three times to obtain these frequent itemsets, but AprioriTid (Algorithm 4.3) scans it only once for the first pass, and makes and uses new datasets $\overline{C}_1$ and $\overline{C}_2$ to count the support of candidates in C_2 and C_3, respectively. Figure 4.2 illustrates how AprioriTid finds frequent itemsets from these datasets. $\overline{C}_2$ is generated while counting the support of each candidate in C_2, whereas $\overline{C}_1$ is generated directly from the given database. Suppose $t = \langle 001, \{\{c\}, \{d\}\}\rangle \in \overline{C}_1$. Then, a candidate cd in C_2 is added to C_t because t.set-of-itemsets ($\{\{c\}, \{d\}\}$) contains both 1-itemsets constituting cd. More precisely, cd is added to C_t because it is a union of two 1-itemsets in t, which means Transaction 001 supports cd. No other candidate is added to C_t as Transaction 001 does not support any other candidate in C_2. Then, the support count of cd is increased by 1, and $\langle 001, \{\{cd\}\}\rangle$ is added to $\overline{C}_2$. Similarly, $\langle 003, \{\{ac\}\}\rangle$ is added to $\overline{C}_2$ because Transaction 003 supports $ac \in C_2$, although an entry corresponding to $\langle 002, \{\{f\}\}\rangle$ of $\overline{C}_1$ is not because Transaction 002 does not support any 2-itemsets. Eventually, $\overline{C}_2$ has 9 entries, as shown in Figure 4.2, whose size is smaller than that of the given database. $\overline{C}_3$ is generated in the same manner during the support counting of candidates in C_3. Since the unique candidate in C_3 is cdf, only the three entries of $\overline{C}_2$, including both cd and cf, whose union is cdf, survive in $\overline{C}_3$. Note that $\overline{C}_3$ is generated, but actually never used because C_4 becomes empty.

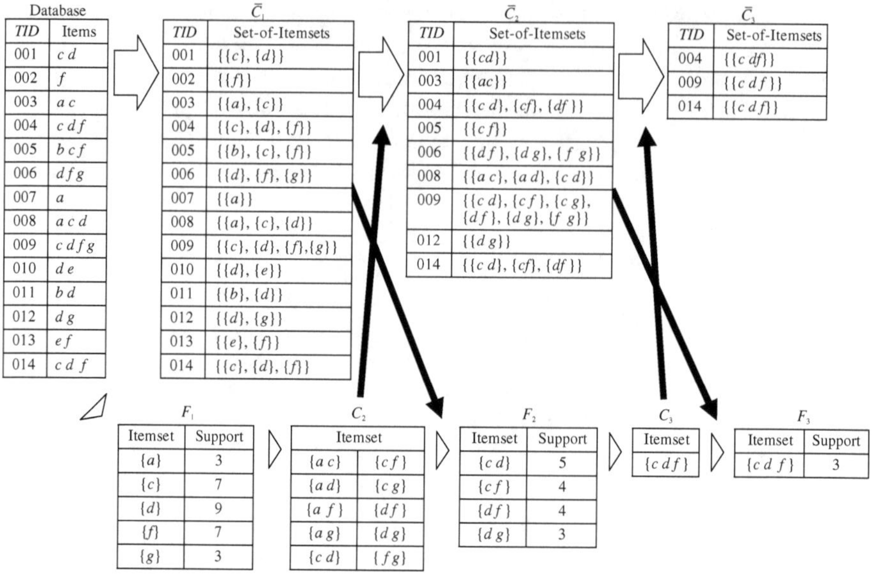

Figure 4.2 Example of AprioriTid.

Association rules (Algorithm 4.2)

Next, association rules are generated from the found frequent itemsets according to Algorithm 4.2 for the given $minconf = 0.6$. Let us consider frequent 2-itemsets, cd, cf, df, and dg, first. It is obvious that only two kinds of rules can be generated from each itemset. Table 4.2 summarizes the resulting rules and their confidence. The association rules 1 and 8 are the outputs by Algorithm 4.2 because they satisfy the $minconf$ constraint. The procedure ap-genrules is called for each of these satisfactory rules, but it outputs nothing because it no longer generates other rules from the 2-itemsets.

Then, Algorithm 4.2 tries to generate association rules from the frequent 3-itemset, cdf. First, it generates three association rules with 1-item consequent as shown in the left half of Table 4.3. Algorithm 4.2 returns all of them as they satisfy the $minconf$ constraint. After that, the procedure ap-genrules is called, taking cdf and $\{c, d, f\}$

TABLE 4.2 Association Rules Generated from Frequent 2-Itemsets

No.	Rule	Confidence	No.	Rule	Confidence
1	$c \Rightarrow d$	0.71	5	$d \Rightarrow f$	0.44
2	$d \Rightarrow c$	0.56	6	$f \Rightarrow d$	0.57
3	$c \Rightarrow f$	0.57	7	$d \Rightarrow g$	0.33
4	$f \Rightarrow c$	0.57	8	$g \Rightarrow d$	1.0

TABLE 4.3 Association Rules Generated from Frequent 3-Itemsets

1-Item Consequent			2-Item Consequent		
No.	**Rule**	**Confidence**	**No.**	**Rule**	**Confidence**
9	$cd \Rightarrow f$	0.60	12	$f \Rightarrow cd$	0.43
10	$cf \Rightarrow d$	0.75	13	$d \Rightarrow cf$	0.33
11	$df \Rightarrow c$	0.75	14	$c \Rightarrow df$	0.43

as its arguments. A set of 2-itemsets $\{cd, cf, df\}$ is derived by the function apriori-gen called within ap-genrules, each of which is used as the consequent of a new association rule. The resulting three rules are shown in the right half of Table 4.3. But, none of them can be the outputs because their confidence is less than the specified $minconf = 0.6$. Since 3-item consequents cannot be obtained from cdf, ap-genrules terminates, and Algorithm 4.2 terminates too because $F_4 = \emptyset$.

4.4.1.2 Sequential Pattern Mining

Next, we find frequent maximal sequential patterns from the same transaction database in Table 4.1 by using AprioriAll (Algorithm 4.4) for *minsup* = 0.3. Figure 4.3 illustrates the flow of the first three phases, that is, sort phase, fitemset phase, and

Original database

TID	SID	TT	Items
001	1	May 03	*c d*
002	1	May 05	*f*
003	4	May 05	*a c*
004	3	May 05	*c d f*
005	2	May 05	*b c f*
006	3	May 06	*d f g*
007	4	May 06	*a*
008	4	May 07	*a c d*
009	3	May 08	*c d f g*
010	1	May 08	*d e*
011	2	May 08	*b d*
012	3	May 09	*d g*
013	1	May 09	*e f*
014	3	May 10	*c d f*

Sorted database

SID	TID	TT	Items
1	001	May 03	*c d*
1	002	May 05	*f*
1	010	May 08	*d e*
1	013	May 09	*e f*
2	005	May 05	*b c f*
2	011	May 08	*b d*
3	004	May 05	*c d f*
3	006	May 06	*d f g*
3	009	May 08	*c d f g*
3	012	May 09	*d g*
3	014	May 10	*c d f*
4	003	May 05	*a c*
4	007	May 06	*a*
4	008	May 07	*a c d*

Frequent itemsets

Fitemset	Mapped To
(*c*)	1
(*d*)	2
(*c d*)	3
(*f*)	4
(*c f*)	5

Transformed database

SID	Sequence	Transformed sequence	After mapping
1	<(*c d*) (*f*) (*d e*) (*e f*)>	<{(c), (*d*), (*c d*)} {(*f*)} {(*d*)} {(*f*)}>	<{1, 2, 3} {4} {2} {4}>
2	<(*b c f*) (*b d*) >	<{(c), (*f*), (*c f*)} {(*d*)} >	<{1, 4, 5} {2} >
3	<(*c d f*) (*d f g*) (*c d f g*) (*d g*) (*c d f*)>	<{(c), (*d*), (*cd*), (*f*) , (*c f*)} {(*d*), (*f*)} {(c), (*d*), (*cd*), (*f*) , (*c f*)} {(*d*)} {(c), (*d*), (*cd*), (*f*) , (*c f*)}>	<{1, 2, 3, 4, 5} {2, 4)} {1, 2, 3, 4, 5} {2} {1, 2, 3, 4, 5}>
4	<(*a c*) (*a*) (*a c d*)>	<{(c)} {(c), (*d*) , (*cd*)}>	<{1} {1, 2 , 3}>

Figure 4.3 Transformation from the original database to the transformed database.

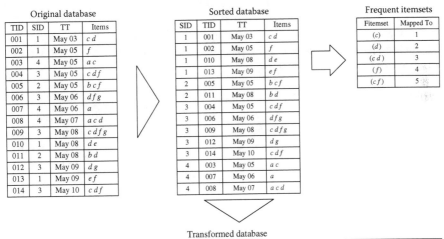

TABLE 4.4 Frequent Sequences and Candidate Sequences

F_1	C_2	F_2	C_3	F_3	C_4	F_4
⟨1⟩	⟨11⟩ ⟨12⟩ ⟨21⟩ ⟨13⟩ ⟨31⟩	⟨11⟩ ⟨12⟩	⟨111⟩ ⟨112⟩ ⟨113⟩ ⟨114⟩	⟨124⟩ ⟨142⟩	⟨1244⟩	⟨1424⟩
⟨2⟩	⟨14⟩ ⟨41⟩ ⟨15⟩ ⟨51⟩ ⟨22⟩	⟨13⟩ ⟨14⟩	⟨122⟩ ⟨132⟩ ⟨124⟩ ⟨142⟩	⟨144⟩ ⟨224⟩	⟨1424⟩	⟨2424⟩
⟨3⟩	⟨23⟩ ⟨32⟩ ⟨24⟩ ⟨42⟩ ⟨25⟩	⟨22⟩ ⟨32⟩	⟨134⟩ ⟨144⟩ ⟨222⟩ ⟨224⟩	⟨242⟩ ⟨324⟩	⟨2244⟩	⟨3424⟩
⟨4⟩	⟨52⟩ ⟨33⟩ ⟨34⟩ ⟨43⟩ ⟨35⟩	⟨24⟩ ⟨42⟩	⟨242⟩ ⟨322⟩ ⟨324⟩ ⟨342⟩	⟨342⟩ ⟨244⟩	⟨2424⟩	
⟨5⟩	⟨53⟩ ⟨44⟩ ⟨45⟩ ⟨54⟩ ⟨55⟩	⟨52⟩ ⟨34⟩	⟨244⟩ ⟨422⟩ ⟨424⟩ ⟨442⟩	⟨424⟩ ⟨344⟩	⟨3244⟩	
		⟨44⟩	⟨522⟩ ⟨344⟩ ⟨444⟩		⟨3424⟩	

transformation phase on this example. In the sort phase, transactions in the database are sorted with sequence-id (SID) as the major key and transaction-time (TT) as the minor key. Then, in the fitemset phase, fitemsets are derived in the similar manner to Apriori. Note that the support of an fitemset is the number of transaction sequences, including the itemset, but not the number of transactions including it. Thus, the resulting set of frequent 1-itemsets in this case is $\{c, d, f\}$. In the transformation phase, each transaction sequence is transformed into a list of sets of fitemsets as shown in the bottom of Figure 4.3 by replacing each transaction in the sequence with a set of fitemsets the transaction contains. Note that the second transaction is dropped in the transaction sequence 4 because it consists of only one nonfrequent itemset $\{a\}$.

AprioriAll generates a set of candidate sequences C_2 from F_1 by calling the function apriori-gen-2. The resulting C_2 is shown in Table 4.4. The function apriori-gen-2 is similar to apriori-gen, but differs in its join operation: The join operation of apriori-gen-2 generates two new k-sequences from two $(k-1)$-sequences whenever they are joinable, while the join operation of apriori-gen generates only one k-itemset from two $(k-1)$-itemsets. For example, when deriving C_2, both two sequences $\langle 12\rangle$ and $\langle 21\rangle$ are generated from $\langle 1\rangle$ and $\langle 2\rangle$. In addition, $\langle 11\rangle$ is also generated by joining the identical sequence $\langle 1\rangle$. This is necessary to generate a sequence in which multiple occurrences of an fitemset is allowed.

Counting the support of each candidate sequence is done in the similar way as Apriori using a hash-tree, and F_2, a set of frequent 2-sequences, is derived as shown in Table 4.4. This F_2 is used to generate a set of candidate sequences C_3 as well. Note that from $\langle 11\rangle$ and $\langle 12\rangle$, a 3-sequence $\langle 112\rangle$ is generated by joining them, but not $\langle 121\rangle$ because its subsequence $\langle 21\rangle$ is not included in F_2. This process consisting of the candidate generation and support counting is repeated until no more frequent sequences are derived. In this example, since no candidate of 5-sequences can be generated from F_4, F_5 becomes empty and thus, the iteration terminates. Finally, AprioriAll outputs $\langle 1424\rangle$, $\langle 2424\rangle$, $\langle 3424\rangle$, $\langle 11\rangle$, $\langle 13\rangle$, and $\langle 52\rangle$ as the maximal frequent sequences as the other frequent sequences are included in one of them.

4.4.2 Performance Evaluation

In this section, we discuss the performance of Apriori with respect to its runtime, the number of derived association rules and frequent itemsets when *minsup*, *minconf*, and the number of transactions are varied. We used the implementation by Christian Borgelt [1] for this assessment because it provides options that allow us to simulate a

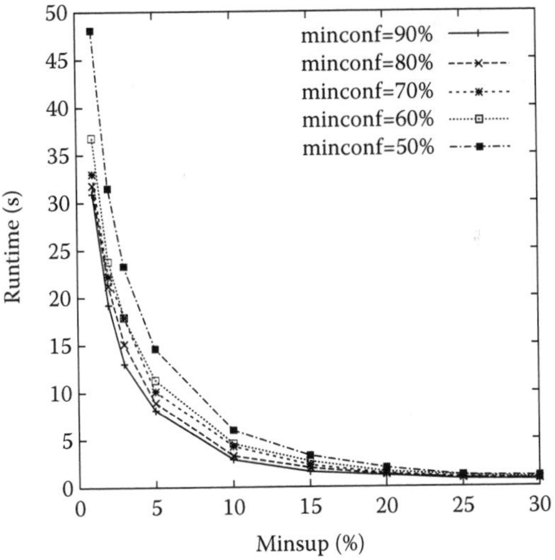

Figure 4.4 Runtime for various *minsup* and *minconf* values.

naive implementation closest to the original Apriori. Thus, we disabled its functions of sorting items with respect to their support and of filtering unused items from transactions.

As a benchmark dataset, we used the Mushroom dataset downloadable from UCI Machine Learning Repository [8], which contains 8124 cases with 23 nominal attributes including a class attribute. Each case is regarded as a transaction, and each attribute value of each case is converted into an item by joining it with the corresponding attribute name, for example, "cap-shape=x," where cap-shape is an attribute name and x is an attribute value. In 2480 cases, the attribute value of one attribute is missing. Since we ignored missing values, the transactions corresponding to them have 22 items, while the others have 23 items. Some attribute values have different meanings for different attributes. For example, "n" means "none" for the attribute "odor," while "brown" for "cap-color." As a result, the number of valid pairs of attribute name and attribute value, that is, number of distinct items, became 118.

First, we show the runtime of Apriori for various *minsup* and *minconf* values in Figure 4.4. All runtimes shown in this section were measured on a PC running Windows XP with 2.8 GHz Pentium IV and 4 GB memory. In these experiments, the maximal number of items per rule is set to 5 for convenience. We also limited the minimal number of items per rule to 2 in order to prevent a rule with no premise from being derived. In addition, a prefix tree was not used to store transactions. From the results, it is obvious that the change of *minconf* does not affect the runtime so much, but the runtime exponentially increases as *minsup* becomes smaller. The similar tendency is observed in Figure 4.5, showing the relation between *minsup* and the number of derived association rules. This is because the number of frequent itemsets exponentially increases as *minsup* becomes smaller, as shown in Figure 4.6.

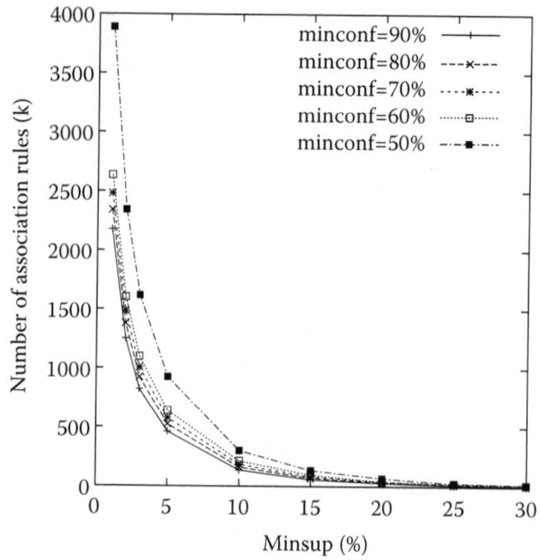

Figure 4.5 Number of association rules derived for various *minsup* and *minconf* values.

These results show that *minsup*, or the antimonotonicity property of itemsets, is very effective to prune nonfrequent itemsets.

Next, we show the relation between the runtime and the number of transactions in Figure 4.7. In this evaluation, we copied the original dataset multiple times (up to

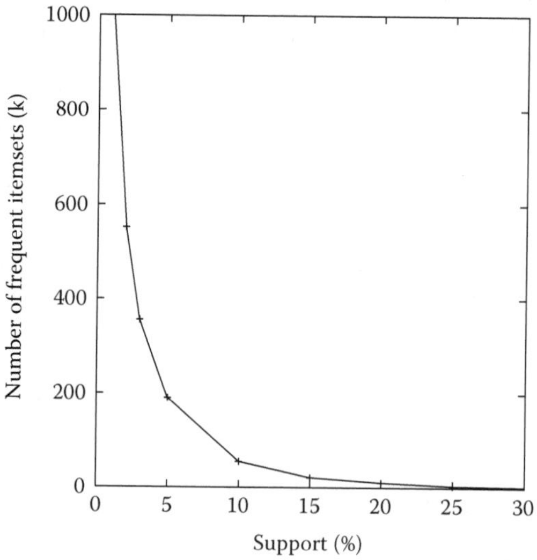

Figure 4.6 Number of frequent itemsets for various *minsup* values.

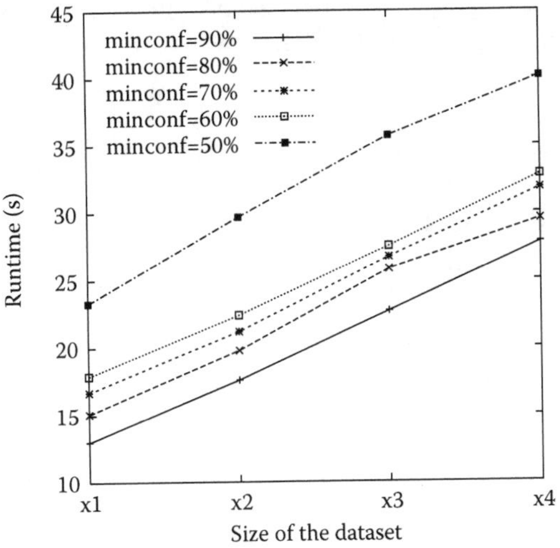

Figure 4.7 Runtime for various sizes of the dataset (*minsup* = 5).

4 times). Note that the fraction of each item remains the same for all datasets, so is the number of resulting association rules (frequent itemsets). Figure 4.7 shows that the runtime linearly increases as the number of transactions becomes larger. Consequently, under a certain distribution of items, *minsup* is much more influential to the runtime than both *minconf* and the number of transactions in Apriori.

Finally, we briefly mention association rules mined through the experiments, especially, for convenience, those which have only one item representing the class attribute in the consequent. The class value is either "edible" (e) or "poisonous" (p). A typical rule found under $minsup = 0.3$ and $minconf = 0.9$ is "odor = n gill-size = b ring-number = o ⇒ class = e," which is the simplest one among those whose consequent is "class = e," confidence is 1.0, and support is maximum (0.331). This rule means a mushroom is edible if its order is none, the size of its gill is broad, and the number of its rings is one. The attributes "odor" and "gill-size" appear as the first and the third test nodes, respectively, in the decision tree learned from this dataset by J48, a decision tree learner available in Weka, under its default setting. A similar rule "odor = n spore-print-color = w gill-size = b ⇒ class = e" can be derived from the decision tree and its confidence is 1.0, too, but it is true for only 528 cases, while the association rule is true for 2689 cases. On the other hand, no rule whose confidence is 1.0 and consequent is "class = p" was found under this setting because $minsup$ was too high. When setting $minsup = 0.2$, 470 such rules were found.

In general we can obtain a small number of association rules in a short runtime for a high *minsup*, but many of them could be trivial. To find more interesting rules, we have to use a smaller *minsup*, but it leads to an unacceptable runtime and a huge number of association rules, which in turn would make it harder to find interesting association rules. More efficient algorithms and better measures are required to find frequent itemsets and interesting association rules, which are the topics of the next section.

4.5 Advanced Topics

Since the first proposal of frequent pattern and association rule mining algorithm by Agrawal and Srikant, there have been many publications on various kinds of improvements, extensions, and applications, ranging from efficient scalable data mining methodologies, to handling a wide diversity of data types, various extended mining tasks, and a variety of new applications. Some of the important advanced topics are briefly described in this section. There are good tutorials and surveys for frequent pattern mining by Han et al. [16] and Goethals [15] that contain a substantial amount of references.

4.5.1 Improvement in Apriori-Type Frequent Pattern Mining

There have been many attempts to devise more efficient algorithms of frequent itemset mining in the framework of Apriori algorithm in that they generate candidates. These include hash-based technique, partitioning, sampling, and using vertical data format.

Hash-based technique can reduce the size of candidate itemsets. Each itemset is hashed into a corresponding bucket by using an appropriate hash function. Since a bucket can contain different itemsets, if its count is less than a minimum support, these itemsets in the bucket can be removed from the candidate sets. DHP [26] uses this idea.

Partitioning can be used to divide the entire mining problem into n smaller ones [29]. The dataset is divided into n nonoverlapping partitions such that each partition fits into main memory and each partition is mined separately. Since any itemset that is potentially frequent must occur as a frequent itemset in at least one of the partitions, all the frequent itemsets found this way are candidates, which can be checked by accessing the entire dataset only once.

Sampling is simply to mine a random sampled small subset of the entire data. Since there is no guarantee that we can find all the frequent itemsets, normal practice is to use a lower support threshold. Trade-off has to be made between accuracy and efficiency.

Vertical data format associates TID with each itemset, whereas Apriori uses a horizontal data format, that is, frequent itemsets are associated with each transaction. With the vertical data format, mining can be performed by taking the intersection of TIDs. The support count is simply the length of the TID set for the itemset. There is no need to scan the database because TID set carries the complete information required for computing support. This technique requires,

Algorithm 4.5 FP-Growth Algorithm: $F[I]$(FP-tree)

$F[I] = \emptyset$;
foreach $i \in \mathcal{I}$ that is in $\mathcal{D}$ in frequency increasing order **do begin**
  $F[I] = F[I] \cup \{I \cup \{i\}\}$;
  $\mathcal{D}^i = \emptyset$;
  $H = \emptyset$;
  foreach $j \in \mathcal{I}$ in $\mathcal{D}$ such that $j < i$ **do begin**
    // (j is more frequent than i)
    Select j for which support $(I \cup \{i, j\}) \geq minsup$;
    $H = H \cup \{j\}$;
  end
  foreach $(Tid, X) \in \mathcal{D}$ with $i \in X$ **do**
    $\mathcal{D}^i = \mathcal{D}^i \cup \{(Tid, \{X \setminus \{i\}\} \cap H)\}$;
  Construct conditional FP-tree from $\mathcal{D}^i$;
  Call $F[I \cup \{i\}]$(conditional FP-tree);
  $F[I] = F[I] \cup F[I \cup \{i\}]$(conditional FP-tree);
end

given a set of candidate itemsets, that their TIDs are available in main memory, which is of course not always the case. However, it is possible to significantly reduce the total size by using a depth-first search. Eclat [43] uses this strategy. In the depth-first approach, it is necessary to store at most the *TID* list of all k-itemsets with the same first $k-1$ items ($k-1$ prefix) at depth d with $k \leq d$ in the main memory.

4.5.2 Frequent Pattern Mining Without Candidate Generation

The most outstanding improvement over Apriori would be a method called *FP-growth* (frequent pattern growth) that succeeded in eliminating candidate generation [17, 18]. It adopts a divide and conquer strategy by (1) compressing the database representing frequent items into a structure called FP-tree (frequent pattern tree) that retains all the essential information and (2) dividing the compressed database into a set of conditional databases, each associated with one frequent itemset and mining each one separately. It scans the database only twice. In the first scan, all the frequent items and their support counts (frequencies) are derived and they are sorted in the order of descending support count in each transaction. In the second scan, items in each transaction are merged into an FP-tree and items (nodes) that appear in common in different transactions are counted. Each node is associated with an item and its count. Nodes with the same label are linked by a pointer called a node-link. Since items are sorted in the descending order of frequency, nodes closer to the root of the FP-tree are shared by more transactions, thus resulting in a very compact representation that stores all the necessary information. Pattern growth algorithm works on FP-tree by choosing an item in the order of increasing frequency and extracting frequent itemsets that contain the chosen item by recursively calling itself on the conditional FP-tree, that is, FP-tree conditioned to the chosen item. FP-growth is an order of magnitude faster than the original Apriori algorithm. The algorithm of FP-growth is given in Algorithm 4.5. $F[\emptyset]$(FP-tree) returns all the frequent itemsets. As noted easily, the divide and conquer strategy mentioned by Han et al. is equivalent to the depth-first search without candidate generation. The $\mathcal{D}^i$ is called i-projected database and generally much smaller than the FP-tree of the whole database. It is, thus, expected that $\mathcal{D}^i$ fits in the main memory even if the latter does not. The idea of pattern growth can also be applicable to closed itemset mining [27] (see Section 4.5.4) and sequential pattern mining [28] (see Section 4.5.8).

4.5.3 Incremental Approach

When the database is not stationary and a new batch of transactions keeps being added, it happens that some items that were frequent become no more frequent (losers) and some other items that were infrequent become frequent (winners). Rerunning Apriori or any other frequent pattern mining algorithm each time the database is updated is not efficient. The FUP algorithm in [12] provides a way to incrementally update the frequent itemsets using Apriori framework. It works efficiently on the updated database since the size of the increment database $\Delta\mathcal{D}$ is generally much smaller than the initial database $\mathcal{D}$.

Let F_k, F'_k be the frequent k-itemsets in $\mathcal{D}$ and $\mathcal{D} \cup \Delta\mathcal{D}$, respectively, and C_k be the candidate frequent itemsets in $\mathcal{D} \cup \Delta\mathcal{D}$. At k-th iteration, C_k can be generated from F'_{k-1} using apriori-gen function. Any itemset in F_k that contains any one of the losers of size $k-1$ (those which are in F_{k-1} but not in F'_{k-1}) as its subset are filtered out from F_k without checking $\Delta\mathcal{D}$. Frequency of the remaining itemsets in F_k are counted over $\Delta\mathcal{D}$ and those frequent in $\mathcal{D} \cup \Delta\mathcal{D}$ are identified (A), and excluded from C_k because we know that they are frequent. The remaining itemsets are those not in F_k. Their frequency is counted over $\Delta\mathcal{D}$ and those not frequent in $\Delta\mathcal{D}$ are removed from C_k because we know that they are infrequent in $\mathcal{D}$. Frequency of the remaining elements in C_k are counted over $\mathcal{D} \cup \Delta\mathcal{D}$ and the frequent ones are retained (B). F'_k is $A \cup B$. As can be seen above, FUP has to scan the updated database for each k, but the size of the C_k is expected to be very small. The experiment shows that it is only about 2 to 5% of that of rerunning Apriori for the updated database, and FUP runs 2 to 16 times faster than Apriori.

4.5.4 Condensed Representation: Closed Patterns and Maximal Patterns

An itemset (pattern) X is a maximal itemset if (1) there exists no itemset X' such that X' is a proper superset of X. An itemset (pattern) X is a closed itemset if (1) there exists no itemset X' such that X' is a proper superset of X and (2) every transaction containing X also contains X'. They are frequent if their support is no less than the *minsup*. A closed itemset satisfies $I(\mathcal{T}(X)) = X$, where $\mathcal{T}(X) = \{t \in \mathcal{D} | X \subseteq t\}$ and $I(S) = \bigcap_{t \in S} t$ for $S \subseteq \mathcal{D}$. For any two itemsets X and Y, if $X \subset Y$ and their support is the same, X is not a closed itemset. A closed itemset is a lossless representation, whereas a maximal itemset is not. Thus, once the closed itemsets are found, all the frequent itemsets can be derived from them. A rule $X \Rightarrow Y$ is an association rule on frequent closed itemsets if (1) both X and $X \cup Y$ are frequent closed itemsets, (2) there does not exist a frequent closed itemset Z such that $X \subset Z \subset (X \cup Y)$, and (3) the confidence of the rule is no less than *minconf*. The complete set of association rules can be generated once frequent closed itemsets are found.

CLOSET partitions the database and decomposes the problem into a set of subproblems, each with the corresponding conditional database, and it is known efficient [27]. First, all the frequent items are derived and sorted in the order of descending support count as f_list $= \langle i_1, i_2, \ldots, i_n \rangle$. The j-th subproblem $(1 \leq j \leq n)$ is to find the complete set of frequent closed itemsets containing i_{n+1-j} but no i_k (for $n+1-j < k \leq n$). The i_{n+1-j} conditional database is the subset of transactions containing i_{n+1-j}, where all the occurrences of infrequent items, item i_{n+1-j}, and items following i_{n+1-j} in the f_list are omitted. The corresponding FP-tree is generated and used for search. Each subproblem is recursively decomposed if necessary. The frequent closed itemsets are identified from the conditional database using the following properties. If X is a frequent closed itemset, there is no item appearing in every transaction in the X-conditional database. If an itemset Y is the maximal set of items appearing in every transaction in the X-conditional database, and $X \cup Y$ is not subsumed by some already found frequent closed itemset with identical support, $X \cup Y$ is a frequent closed itemset. As in FP-growth, further optimization is possible.

LCM is another algorithm, known to be the most efficient, to find the closed patterns (itemsets) [34]. It derives frequent closed itemsets via a closure operation without generating nonclosed itemsets. A closure of an itemset X, denoted by $Clo(X)$, is the unique smallest closed itemset including X, that is, $I(\mathcal{T}(X))$. Without loss of generality, we assume all items in a transaction database are uniquely indexed by contiguous natural numbers. Then, $X(i) = X \cap \{1, \ldots, i\}$ is called the *i-prefix* of X, which is the subset of X having only elements no greater than i. The *core index* of a closed itemset X, denoted by $core\_i(X)$, is the minimum index i such that $\mathcal{T}(X(i)) = \mathcal{T}(X)$. LCM generates, from a frequent closed itemset X, another frequent closed itemset Y such that $Y = Clo(X \cup \{i\})$ and $X(i-1) = Y(i-1)$, where i is an item that satisfies $i \notin X$ and $i > core\_i(X)$. Y is called the *prefix-preserving closure extension*, or ppc-extension for short, of X. LCM recursively applies this closure operation to closed itemsets from an empty itemset to larger ones in a depth-first manner. Completeness and nonredundancy of the enumeration of closed itemsets by LCM are guaranteed by the following property: If Y is a nonempty closed itemset, then there is just one closed itemset X such that Y is a ppc-extension of X. Since LCM generates a new frequent closed itemset Y from $\mathcal{T}(X)$ and a subset of $\mathcal{I}$, its time complexity to enumerate all frequent closed itemsets for X is $O(||\mathcal{T}(X)|| \times |\mathcal{I}|)$, where $||\mathcal{T}(X)||$ is the summation of size of each transaction included in $\mathcal{T}(X)$. Let $\mathcal{C}$ be a set of all frequent closed itemsets in $\mathcal{D}$. Then, the time complexity of LCM is linear in $|\mathcal{C}|$ with a factor depending on $||\mathcal{T}|| \times |\mathcal{I}|$. In fact, to improve the computation time and memory use, LCM incorporates three techniques: occurrence deliver, anytime database reduction, and fast prefix-preserving test. Occurrence deliver constructs

$\mathcal{T}(X \cup \{i\})$ for all i by scanning $\mathcal{T}(X)$ only once instead of scanning it for each i. Anytime database reduction reduces the size of the database by removing unnecessary transactions and items from it each time before an iteration starts with the current closed itemset to reduce both the computation time and memory use. Fast prefix-preserving test significantly reduces the number of items to be accessed to test the equality $X(i-1) = Y(i-1)$ by checking only items j such that $j < i, j \notin X(i-1)$ and they are included in the transaction of the minimum size in $\mathcal{T}(X \cup \{i\})$ instead of actually generating a closure when performing a ppc-extention. If an item j is included in every transaction in $\mathcal{T}(X \cup \{i\})$, then j is included in $Clo(X \cup \{i\})$, thus $X(i-1) \neq Y(i-1)$.

4.5.5 Quantitative Association Rules

When the item has a continuous numeric value, current frequent itemset mining algorithms are not applicable unless the values are discretized and appropriate intervals defined. This is known as *quantitative frequent itemset (QFI) mining*. The items can be both categorical and numeric. An example is {⟨ Age: [30,39] ⟩, ⟨ House-owner: Yes ⟩, ⟨ Married: Yes ⟩}, where an item is represented as ⟨ attribute: its value (range) ⟩. QFI mining was initially proposed in the study of mining quantitative association rules [31], but later density-based subspace clustering has commonly been applied because a QFI is viewed as an axis-parallel hyper-rectangular containing a cluster of transactions in a numeric attribute space. SUBCLUE [20] and QFIMiner [36] are two such examples. QFIMiner finds in $O(N \log N)$ all dense clusters of no less than *minsup* in all subspaces formed by both numeric and categorical attributes, where N is the number of transactions. An optimal value interval for each numeric item in each frequent itemset is obtained by Apriori-like level-wise algorithm with the antimonotonicity property of dense clusters. QFIMiner is shown to be faster than SUBCLUE and scales very well.

4.5.6 Using Other Measure of Importance/Interestingness

The problem of support-confidence framework is that there is no valid means to determine appropriate values for *minsup* and *minconf*. Especially setting *minsup* too high will miss important rules and setting it too low will generate too many rules. In fact, it is possible that a rule with infrequent itemsets is of great interest for some applications. Further, this framework fails to capture the notion of correlation. It can happen that a rule $X \Rightarrow Y$ which satisfies both *minsup* and *minconf* constraints has no correlation between X and Y, that is, support(X) $\times$ support(Y) = support($X \cup Y$).

Therefore, an alternative approach is to use other measures that account for importance or interestingness of a rule and select rules that have high score for these measures. Support and confidence can still be used as a constraint (setting *minsup* and *minconf* to 0 means not to use them at all). These measures include lift, leverage, redundancy, productivity, and well-known statistical measures such as chi-square, correlation coefficient, information gain, and so on.

Lift and leverage represent the ratio and the difference between the support and the support that would be expected if X and Y were independent, respectively. They try to find rules with strong correlations between X and Y.

$$\begin{aligned}
\text{lift}(X \Rightarrow Y) &= \frac{\text{confidence}(X \Rightarrow Y)}{\text{confidence}(\emptyset \Rightarrow Y)} = \frac{\text{support}(X \Rightarrow Y)}{\text{support}(X) \times \text{support}(Y)} \\
\text{leverage}(X \Rightarrow Y) &= \text{support}(X \Rightarrow Y) - \text{support}(X) \times \text{support}(Y) \\
&= \text{support}(X) \times (\text{confidence}(X \Rightarrow Y) - \text{support}(Y))
\end{aligned}$$

Redundant rule constraint discards a rule $X \Rightarrow Y$ if $\exists Z \in X$: support$(X \Rightarrow Y) =$ support$(X - [Z] \Rightarrow Y)$. A more powerful constraint is productive constraint. A rule is said to be productive if its improvement is greater than 0, where the rule's improvement is defined as

$$\text{improvement}(X \Rightarrow Y) = \text{confidence}(X \Rightarrow Y) - \max_{Z \subset X}(\text{confidence}(Z \Rightarrow Y)).$$

The improvement of a redundant rule cannot be greater than 0 and hence a constraint that rules must be productive discards all redundant rules. Further, it can discard rules that include items in the antecedent that are independent of the consequent, given the remaining items in the antecedent.

Statistical measures are useful in finding discriminative patterns (itemsets). However, these measures do not satisfy the antimonotonicity property, and finding the best k patterns or rules is not that easy. If a measure is convex with respect to its arguments, it is possible to estimate its upperbound for supersets of a pattern X (itemset) for a fixed conclusion Y (normally, a class value) [23] and use this to prune the search space. Statistical measures mentioned above satisfy this property.

Webb's KORD algorithm [39] finds k-optimal rules through the space of pairs X and Y (without fixing Y) and uses leverage as a measure to optimize using various pruning strategies.

4.5.7 Class Association Rules

When a transaction t is associated with a class cl, it is natural to use association rules for classification purpose. The association rules mined for classification purpose are called *class association rules* (CARs). CARs have the form $\{\langle p_1 : q_1\rangle, \langle p_2 : q_2\rangle, \ldots, \langle p_m : q_m\rangle\} \Rightarrow cl$. Here a numeric item has a numeric interval value, whereas a categorical item has a categorical value. Let $\mathcal{D}_{cl}$ be a set of all instances having a class cl in $\mathcal{D}$. CBA [22], CMAR [21], and CAEP [14] are the representative CAR-based classification systems. Especially, CAEP introduces a notion of emergent patterns and uses the strength of all CARs. Let the support of an itemset a by $\mathcal{D}_{cl}$ be $\text{support}_{\mathcal{D}_{cl}}(a) = |\{t \in \mathcal{D}_{cl} | a \in t\}|/|\mathcal{D}_{cl}|$. A set of QFIs, FQFI$(cl)$, in which every itemset a satisfies $\text{support}_{\mathcal{D}_{cl}}(a) \geq minsup$, is derived for every cl from $\mathcal{D}_{cl}$. Next, for every $a \in$ FQFI(cl), the *growth rate* defined by $growth\_rate_{\overline{\mathcal{D}}_{cl} \rightarrow \mathcal{D}_{cl}}(a) = \text{support}_{\mathcal{D}_{cl}}(a)/\text{support}_{\overline{\mathcal{D}}_{cl}}(a)$ is calculated for each class cl, where $\overline{\mathcal{D}}_{cl} = \mathcal{D} - \mathcal{D}_{cl}$ represents the opponent instances of cl. When the growth rate of a is not less than its threshold $\rho(\geq 1)$, that is, $growth\_rate_{\overline{\mathcal{D}}_{cl} \rightarrow \mathcal{D}_{cl}}(a) \geq \rho$, a is called an *emergent pattern* (EP) and is selected for a rule body where its head is the class cl, that is, $a \Rightarrow cl$. Let FEP(cl) be a set of all EPs selected from FQFI(cl) under this measure. The underlying principle here is to select the rule bodies that are strong enough to differentiate the class cl from the others. The strength of an EP a is measured by the relative difference between $\text{support}_{\mathcal{D}_{cl}}(a)$ and $\text{support}_{\overline{\mathcal{D}}_{cl}}(a)$: $\text{support}_{\mathcal{D}_{cl}}(a)/(\text{support}_{\mathcal{D}_{cl}}(a) + \text{support}_{\overline{\mathcal{D}}_{cl}}(a)) = growth\_rate_{\overline{\mathcal{D}}_{cl}\rightarrow\mathcal{D}_{cl}}(a)/(growth\_rate_{\overline{\mathcal{D}}_{cl}\rightarrow\mathcal{D}_{cl}}(a) + 1)$. This can be aggregated to define the *aggregate score* defined by $score(t, cl) = \sum_{a\subseteq t, a\in FEP(cl)} \frac{growth\_rate(a)}{growth\_rate(a)+1} * \text{support}_{\mathcal{D}_{cl}}(a)$ which represents the possibility of t to be classified into cl by EPs in FEP(cl). Since the distribution of the number of EPs is not uniform over cl, instances may get higher scores for some classes. Another factor, called a *base score*, which is defined to be the median of all aggregate scores in $\{score(t, cl)|t \in \mathcal{D}_{cl}\}$, is introduced to offset this bias, giving the normalized score defined by $norm\_score(t, cl) = \frac{score(t,cl)}{base\_score(cl)}$. The cl for which the normalized score is maximum is assigned to the class of t. This was shown to perform very well.

The problem with CAEP is that it discretizes each numeric attribute by an entropy measure without taking account of the dependency that exists in multiple attributes, and thus a cluster of instances having the same class can often be fragmented. Natural solution is to combine QFIMiner and CAEP, which is LSC-CAEP [37, 36].

4.5.8 Using Richer Expression: Sequences, Trees, and Graphs

Mining frequent itemsets started with a simple transaction dataset, but later it has been generalized to be able to deal with richer expression such as sequences, trees, and graphs. The pioneering work to mine sequential patterns by Agrawal and Srikant has already been discussed in Section 4.2.2. PrefixSpan [28] is another representative algorithm in frequent sequential pattern mining, which is a pattern-growth based algorithm and adopts a divide and conquer strategy similar to FP-growth to avoid unfruitful enumeration of smaller candidates to find larger patterns. PrefixSpan, first, finds sequential patterns consisting of only one item, and then, for each of them, say i_k, extracts a set of sequences containing it, that is, the $\langle i_k\rangle$-projected database. From each such projected database, PrefixSpan finds frequent sequential patterns of size 2 having $\langle i_k\rangle$ as their prefix, and again generates a projected database for each size 2 pattern newly found to find sequential patterns of size 3. This process is recursively repeated until no more sequential patterns are found.

A tree is characterized by V, a set of vertices, and E, a set of edges. A labeled tree assigns a set of labels L to either one or both of vertices and edges. An edge connects a vertex to another one. Every two vertices in a tree are reachable through one or more edges, but there is no cyclic path. TreeMinerV [44] and FREQT [7] are representative algorithms to mine subtrees frequently appearing in a collection of trees. They were independently proposed, but share the same level-wise strategy to enumerate frequent subtrees, which finds frequent subtrees having $k + 1$ vertices (($k + 1$)-subtrees) from k-subtrees by adding one edge to every possible position on a specific path called the rightmost path of each k-subtree with a vertex corresponding to the other end of the edge. Dryade [33] is a tree mining algorithm that can find frequent closed subtrees. A closed subtree is a maximal subtree among those having the same frequency. Unlike the other tree mining algorithms, Dryade assembles frequent closed subtrees level by level from a set of basic units called *tiles*, which are one depth closed subtrees.

A *graph* is a super class of trees and can have cyclic paths. AGM [19] is the first algorithm that mines frequent subgraphs from a collection of graphs by a complete search. It is based on Apriori and generates a candidate subgraph of size k (k-subgraph) from two known frequent ($k-1$)-subgraphs which share the same ($k-2$)-subgraph. Since there is no edge information available between the two ($k-1$)-th vertices, all the possibilities are considered. AGM generates two k-subgraphs from a pair of ($k-1$)-subgraphs, one with an edge between them and the other without an edge (this is a case where there are no labels defined for edges). Although Apriori-based approach enables to conduct a systematic complete search of frequent subgraphs, it has to generate a large number of candidates that do not actually exist in a given set of graphs. AGM uses adjacency matrix to represent a graph and introduces a notion of canonical form to solve subgraph isomorphism which is known to be NP-complete. gSpan [41] is one representative pattern-growth-based subgraph mining algorithm. It finds frequent subgraphs in a depth-first manner by adding an edge to each possible position on the rightmost path of a known frequent subgraph. gSpan takes into account only the edges that actually exist in a given set of graphs, so it never generates candidates that do not actually exist. GBI [42] and SUBDUE [13] are greedy algorithms to find frequent subgraphs, which recursively replace every occurrence of a typical subgraph in a graph with a new vertex. The typicality is defined by a measure based on frequency, for example, information gain in GBI and the minimum description length in SUBDUE. DT-ClGBI [25] generates a decision tree that classifies unknown graphs from a set of training graphs with known classes. It invokes a graph mining algorithm, Cl-GBI [24], an extension of GBI, at every test node of the decision tree. The resulting frequent subgraphs are used as attributes of graphs, and the most discriminative one is chosen to split the set of graphs that reached the node into two subsets: those which include the subgraph and the others.

4.6 Summary

Experimenting with Apriori-like algorithm is the first thing that data miners try to do. In this chapter the basic concepts and algorithms of Apriori family (Apriori, AprioriTid, AprioriAll) were introduced first and then their working mechanisms were explained with illustrative examples, followed by a performance evaluation of Apriori using a typical freely available implementation. Since Apriori is so fundamental and easy to implement, there are many variants of it. The limitation of Apriori approach is discussed and an overview of recent important advancement in frequent pattern mining methodologies is provided. There are other topics that cannot be covered in this chapter. These include use of constraints, colossal patterns, noise handling, and top-k representatives.

4.7 Exercises

1. Prove that Apriori can derive all frequent itemsets from a given transaction database.
2. Prove the following relation:

$$\text{support}(X \cup Y \cup Z) \geq \text{support}(X \cup Y) + \text{support}(X \cup Z) - \text{support}(X),$$

   where X, Y, and Z are itemsets in a database.
3. Given the database shown in Table 4.5, find all frequent itemsets using Apriori and AprioriTid for $minsup = 0.3$ and compare their efficiency.
4. Explain the relation between a hash-tree and a trie.
5. Draw an FP-tree for the database shown in Table 4.5 and explain how frequent itemsets are derived from the FP-tree.
6. Download and install Weka on your computer, and mine association rules by using Apriori from the Soybean dataset included in the Weka's package for various metrics to evaluate association rules using the same minimum threshold (fix the other parameters). Then, report how the resulting association rules change according to the metrics.
7. Draw a prefix tree to store the database in Section 4.4 with reference to [10] and explain how the efficiency of frequency counting can be improved in this case.
8. In an FP-tree, items in a transaction are sorted in the order of descending support count, while in a prefix tree for Apriori they are sorted in the order of ascending support count. Discuss the reason why they adopt the different orders.
9. When a transaction database has a small number of very long transactions, Apriori-based algorithms take much time to mine frequent itemsets. Explain the reason why they need so much time and propose an efficient method of mining closed itemsets from such a database.

TABLE 4.5 Database for Exercise 3

TID	Items
T01	Cheese, Milk, Egg
T02	Apple, Cheese
T03	Apple, Bread, Cheese, Orange, Grape
T04	Bread, Egg, Orange
T05	Cheese, Milk, Grape
T06	Apple, Cheese, Egg, Orange
T07	Bread, Cheese, Orange
T08	Cheese, Egg, Grape
T09	Bread, Cheese, Egg, Grape
T10	Bread, Cheese, Grape

TABLE 4.6 Sequence Database for Exercise 10

SID	Transaction Sequences
S01	$\langle(bc)(d)(ab)(def)\rangle$
S02	$\langle(abc)(cf)(df)\rangle$
S03	$\langle(cef)(df)(ab)(f)\rangle$
S04	$\langle(be)(ac)(cdf)\rangle$

10. Given the sequence database shown in Table 4.6, find frequent sequential patterns by AprioriAll for $minsup = 0.5$.

References

[1] http://www.borgelt.net/apriori.html.

[2] http://www.cs.bme.hu/~bodon/en/apriori/.

[3] R. Agrawal and R. Srikant. Fast algorithms for mining association rules. In *Proc. of the 20th International Conference on Very Large Data Bases (VLDB 1994)*, pages 487–499, 1994.

[4] R. Agrawal and R. Srikant. Fast algorithms for mining association rules. IBM Research Report RJ9839, IBM Research Division, Almaden Research Center, 1994.

[5] R. Agrawal and R. Srikant. Mining sequential patterns. IBM Research Report RJ9910, IBM Research Division, Almaden Research Center, 1994.

[6] R. Agrawal and R. Srikant. Mining sequential patterns. In *Proc. of the 11th International Conference on Data Engineering (ICDE 1995)*, pages 3–14, 1995.

[7] T. Asai, K. Abe, S. Kawasoe, H. Arimura, H. Sakamoto, and S. Arikawa. Efficient substructure discovery from large semi-structured data. In *Proc. of the 2nd SIAM International Conference on Data Mining*, pages 158–174, 2002.

[8] C. Blake and C. Merz. UCI repository of machine learning databases, 1998. http://www.ics.uci.edu/~mlearn/MLRepository.html.

[9] F. Bodon. Surprising results of trie-based fim algorithms. In *Proc. of the IEEE ICDM Workshop on Frequent Itemset Mining Implementations (FIMI'04)*, volume 126 of *CEUR Workshop Proceedings*, 2004. http://ftp.informatik.rwth-aachen.de/Publications/CEUR-WS/Vol-126/bodon.pdf.

[10] C. Borgelt. Efficient implementations of Apriori and Eclat. In *Proc. of the IEEE ICDM Workshop on Frequent Itemset Mining Implementations (FIMI'03)*,

volume 90 of *CEUR Workshop Proceedings*, 2003. http://ftp.informatik.rwth-aachen.de/Publications/CEUR-WS/Vol-90/borgelt.pdf.

[11] S. Brin, R. Motwani, J. D. Ullman, and S. Tsur. Dynamic itemset counting and implication rules for market basket data. In *Proc. of ACM SIGMOD International Conference on Management of Data (SIGMOD 1997)*, pages 255–264, 1997.

[12] D. W. Cheung, J. Han, and C. Y. Wong. Maintenance of discovered association rules in large databases: An incremental updating technique. In *Proc. of the 1996 ACM SIGMOD International Conference on Management of Data*, pages 13–23, 1996.

[13] D. J. Cook and L. B. Holder. Substructure discovery using minimum description length and background knowledge. *Journal of Artificial Intelligence Research*, Vol.1, pages 231–255, 1994.

[14] G. Dong, X. Zhang, L. Wong, and J. Li. Caep: Classification by aggregating emerging patterns. In *Proc. of the 2nd International Conference on Discovery Science (DS '99), LNAI 1721,* Springer, pages 30–42, 1999.

[15] B. Goethals. Survey on frequent pattern mining, 2003. http://www.adrem.ua.ac.be/bibrem/pubs/fpm_survey.pdf

[16] J. Han, H. Cheng, D. Xin, and X. Yan. Frequent pattern mining: Current status and future direction. *Data Mining and Knowledge Discovery*, Vol. 15, No. 1, pages 55–86, 2007.

[17] J. Han, J. Pei, and Y. Yin. Mining frequent patterns without candidate generation. In *Proc. of the 2000 ACM SIGMOD International Conference on Management of Data*, pages 1–12, 2000.

[18] J. Han, J. Pei, Y. Yin, and R. Mao. Mining frequent patterns without candidate generation: A frequent-pattern tree approach. *Data Mining and Knowledge Discovery*, Vol. 8, No. 1, pages 53–87, 2004.

[19] A. Inokuchi, T. Washio, and H. Motoda. General framework for mining frequent subgraphs from labeled graphs. *Fundamenta Informaticae*, Vol. 66, No. 1-2, pages 53–82, 2005.

[20] K. Kailing, H. Kriegel, and P. Kroger. Density-connected subspace clustering for high-dimensional data. In *Proc. of the 4th SIAM International Conference on Data Mining*, pages 246–257, 2004.

[21] W. Li, J. Han, and J. Pei. Cmar: Accurate and efficient classification based on multiple class-association rules. In *Proc. of the 1st IEEE International Conference on Data Mining (ICDM '01)*, pages 369–376, 2001.

[22] B. Liu, W. Hsu, and Y. Ma. Integrating classification and association rule mining. In *Proc. of the 4th International Conference on Knowledge Discovery and Data Mining (KDD-98)*, pages 80–86, 1998.

[23] S. Morishita and J. Sese. Traversing lattice itemset with statistical metric pruning. In *Proc. of the 19th ACM SIGMOD-SIGACT-SIGART Symposium on Principles of Database Systems (PODS 2000)*, pages 226–236, 2000.

[24] P. C. Nguyen, K. Ohara, H. Motoda, and T. Washio. Cl-GBI: A novel approach for extracting typical patterns from graph-structured data. In *Proc. of the 9th Pacific-Asia Conference on Advances in Knowledge Discovery and Data Mining (PAKDD 2005)*, pages 639–649, 2005.

[25] K. Ohara, P. C. Nguyen, A. Mogi, H. Motoda, and T. Washio. Constructing decision trees based on chunkingless graph-based induction. In L. B. Holder and D. J. Cook, editors, *Mining Graph Data*, pages 203–226. Wiley-Interscience, 2006.

[26] J. Park, M. Chen, and P. Yu. An effective hash-based algorithm for mining association rules. In *Proc. of the 1995 ACM SIGMOD International Conference on Management of Data*, pages 175–186, 1995.

[27] J. Pei, J. Han, and R. Mao. Closet: An efficient algorithm for mining frequent closed itemsets. In *Proc. of the 2000 ACM-SIGMOD International Workshop on Data Mining and Knowledge Discovery*, pages 11–20, 2000.

[28] J. Pei, J. Han, B. Mortazavi-Asl, H. Pinto, Q. Chen, U. Dayal, and M. C. Hsu. PrefixSpan: Mining sequential patterns efficiently by prefix projected pattern growth. In *Proc. of the 17th International Conference on Data Engineering (ICDE 2001)*, pages 215–224, 2001.

[29] A. Savasere, E. Omiecinski, and S. Navathe. An efficient algorithm for mining association rules in large databases. In *Proc. of the 21th International Conference on Very Large Data Bases (VLDB 1995)*, pages 432–444. Morgan Kaufmann, 1995.

[30] R. Srikant and R. Agrawal. Mining generalized association rules. In *Proc. of the 21th International Conference on Very Large Data Bases (VLDB 1995)*, pages 407–419, 1995.

[31] R. Srikant and R. Agrawal. Mining quantitative association rules in large relational tables. In *Proc. of the 1996 ACM SIGMOD International Conference on Management of Data*, pages 1–12, 1996.

[32] R. Srikant and R. Agrawal. Mining sequential patterns: Generalization and performance improvement. In *Proc. of the 5th International Conference on Extending Database Technology*, pages 3–17, 1996.

[33] A. Termier, M. C. Rousset, and M. Sebag. Dryade: A new approach for discovering closed frequent trees in heterogeneous tree databases. In *Proc. of the 4th IEEE International Conference on Data Mining (ICDM '04)*, pages 543–546, 2004.

[34] T. Uno, T. Asai, Y. Uchida, and H. Arimura. An efficient algorithm for enumerating frequent closed patterns in transaction databases. In *Proc. of the 7th*

International Conference on Discovery Science (DS '04), LNAI 3245, Springer, pages 16–30, 2004.

[35] T. Washio, H. Matsuura, and H. Motoda. Mining association rules for estimation and prediction. In *Proc. of the 2nd Pacific Asia Conference on Knowledge Discovery and Data Mining (PAKDD 1998)*, pages 417–419, 1998.

[36] T. Washio, Y. Mitsunaga, and H. Motoda. Mining quantitative frequent itemsets using adaptive density-based subspace clustering. In *Proc. of the 5th IEEE International Conference on Data Mining (ICDM '05)*, pages 793–796, 2005.

[37] T. Washio, K. Nakanishi, and H. Motoda. Deriving class association rules based on levelwise subspace clustering. In *Proc. of the 9th European Conference on Principles and Practice of Knowledge Discovery in Databases (PKDD 2005), LNAI 3721*, Springer, pages 692–700, 2005.

[38] G. Webb. Efficient search for association rules. In *Proc. of the 6th ACM SIGKDD International Conference on Knowledge Discovery and Data Mining*, pages 99–107, 2000.

[39] G. Webb and S. Zhang. K-optimal rule discovery. *Data Mining and Knowledge Discovery*, Vol. 10, No. 1, pages 39–79, 2005.

[40] I. H. Witten and E. Frank. *Data Mining: Practical Machine Learning Tools and Techniques, 2nd Edition.* Morgan Kaufmann, San Francisco, 2005. http://www.cs.waikato.ac.nz/ml/weka/.

[41] X. Yan and J. Han. gSpan: Graph-based substructure pattern mining. In *Proc. of the 2nd IEEE International Conference on Data Mining (ICDM'02)*, pages 721–724, 2002.

[42] K. Yoshida and H. Motoda. Clip: Concept learning from inference pattern. *Journal of Artificial Intelligence*, Vol. 75, No. 1, pages 63–92, 1995.

[43] M. Zaki. Scalable algorithms for association mining. *IEEE Transactions on Knowledge and Data Engineering*, Vol. 12, No. 3, pages 372–390, 2000.

[44] M. J. Zaki. Efficiently mining frequent trees in a forest. In *Proc. of the 8th ACM SIGKDD International Conference on Knowledge Discovery and Data Mining (KDD '02)*, pages 71–80, 2002.

Chapter 5

EM

Geoffrey J. McLachlan and Shu-Kay Ng

Contents

Abstract The expectation-maximization (EM) algorithm is a broadly applicable approach to the iterative computation of maximum likelihood (ML) estimates, useful in a variety of incomplete-data problems. In particular, the EM algorithm simplifies considerably the problem of fitting finite mixture models by ML, where mixture models are used to model heterogeneity in cluster analysis and pattern recognition contexts. The EM algorithm has a number of appealing properties, including its numerical stability, simplicity of implementation, and reliable global convergence. There are also extensions of the EM algorithm to tackle complex problems in various data mining applications. It is, however, highly desirable if its simplicity and stability can be preserved.

5.1 Introduction

The expectation-maximization (EM) algorithm has been of considerable interest in recent years in the development of algorithms in various application areas such as data mining, machine learning, and pattern recognition [20, 27, 28]. The seminal paper of Dempster et al. [8] on the EM algorithm greatly stimulated interest in the use of finite mixture distributions to model heterogeneous data. This is because the fitting of mixture models by maximum likelihood (ML) is a classic example of a problem that is simplified considerably by the EM's conceptual unification of ML estimation from data that can be viewed as being incomplete [20]. Maximum likelihood estimation and likelihood-based inference are of central importance in statistical theory and data analysis. Maximum likelihood estimation is a general-purpose method with attractive properties [6, 13, 31]. Finite mixture distributions provide a flexible and mathematical-based approach to the modeling and clustering of data observed on random phenomena. We focus here on the use of the EM algorithm for the fitting of finite mixture models via the ML approach.

With the mixture model-based approach to clustering, the observed p-dimensional data $\boldsymbol{y}_1, \ldots, \boldsymbol{y}_n$ are assumed to have come from a mixture of an initially specified number g of component densities in some unknown proportions $\pi_1, \ldots, \pi_g$, which sum to 1. The mixture density of $\boldsymbol{y}_j$ is expressed as

$$f(\boldsymbol{y}_j; \boldsymbol{\Psi}) = \sum_{i=1}^{g} \pi_i f_i(\boldsymbol{y}_j; \boldsymbol{\theta}_i) \qquad (j = 1, \ldots, n) \tag{5.1}$$

where the component density $f_i(\boldsymbol{y}_j; \boldsymbol{\theta}_i)$ is specified up to a vector $\boldsymbol{\theta}_i$ of unknown parameters $(i = 1, \ldots, g)$. The vector of all the unknown parameters is given by

$$\boldsymbol{\Psi} = \left(\pi_1, \ldots, \pi_{g-1}, \boldsymbol{\theta}_1^T, \ldots, \boldsymbol{\theta}_g^T\right)^T$$

where the superscript T denotes vector transpose. The parameter vector $\boldsymbol{\Psi}$ can be estimated by ML. The objective is to maximize the likelihood $L(\boldsymbol{\Psi})$, or equivalently, the log likelihood $\log L(\boldsymbol{\Psi})$, as a function of $\boldsymbol{\Psi}$, over the parameter space. That is, the ML estimate of $\boldsymbol{\Psi}$, $\hat{\boldsymbol{\Psi}}$, is given by an appropriate root of the log likelihood equation,

$$\partial \log L(\boldsymbol{\Psi})/\partial \boldsymbol{\Psi} = \mathbf{0} \tag{5.2}$$

where

$$\log L(\boldsymbol{\Psi}) = \sum_{j=1}^{n} \log f(\boldsymbol{y}_j; \boldsymbol{\Psi})$$

is the log likelihood function for $\boldsymbol{\Psi}$ formed under the assumption of independent data $\boldsymbol{y}_1, \ldots, \boldsymbol{y}_n$. The aim of ML estimation [13] is to determine an estimate $\hat{\boldsymbol{\Psi}}$ for each n, so that it defines a sequence of roots of Equation (5.2) that is consistent and asymptotically efficient. Such a sequence is known to exist under suitable regularity conditions [7]. With probability tending to one, these roots correspond to local maxima in the interior of the parameter space. For estimation models in general, the likelihood usually has a global maximum in the interior of the parameter space. Then typically a sequence of roots of Equation (5.2) with the desired asymptotic properties is provided by taking $\hat{\boldsymbol{\Psi}}$ for each n to be the root that globally maximizes $L(\boldsymbol{\Psi})$; in this case, $\hat{\boldsymbol{\Psi}}$ is the MLE [18]. We shall henceforth refer to $\hat{\boldsymbol{\Psi}}$ as the MLE, even in situations where it may not globally maximize the likelihood. Indeed, in the example on mixture models to be presented in Section 5.4.1, the likelihood is unbounded. However, there may still exist under the usual regularity conditions a sequence of roots of Equation (5.2) with the properties of consistency, efficiency, and asymptotic normality [16].

5.2 Algorithm Description

The EM algorithm is an iterative algorithm, in each iteration of which there are two steps, the Expectation step (E-step) and the Maximization step (M-step). A brief history of the EM algorithm can be found in [18]. Within the incomplete-data framework of the EM algorithm, we let $\boldsymbol{y} = (\boldsymbol{y}_1^T, \ldots, \boldsymbol{y}_n^T)^T$ denote the vector containing the observed data and we let $\boldsymbol{z}$ denote the vector containing the incomplete data. The complete-data vector is declared to be

$$\boldsymbol{x} = (\boldsymbol{y}^T, \boldsymbol{z}^T)^T$$

The EM algorithm approaches the problem of solving the "incomplete-data" log likelihood Equation (5.2) indirectly by proceeding iteratively in terms of the "complete-data" log likelihood, $\log L_c(\boldsymbol{\Psi})$. As it depends explicitly on the unobservable data $\boldsymbol{z}$, the E-step is performed on which $\log L_c(\boldsymbol{\Psi})$ is replaced by the so-called Q-function, which is its conditional expectation given $\boldsymbol{y}$, using the current fit for $\boldsymbol{\Psi}$. More specifically, on the $(k+1)$th iteration of the EM algorithm, the E-step computes

$$Q(\boldsymbol{\Psi}; \boldsymbol{\Psi}^{(k)}) = E_{\boldsymbol{\Psi}^{(k)}}\{\log L_c(\boldsymbol{\Psi})|\boldsymbol{y}\}$$

where $E_{\boldsymbol{\Psi}^{(k)}}$ denotes expectation using the parameter vector $\boldsymbol{\Psi}^{(k)}$. The M-step updates the estimate of $\boldsymbol{\Psi}$ by that value $\boldsymbol{\Psi}^{(k+1)}$ of $\boldsymbol{\Psi}$ that maximizes the Q-function, $Q(\boldsymbol{\Psi}; \boldsymbol{\Psi}^{(k)})$, with respect to $\boldsymbol{\Psi}$ over the parameter space [18]. The E- and M-steps are alternated repeatedly until the changes in the log likelihood values are less than some specified threshold. As mentioned in Section 5.1, the EM algorithm is numerically stable with each EM iteration increasing the likelihood value as

$$L(\boldsymbol{\Psi}^{(k+1)}) \geq L(\boldsymbol{\Psi}^{(k)})$$

It can be shown that both the E- and M-steps will have particularly simple forms when the complete-data probability density function is from an exponential family [18]. Often in practice, the solution to the M-step exists in closed form. In those instances where it does not, it may not be feasible to attempt to find the value of $\boldsymbol{\Psi}$ that globally maximizes the function $Q(\boldsymbol{\Psi}; \boldsymbol{\Psi}^{(k)})$. For such situations, a generalized EM (GEM) algorithm [8] may be adopted for which the M-step requires $\boldsymbol{\Psi}^{(k+1)}$ to be chosen such that $\boldsymbol{\Psi}^{(k+1)}$ increases the Q-function $Q(\boldsymbol{\Psi}; \boldsymbol{\Psi}^{(k)})$ over its value at $\boldsymbol{\Psi} = \boldsymbol{\Psi}^{(k)}$. That is,

$$Q(\boldsymbol{\Psi}^{(k+1)}; \boldsymbol{\Psi}^{(k)}) \geq Q(\boldsymbol{\Psi}^{(k)}; \boldsymbol{\Psi}^{(k)})$$

holds; see [18].

Some of the drawbacks of the EM algorithm are (a) it does not automatically produce an estimate of the covariance matrix of the parameter estimates. This disadvantage, however, can easily be removed by using appropriate methodology associated with the EM algorithm [18]; (b) it is sometimes very slow to converge; and (c) in some problems, the E- or M-steps may be analytically intractable. We shall briefly address the last two issues in Section 5.5.

5.3 Software Implementation

The EMMIX program: McLachlan et al. [22] have developed the program EMMIX as a general tool to fit mixtures of multivariate normal or t-distributed components by ML via the EM algorithm to continuous multivariate data. It also includes many other features that were found to be of use when fitting mixture models. These include the provision of starting values for the application of the EM algorithm, the provision of standard errors for the fitted parameters in the mixture model via various methods, and the determination of the number of components; see below.

Starting values for EM algorithm: With applications where the log likelihood equation has multiple roots corresponding to local maxima, the EM algorithm should be applied from a wide choice of starting values in any search for all local maxima. In the context of finite mixture models, an initial parameter value can be obtained using the k-means clustering algorithm, hierarchical clustering methods, or random partitions of the data [20]. With the EMMIX program, there is an additional option for random starts whereby the user can first subsample the data before using a random start based on the subsample each time. This is to limit the effect of the central limit theorem, which would have the randomly selected starts being similar for each component in large samples [20].

Provision of standard errors: Several methods have been suggested in the EM literature for augmenting the EM computation with some computation for obtaining an estimate of the covariance matrix of the computed ML estimates; see [11, 15, 18]. Alternatively, standard error estimation may be obtained with the EMMIX program using the bootstrap resampling approach implemented parametrically or nonparametrically [18, 20].

Number of components: We can make a choice as to an appropriate value of the number of components (clusters) g by consideration of the likelihood function. In the absence of any prior information as to the number of clusters present in the data, we can monitor the increase in log likelihood function as the value of g increases. At any stage, the choice of $g = g_0$ versus $g = g_0 + 1$ can be made by either performing the likelihood ratio test or using some information-based criterion, such as the Bayesian Information Criterion (BIC). Unfortunately, regularity conditions do not hold for the likelihood ratio test statistic λ to have its usual null distribution of chi-squared with degrees of freedom equal to the difference d in the number of parameters for $g = g_0+1$ and $g = g_0$ components in the mixture model. The EMMIX program provides a bootstrap resampling approach to assess the null distribution (and hence the p-value) of the statistic $(-2 \log \lambda)$. Alternatively, one can apply BIC, although regularity conditions do not hold for its validity here. The use of BIC leads to the selection of $g = g_0+1$ over $g = g_0$ if $-2 \log \lambda$ is greater than $d \log(n)$.

Other mixture software: There are some other EM-based software for mixture modeling via ML. For example, Fraley and Raftery [9] have developed the MCLUST program for hierarchical clustering on the basis of mixtures of normal components under various parameterizations of the component-covariance matrices. It is interfaced to the S-PLUS commercial software and has the option to include an additional component in the model for background (Poisson) noise. The reader is referred to the appendix in McLachlan and Peel [20] for the availability of software for the fitting of mixture models.

5.4 Illustrative Examples

We give in this section two examples to demonstrate how the EM algorithm can be conveniently applied to find the ML estimates in some commonly occurring situations in data mining. Both examples concern the application of the EM algorithm for the ML estimation of finite mixture models, which is widely adopted to model heterogeneous data [20]. They illustrate how an incomplete-data formulation is used to derive the EM algorithm for computing ML estimates.

5.4.1 Example 5.1: Multivariate Normal Mixtures

This example concerns the application of the EM algorithm for the ML estimation of finite mixture models with multivariate normal components [20]. With reference to Equation (5.1), the mixture density of $\boldsymbol{y}_j$ is given by

$$f(\boldsymbol{y}_j; \boldsymbol{\Psi}) = \sum_{i=1}^{g} \pi_i \phi(\boldsymbol{y}_j; \boldsymbol{\mu}_i, \boldsymbol{\Sigma}_i) \quad (j = 1, \ldots, n) \tag{5.3}$$

where $\phi(\boldsymbol{y}_j; \boldsymbol{\mu}_i, \boldsymbol{\Sigma}_i)$ denotes the p-dimensional multivariate normal distribution with mean $\boldsymbol{\mu}_i$ and covariance matrix $\boldsymbol{\Sigma}_i$. Here the vector $\boldsymbol{\Psi}$ of unknown parameters consists of the mixing proportions $\pi_1, \ldots, \pi_{g-1}$, the elements of the component means $\boldsymbol{\mu}_i$, and the distinct elements of the component-covariance matrices $\boldsymbol{\Sigma}_i$. The log likelihood for $\boldsymbol{\Psi}$ is then given by

$$\log L(\boldsymbol{\Psi}) = \sum_{j=1}^{n} \log \left\{ \sum_{i=1}^{g} \pi_i \phi(\boldsymbol{y}_j; \boldsymbol{\mu}_i, \boldsymbol{\Sigma}_i) \right\}$$

Solutions of the log likelihood equation corresponding to local maxima can be found iteratively by application of the EM algorithm.

Within the EM framework, each $\boldsymbol{y}_j$ is conceptualized to have arisen from one of the g components of the mixture model [Equation (5.3)]. We let $\boldsymbol{z}_1, \ldots, \boldsymbol{z}_n$ denote the unobservable component-indicator vectors, where the ith element z_{ij} of $\boldsymbol{z}_j$ is taken to be one or zero according as the jth observation $\boldsymbol{y}_j$ does or does not come from the ith component. The observed-data vector $\boldsymbol{y}$ is viewed as being incomplete, as the associated component-indicator vectors, $\boldsymbol{z}_1, \ldots, \boldsymbol{z}_n$, are not available. The complete-data vector is therefore $\boldsymbol{x} = (\boldsymbol{y}^T, \boldsymbol{z}^T)^T$, where $\boldsymbol{z} = (\boldsymbol{z}_1^T, \ldots, \boldsymbol{z}_n^T)^T$. The complete-data log likelihood for $\boldsymbol{\Psi}$ is given by

$$\log L_c(\boldsymbol{\Psi}) = \sum_{i=1}^{g} \sum_{j=1}^{n} z_{ij}\{\log \pi_i + \log \phi(\boldsymbol{y}_j; \boldsymbol{\mu}_i, \boldsymbol{\Sigma}_i)\} \tag{5.4}$$

The EM algorithm is applied to this problem by treating the z_{ij} in Equation (5.4) as missing data. On the $(k+1)$th iteration, the E-step computes the Q-function, $Q(\boldsymbol{\Psi}; \boldsymbol{\Psi}^{(k)})$, which is the conditional expectation of the complete-data log likelihood given $\boldsymbol{y}$ and the current estimates $\boldsymbol{\Psi}^{(k)}$. As the complete-data log likelihood [Equation (5.4)] is linear in the missing data z_{ij}, we simply have to calculate the current conditional expectation of Z_{ij} given the observed data $\boldsymbol{y}$, where Z_{ij} is the random variable corresponding to z_{ij}. That is,

$$\begin{aligned} E_{\boldsymbol{\Psi}^{(k)}}(Z_{ij}|\boldsymbol{y}) &= \mathrm{pr}_{\boldsymbol{\Psi}^{(k)}}\{Z_{ij} = 1|\boldsymbol{y}\} \\ &= \tau_i(\boldsymbol{y}_j; \boldsymbol{\Psi}^{(k)}) \\ &= \pi_i^{(k)}\phi\left(\boldsymbol{y}_j; \boldsymbol{\mu}_i^{(k)}, \boldsymbol{\Sigma}_i^{(k)}\right) \bigg/ \sum_{h=1}^{g} \pi_h^{(k)}\phi\left(\boldsymbol{y}_j; \boldsymbol{\mu}_h^{(k)}, \boldsymbol{\Sigma}_h^{(k)}\right) \end{aligned} \tag{5.5}$$

for $i = 1, \ldots, g$; $j = 1, \ldots, n$. The quantity $\tau_i(\boldsymbol{y}_j; \boldsymbol{\Psi}^{(k)})$ is the posterior probability that the jth observation $\boldsymbol{y}_j$ belongs to the ith component of the mixture. From Equations (5.4) and (5.5), it follows that

$$Q(\boldsymbol{\Psi}; \boldsymbol{\Psi}^{(k)}) = \sum_{i=1}^{g} \sum_{j=1}^{n} \tau_i(\boldsymbol{y}_j; \boldsymbol{\Psi}^{(k)})\{\log \pi_i + \log \phi(\boldsymbol{y}_j; \boldsymbol{\mu}_i, \boldsymbol{\Sigma}_i)\} \tag{5.6}$$

For mixtures with normal component densities, it is computationally advantageous to work in terms of the sufficient statistics [26] given by

$$\begin{aligned} T_{i1}^{(k)} &= \sum_{j=1}^{n} \tau_i(\boldsymbol{y}_j; \boldsymbol{\Psi}^{(k)}) \\ \boldsymbol{T}_{i2}^{(k)} &= \sum_{j=1}^{n} \tau_i(\boldsymbol{y}_j; \boldsymbol{\Psi}^{(k)})\boldsymbol{y}_j \\ \boldsymbol{T}_{i3}^{(k)} &= \sum_{j=1}^{n} \tau_i(\boldsymbol{y}_j; \boldsymbol{\Psi}^{(k)})\boldsymbol{y}_j\boldsymbol{y}_j^T \end{aligned} \tag{5.7}$$

For normal components, the M-step exists in closed form and is simplified on the basis of the sufficient statistics in Equation (5.7) as

$$\begin{aligned} \pi_i^{(k+1)} &= T_{i1}^{(k)}/n \\ \boldsymbol{\mu}_i^{(k+1)} &= \boldsymbol{T}_{i2}^{(k)}/T_{i1}^{(k)} \\ \boldsymbol{\Sigma}_i^{(k+1)} &= \left\{\boldsymbol{T}_{i3}^{(k)} - T_{i1}^{(k)^{-1}}\boldsymbol{T}_{i2}^{(k)}\boldsymbol{T}_{i2}^{(k)^T}\right\}/T_{i1}^{(k)} \end{aligned} \tag{5.8}$$

see [20, 26]. In the case of unrestricted component-covariance matrices $\mathbf{\Sigma}_i$, $L(\mathbf{\Psi})$ is unbounded, as each data point gives rise to a singularity on the edge of the parameter space [16, 20]. Consideration has to be given to the problem of relatively large (spurious) local maxima that occur as a consequence of a fitted component having a very small (but nonzero) generalized variance (the determinant of the covariance matrix). Such a component corresponds to a cluster containing a few data points either relatively close together or almost lying in a lower dimensional subspace in the case of multivariate data.

In practice, the component-covariance matrices $\mathbf{\Sigma}_i$ can be restricted to being the same, $\mathbf{\Sigma}_i = \mathbf{\Sigma}$ $(i = 1, \ldots, g)$, where $\mathbf{\Sigma}$ is unspecified. In this case of homoscedastic normal components, the updated estimate of the common component-covariance matrix $\mathbf{\Sigma}$ is given by

$$\mathbf{\Sigma}^{(k+1)} = \sum_{i=1}^{g} T_{i1}^{(k)} \mathbf{\Sigma}_i^{(k+1)} / n \tag{5.9}$$

where $\mathbf{\Sigma}_i^{(k+1)}$ is given by Equation (5.8), and the updates of π_i and $\boldsymbol{\mu}_i$ are as above in the heteroscedastic case [Equation (5.8)].

The well-known set of *Iris* data is available at the UCI Repository of machine learning databases [1]. The data consist of measurements of the length and width of both sepals and petals of 50 plants for each of the three types of *Iris* species *setosa*, *versicolor*, and *virginica*. Here, we cluster these four-dimensional data, ignoring the known classification of the data, by fitting a mixture of $g = 3$ normal components with heteroscedastic diagonal component-covariance matrices using the EMMIX program [22]. The vector of unknown parameters $\mathbf{\Psi}$ now consists of the mixing proportions π_1, π_2, the elements of the component means $\boldsymbol{\mu}_i$, and the diagonal elements of the component-covariance matrices $\mathbf{\Sigma}_i$ $(i = 1, 2, 3)$. An initial value $\mathbf{\Psi}^{(0)}$ is chosen to be

$$\begin{aligned}
\pi_1^{(0)} &= 0.31, \ \pi_2^{(0)} = 0.33, \ \pi_3^{(0)} = 0.36 \\
\boldsymbol{\mu}_1^{(0)} &= (5.0, 3.4, 1.5, 0.2)^T, \ \boldsymbol{\mu}_2^{(0)} = (5.8, 2.7, 4.2, 1.3)^T \\
\boldsymbol{\mu}_3^{(0)} &= (6.6, 3.0, 5.5, 2.0)^T \\
\mathbf{\Sigma}_1^{(0)} &= \mathrm{diag}(0.1, 0.1, 0.03, 0.01) \quad \mathbf{\Sigma}_2^{(0)} = \mathrm{diag}(0.2, 0.1, 0.2, 0.03) \\
\mathbf{\Sigma}_3^{(0)} &= \mathrm{diag}(0.3, 0.1, 0.3, 0.1)
\end{aligned}$$

which is obtained through the use of k-means clustering method. With the EMMIX program, the default stopping criterion is that the change in the log likelihood from the current iteration and the log likelihood from 10 iterations previously differs by less than 0.000001 of the current log likelihood [22]. The results of the EM algorithm are presented in Table 5.1. The MLE of $\mathbf{\Psi}$ can be taken to be the value of $\mathbf{\Psi}^{(k)}$ on iteration $k = 29$. Alternatively, the EMMIX program offers automatic starting values for the application of the EM algorithm. As an example, an initial value $\mathbf{\Psi}^{(0)}$ is determined from 10 random starts (using 70% subsampling of the data), 10 k-means starts, and 6 hierarchical methods; see Section 5.3 and [22]. The final estimates of $\mathbf{\Psi}$ are the same as those given in Table 5.1.

TABLE 5.1 Results of the EM Algorithm for Example 5.1

Iteration	$\pi_i^{(k)}$	$\boldsymbol{\mu}_i^{(k)T}$	**Diagonal Elements of** $\boldsymbol{\Sigma}_i^{(k)}$	**Log Likelihood**
0	0.310	(5.00, 3.40, 1.50, 0.20)	(0.100, 0.100, 0.030, 0.010)	−317.98421
	0.330	(5.80, 2.70, 4.20, 1.30)	(0.200, 0.100, 0.200, 0.030)	
	0.360	(6.60, 3.00, 5.50, 2.00)	(0.300, 0.100, 0.300, 0.100)	
1	0.333	(5.01, 3.43, 1.46, 0.25)	(0.122, 0.141, 0.030, 0.011)	−306.90935
	0.299	(5.82, 2.70, 4.20, 1.30)	(0.225, 0.089, 0.212, 0.034)	
	0.368	(6.62, 3.01, 5.48, 1.98)	(0.322, 0.083, 0.325, 0.088)	
2	0.333	(5.01, 3.43, 1.46, 0.25)	(0.122, 0.141, 0.030, 0.011)	−306.87370
	0.300	(5.83, 2.70, 4.21, 1.30)	(0.226, 0.087, 0.218, 0.034)	
	0.367	(6.62, 3.01, 5.47, 1.98)	(0.323, 0.083, 0.328, 0.087)	
10	0.333	(5.01, 3.43, 1.46, 0.25)	(0.122, 0.141, 0.030, 0.011)	−306.86234
	0.303	(5.83, 2.70, 4.22, 1.30)	(0.227, 0.087, 0.224, 0.035)	
	0.364	(6.62, 3.02, 5.48, 1.99)	(0.324, 0.083, 0.328, 0.086)	
20	0.333	(5.01, 3.43, 1.46, 0.25)	(0.122, 0.141, 0.030, 0.011)	−306.86075
	0.304	(5.83, 2.70, 4.22, 1.30)	(0.228, 0.087, 0.225, 0.035)	
	0.363	(6.62, 3.02, 5.48, 1.99)	(0.324, 0.083, 0.327, 0.086)	
29	0.333	(5.01, 3.43, 1.46, 0.25)	(0.122, 0.141, 0.030, 0.011)	−306.86052
	0.305	(5.83, 2.70, 4.22, 1.30)	(0.229, 0.087, 0.225, 0.035)	
	0.362	(6.62, 3.02, 5.48, 1.99)	(0.324, 0.083, 0.327, 0.085)	

5.4.2 Example 5.2: Mixtures of Factor Analyzers

McLachlan and Peel [21] adopt a mixture of factor analyzers model to cluster the so-called wine data set, which is available at the UCI Repository of machine learning databases [1]. These data give the results of a chemical analysis of wines grown in the same region in Italy, but derived from three different cultivars. The analysis determined the quantities of $p = 13$ consituents found in each of $n = 178$ wines. To cluster this data set, a three-component normal mixture model can be adopted. However, as $p = 13$ in this problem, the (unrestricted) covariance matrix $\boldsymbol{\Sigma}_i$ has 91 parameters for each i $(i = 1, 2, 3)$, which means that the total number of parameters is very large relative to the sample size of $n = 178$. A mixture of factor analyzers can be used to reduce the number of parameters to be fitted. In a mixture of factor analyzers, each observation $\boldsymbol{Y}_j$ is modeled as

$$\boldsymbol{Y}_j = \boldsymbol{\mu}_i + \boldsymbol{B}_i \boldsymbol{U}_{ij} + \boldsymbol{\epsilon}_{ij}$$

with probability π_i $(i = 1, \ldots, g)$ for $j = 1, \ldots, n$, where $\boldsymbol{U}_{ij}$ is a q-dimensional $(q < p)$ vector of latent or unobservable variables called *factors* and $\boldsymbol{B}_i$ is a $p \times q$ matrix of factor loadings (parameters). The factors $\boldsymbol{U}_{i1}, \ldots, \boldsymbol{U}_{in}$ are distributed independently $N(\boldsymbol{0}, \boldsymbol{I}_q)$, independently of the $\boldsymbol{\epsilon}_{ij}$, which are distributed independently

$N(\mathbf{0}, \boldsymbol{D}_i)$, where $\boldsymbol{I}_q$ is the $q \times q$ identity matrix and $\boldsymbol{D}_i$ is a $p \times p$ diagonal matrix $(i = 1, \ldots, g)$. That is,

$$f(\boldsymbol{y}_j; \boldsymbol{\Psi}) = \sum_{i=1}^{g} \pi_i \phi(\boldsymbol{y}_j; \boldsymbol{\mu}_i, \boldsymbol{\Sigma}_i)$$

where

$$\boldsymbol{\Sigma}_i = \boldsymbol{B}_i \boldsymbol{B}_i^T + \boldsymbol{D}_i \qquad (i = 1, \ldots, g)$$

The vector of unknown parameters $\boldsymbol{\Psi}$ now consists of the elements of the $\boldsymbol{\mu}_i$, the $\boldsymbol{B}_i$, and the $\boldsymbol{D}_i$, along with the mixing proportions π_i $(i = 1, \ldots, g-1)$.

The alternating expectation conditional-maximization (AECM) algorithm [24] can be used to fit the mixture of factor analyzers model by ML; see Section 5.5. The unknown parameters are partitioned as $(\boldsymbol{\Psi}_1^T, \boldsymbol{\Psi}_2^T)^T$, where $\boldsymbol{\Psi}_1$ contains the π_i $(i = 1, \ldots, g-1)$ and the elements of $\boldsymbol{\mu}_i$ $(i = 1, \ldots, g)$. The subvector $\boldsymbol{\Psi}_2$ contains the elements of $\boldsymbol{B}_i$ and $\boldsymbol{D}_i$ $(i = 1, \ldots, g)$. The AECM algorithm is an extension of the expectation-conditional maximization (ECM) algorithm [23], where the specification of the complete-data is allowed to be different on each conditional maximization (CM) step. In this application, one iteration consists of two cycles corresponding to the partition of $\boldsymbol{\Psi}$ into $\boldsymbol{\Psi}_1$ and $\boldsymbol{\Psi}_2$, and there is one E-step and one CM-step for each cycle. For the first cycle of the AECM algorithm, we specify the missing data to be just the component-indicator vectors, $\boldsymbol{z}_1, \ldots, \boldsymbol{z}_n$; see Equation (5.4). The E-step on the first cycle on the $(k+1)$th iteration is essentially the same as given in Equations (5.5) and (5.6). The first CM-step computes the updated estimate $\boldsymbol{\Psi}_1^{(k+1)}$ as

$$\pi_i^{(k+1)} = \sum_{j=1}^{n} \tau_{ij}^{(k)} / n$$

and

$$\boldsymbol{\mu}_i^{(k+1)} = \sum_{j=1}^{n} \tau_{ij}^{(k)} \boldsymbol{y}_j \Big/ \sum_{j=1}^{n} \tau_{ij}^{(k)}$$

for $i = 1, \ldots, g$. For the second cycle for the updating of $\boldsymbol{\Psi}_2$, we specify the missing data to be the factors $\boldsymbol{U}_{i1}, \ldots, \boldsymbol{U}_{in}$, as well as the component-indicator vectors, $\boldsymbol{z}_1, \ldots, \boldsymbol{z}_n$. On setting $\boldsymbol{\Psi}^{(k+1/2)}$ equal to $(\boldsymbol{\Psi}_1^{(k+1)^T}, \boldsymbol{\Psi}_2^{(k)^T})^T$, the E-step on the second cycle calculates the conditional expectations as

$$E_{\boldsymbol{\Psi}^{(k+1/2)}}\{Z_{ij}(\boldsymbol{U}_{ij} - \boldsymbol{\mu}_i) | \boldsymbol{y}_j\} = \tau_{ij}^{(k+1/2)} \boldsymbol{\gamma}_i^{(k)^T} (\boldsymbol{y}_j - \boldsymbol{\mu}_i)$$

and

$$\begin{aligned} &E_{\boldsymbol{\Psi}^{(k+1/2)}}\{Z_{ij}(\boldsymbol{U}_{ij} - \boldsymbol{\mu}_i)(\boldsymbol{U}_{ij} - \boldsymbol{\mu}_i)^T | \boldsymbol{y}_j\} \\ &= \tau_{ij}^{(k+1/2)} \{\boldsymbol{\gamma}_i^{(k)^T} (\boldsymbol{y}_j - \boldsymbol{\mu}_i)(\boldsymbol{y}_j - \boldsymbol{\mu}_i)^T \boldsymbol{\gamma}_i^{(k)} + \boldsymbol{\Omega}_i^{(k)}\} \end{aligned}$$

where

$$\boldsymbol{\gamma}_i^{(k)} = \left(\boldsymbol{B}_i^{(k)} \boldsymbol{B}_i^{(k)^T} + \boldsymbol{D}_i^{(k)}\right)^{-1} \boldsymbol{B}_i^{(k)}$$

and

$$\boldsymbol{\Omega}_i^{(k)} = \boldsymbol{I}_q - \boldsymbol{\gamma}_i^{(k)^T} \boldsymbol{B}_i^{(k)}$$

for $i = 1, \ldots, g$. The E-step above uses the result that the conditional distribution of $\boldsymbol{U}_{ij}$ given $\boldsymbol{y}_j$ and $z_{ij} = 1$ is given by

$$\boldsymbol{U}_{ij} | \boldsymbol{y}_j, z_{ij} = 1 \sim N\left(\boldsymbol{\gamma}_i^T (\boldsymbol{y}_j - \boldsymbol{\mu}_i), \boldsymbol{\Omega}_i\right)$$

for $i = 1, \ldots, g$; $j = 1, \ldots, n$. The CM-step on the second cycle provides the updated estimate $\boldsymbol{\Psi}_2^{(k+1)}$ as

$$\boldsymbol{B}_i^{(k+1)} = \boldsymbol{V}_i^{(k+1/2)} \boldsymbol{\gamma}_i^{(k)} \left(\boldsymbol{\gamma}_i^{(k)^T} \boldsymbol{V}_i^{(k+1/2)} \boldsymbol{\gamma}_i^{(k)} + \boldsymbol{\Omega}_i^{(k)}\right)^{-1}$$

and

$$\boldsymbol{D}_i^{(k+1)} = \operatorname{diag}\left\{\boldsymbol{V}_i^{(k+1/2)} - \boldsymbol{B}_i^{(k+1)} \boldsymbol{H}_i^{(k+1/2)} \boldsymbol{B}_i^{(k+1)^T}\right\}$$

where

$$\boldsymbol{V}_i^{(k+1/2)} = \frac{\sum_{j=1}^n \tau_{ij}^{(k+1/2)} (\boldsymbol{y}_j - \boldsymbol{\mu}_i^{(k+1)})(\boldsymbol{y}_j - \boldsymbol{\mu}_i^{(k+1)})^T}{\sum_{j=1}^n \tau_{ij}^{(k+1/2)}}$$

and

$$\boldsymbol{H}_i^{(k+1/2)} = \boldsymbol{\gamma}_i^{(k)^T} \boldsymbol{V}_i^{(k+1/2)} \boldsymbol{\gamma}_i^{(k)} + \boldsymbol{\Omega}_i^{(k)}$$

As an illustration, a mixture of factor analyzers model with different values of q is fitted to the wine data set, ignoring the known classification of the data. To determine the initial estimate of $\boldsymbol{\Psi}$, the EMMIX program is used to fit the normal mixture model with unrestricted component-covariance matrices using ten random starting values (with 70% subsampling of the data). The estimates of π_i and $\boldsymbol{\mu}_i$ so obtained are used as the initial values for π_i and $\boldsymbol{\mu}_i$ in the AECM algorithm. The estimate of $\boldsymbol{\Sigma}_i$ so obtained (denoted as $\boldsymbol{\Sigma}_i^{(0)}$) is used to determine the initial estimate of $\boldsymbol{D}_i$, where $\boldsymbol{D}_i^{(0)}$ is taken to be the diagonal matrix formed from the diagonal elements of $\boldsymbol{\Sigma}_i^{(0)}$. An initial estimate of $\boldsymbol{B}_i$ can be obtained using the method described in [20]. The results of the AECM algorithm from $q = 1$ to $q = 8$ are presented in Table 5.2. We have also reported the value of minus twice the likelihood ratio test statistic λ (i.e., twice the increase in the log likelihood), as we proceed from fitting a mixture of q factor analyzers to one with $q + 1$ component factors. For a given level of the number of components g, regularity conditions hold for the asymptotic null distribution of $-2 \log \lambda$ to be chi-squared with d degrees of freedom, where d is the difference between the number of parameters under the null and alternative hypotheses for the value of q. It can be seen from Table 5.2 that the apparent error rate of the outright clustering is smallest for $q = 2$ and 3. However, this error rate is unknown in a clustering context and so cannot be used as a guide to the choice of q. Concerning the use of the likelihood ratio test to decide on the number of factors q, the test of $q = q_0 = 6$ versus $q = q_0 + 1 = 7$ is not significant ($P = 0.28$), on taking $-2 \log \lambda$ to be chi-squared with $d = g(p - q_0) = 21$ degrees of freedom under the null hypothesis that $q = q_0 = 6$.

TABLE 5.2 Results of the AECM Algorithm for Example 5.2

q	Log Likelihood	Error (%Error)	$-2 \log \lambda$
1	−3102.254	2 (1.12)	—
2	−2995.334	1 (0.56)	213.8
3	−2913.122	1 (0.56)	164.4
4	−2871.655	3 (1.69)	82.93
5	−2831.860	4 (2.25)	79.59
6	−2811.290	4 (2.25)	41.14
7	−2799.204	4 (2.25)	24.17
8	−2788.542	4 (2.25)	21.32

5.5 Advanced Topics

In this section, we consider some extensions of the EM algorithm to handle problems with more difficult E-step and/or M-step computations, and to tackle problems of slow convergence. Moreover, we present a brief account of the applications of the EM algorithm in the context of Hidden Markov Models (HMMs), which provide a convenient way of formulating an extension of a mixture model to allow for dependent data.

In some applications of the EM algorithm such as with generalized linear mixed models, the E-step is complex and does not admit a close-form solution to the Q-function. In this case, the E-step may be executed by a Monte Carlo (MC) process. At the $(k+1)$th iteration, the E-step involves

- simulation of M independent sets of realizations of the missing data $\boldsymbol{Z}$ from the conditional distribution $g(\boldsymbol{z}|\boldsymbol{y}; \boldsymbol{\Psi}^{(k)})$
- approximation of the Q-function by

$$Q(\boldsymbol{\Psi}; \boldsymbol{\Psi}^{(k)}) \approx Q_M(\boldsymbol{\Psi}; \boldsymbol{\Psi}^{(k)}) = \frac{1}{M} \sum_{m=1}^{M} \log L_c(\boldsymbol{\Psi}; \boldsymbol{y}, \boldsymbol{z}^{(m_k)})$$

  where $\boldsymbol{z}^{(m_k)}$ is the mth set of missing values based on $\boldsymbol{\Psi}^{(k)}$

In the M-step, the Q-function is maximized over $\boldsymbol{\Psi}$ to obtain $\boldsymbol{\Psi}^{(k+1)}$. This variant is known as the *Monte Carlo EM (MCEM)* algorithm [33]. As an MC error is introduced at the E-step, the monotonicity property is lost. But in certain cases, the algorithm gets close to a maximizer with a high probability [4]. The problems of specifying M and monitoring convergence are of central importance in the routine use of the algorithm; see [4, 18, 33].

With the EM algorithm, the M-step involves only complete-data ML estimation, which is often computationally simple. However, in some applications, such as that in mixtures of factor analyzers (Section 5.4.2), the M-step is rather complicated.

The ECM algorithm [23] is a natural extension of the EM algorithm in situations where the maximization process on the M-step is relatively simple when conditional on some function of the parameters under estimation. The ECM algorithm takes advantage of the simplicity of complete-data conditional maximization by replacing a complicated M-step of the EM algorithm with several computationally simpler CM steps. In particular, the ECM algorithm preserves the appealing convergence properties of the EM algorithm [18, 23]. The AECM algorithm [24] mentioned in Section 5.4.2 allows the specification of the complete-data to vary where necessary over the CM-steps within and between iterations. This flexible data augmentation and model reduction scheme is eminently suitable for applications like mixtures of factor analyzers where the parameters are large in number.

Massively huge data sets of millions of multidimensional observations are now commonplace. There is an ever increasing demand on speeding up the convergence of the EM algorithm to large databases. But at the same time, it is highly desirable if its simplicity and stability can be preserved. An incremental version of the EM algorithm was proposed by Neal and Hinton [25] to improve the rate of convergence of the EM algorithm. This incremental EM (IEM) algorithm proceeds by dividing the data into B blocks and implementing the (partial) E-step for only a block of data at a time before performing an M-step. That is, a "scan" of the IEM algorithm consists of B partial E-steps and B full M-steps [26]. It can be shown from Exercises 6 and 7 in Section 5.6 that the IEM algorithm in general converges with fewer scans and hence faster than the EM algorithm. The IEM algorithm also increases the likelihood at each scan; see the discussion in [27].

In the mixture framework with observations $\boldsymbol{y}_1, \ldots, \boldsymbol{y}_n$, the unobservable component-indicator vector $\boldsymbol{z} = (\boldsymbol{z}_1^T, \ldots, \boldsymbol{z}_n^T)^T$ can be termed as the "hidden variable." In speech recognition applications, the $\boldsymbol{z}_j$ may be unknown serially dependent prototypical spectra on which the observed speech signals $\boldsymbol{y}_j$ depend $(j = 1, \ldots, n)$. Hence the sequence or set of hidden values $\boldsymbol{z}_j$ cannot be regarded as independent. In the automatic speech recognition applications or natural language processing (NLP) tasks, a stationary Markovian model over a finite state space is generally formulated for the distribution of the hidden variable $\boldsymbol{Z}$ [18]. As a consequence of the dependent structure of $\boldsymbol{Z}$, the density of $\boldsymbol{Y}_j$ will not have its simple representation [Equation (5.1)] of a mixture density as in the independence case. However, $\boldsymbol{Y}_1, \ldots, \boldsymbol{Y}_n$ are assumed conditionally independent given $\boldsymbol{z}_1, \ldots, \boldsymbol{z}_n$; that is

$$f(\boldsymbol{y}_1, \ldots, \boldsymbol{y}_n | \boldsymbol{z}_1, \ldots, \boldsymbol{z}_n; \boldsymbol{\theta}) = \prod_{j=1}^{n} f(\boldsymbol{y}_j | \boldsymbol{z}_j; \boldsymbol{\theta})$$

where $\boldsymbol{\theta}$ denotes the vector containing the unknown parameters in these conditional distributions that are known a priori to be distinct. The application of the EM algorithm to this problem is known as the *Baum–Welch algorithm* in the HMM literature. Baum and his collaborators formulated this algorithm before the appearance of the EM algorithm in Dempster et al. [8] and established the convergence properties for this algorithm; see [2] and the references therein. The E-step can be implemented exactly, but it does require a forward and backward recursion through the data [18]. The M-step can be implemented in closed form, using formulas which are a combination of the MLEs for the multinomial parameters and Markov chain transition probabilities; see [14, 30].

5.6 Exercises

Ten exercises are given in this section. They arise in various scientific fields in the contexts of data mining and pattern recognition, in which the EM algorithm or its variants have been applied. The exercises include problems where the incompleteness of the data is perhaps not as natural or evident as in the two illustrative examples in Section 5.4.

1. Böhning et al. [3] consider a cohort study on the health status of 602 preschool children from 1982 to 1985 in northest Thailand [32]. The frequencies of illness spells (fever, cough, or both) during the study period are presented in Table 5.3. A three-component mixture of Poisson distributions is fitted to the data. The log likelihood function is given by

$$\log L(\boldsymbol{\Psi}) = \sum_{j=1}^{n} \log \left\{ \sum_{i=1}^{3} \pi_i f(y_j, \theta_i) \right\}$$

where $\boldsymbol{\Psi} = (\pi_1, \pi_2, \theta_1, \theta_2, \theta_3)^T$ and

$$f(y_j, \theta_i) = \exp(-\theta_i)\theta_i^{y_j}/y_j! \qquad (i = 1, 2, 3)$$

With reference to Section 5.4.1, let

$$\tau_i(y_j; \boldsymbol{\Psi}^{(k)}) = \pi_i^{(k)} f\left(y_j, \theta_i^{(k)}\right) \Big/ \sum_{h=1}^{3} \pi_h^{(k)} f\left(y_j, \theta_h^{(k)}\right) \qquad (i = 1, 2, 3)$$

denote the posterior probability that y_j belongs to the ith component. Show that the M-step updates the estimates as

$$\pi_i^{(k+1)} = \sum_{j=1}^{n} \tau_i(y_j; \boldsymbol{\Psi}^{(k)})/n \qquad (i = 1, 2)$$

$$\theta_i^{(k+1)} = \sum_{j=1}^{n} \tau_i(y_j; \boldsymbol{\Psi}^{(k)}) y_j \big/ \left(n\pi_i^{(k+1)}\right) \qquad (i = 1, 2, 3)$$

Using the initial estimates $\pi_1 = 0.6, \pi_2 = 0.3, \theta_1 = 2, \theta_2 = 9$, and $\theta_3 = 17$, find the MLE of $\boldsymbol{\Psi}$.

TABLE 5.3 Frequencies of Illness Spells for a Cohort Sample of Preschool Children in Northest Thailand

No. of Illnesses	Frequency	No. of Illnesses	Frequency	No. of Illnesses	Frequency
0	120	8	25	16	6
1	64	9	19	17	5
2	69	10	18	18	1
3	72	11	18	19	3
4	54	12	13	20	1
5	35	13	4	21	2
6	36	14	3	23	1
7	25	15	6	24	2

2. The fitting of mixtures of (multivariate) t distributions was proposed by McLachlan and Peel [19] to provide a more robust approach to the fitting of normal mixture models. A g-component mixture of t distributions is given by

$$f(\boldsymbol{y}_j; \boldsymbol{\Psi}) = \sum_{i=1}^{g} \pi_i f(\boldsymbol{y}_j; \boldsymbol{\mu}_i, \boldsymbol{\Sigma}_i, \nu_i)$$

where the component density $f(\boldsymbol{y}_j; \boldsymbol{\mu}_i, \boldsymbol{\Sigma}_i, \nu_i)$ has a multivariate t distribution with location $\boldsymbol{\mu}_i$, positive definite inner product matrix $\boldsymbol{\Sigma}_i$, and ν_i degrees of freedom ($i = 1, \ldots, g$); see [19, 29]. The vector of unknown parameters is

$$\boldsymbol{\Psi} = (\pi_1, \ldots, \pi_{g-1}, \boldsymbol{\theta}^T, \boldsymbol{\nu}^T)^T$$

where $\boldsymbol{\nu} = (\nu_1, \ldots, \nu_g)^T$ are the degrees of freedom for the t distributions, and $\boldsymbol{\theta} = (\boldsymbol{\theta}_1^T, \ldots, \boldsymbol{\theta}_g^T)^T$, and where $\boldsymbol{\theta}_i$ contains the elements of $\boldsymbol{\mu}_i$ and the distinct elements of $\boldsymbol{\Sigma}_i$ ($i = 1, \ldots, g$). With reference to Section 5.4.1, the observed data augmented by the component-indicator vectors $\boldsymbol{z}_1, \ldots, \boldsymbol{z}_n$ are viewed as still being incomplete. Additional missing data, $u_1, \ldots, u_n$, are introduced into the complete-data vector, that is,

$$\boldsymbol{x} = \left(\boldsymbol{y}^T, \boldsymbol{z}_1^T, \ldots, \boldsymbol{z}_n^T, u_1, \ldots, u_n\right)^T$$

where $u_1, \ldots, u_n$ are defined so that, given $z_{ij} = 1$,

$$\boldsymbol{Y}_j | u_j, z_{ij} = 1 \sim N(\boldsymbol{\mu}_i, \boldsymbol{\Sigma}_i / u_j)$$

independently for $j = 1, \ldots, n$, and

$$U_j | z_{ij} = 1 \sim \text{gamma}\left(\tfrac{1}{2}\nu_i, \tfrac{1}{2}\nu_i\right)$$

Show that the complete-data log likelihood can be written in three terms as

$$\log L_c(\boldsymbol{\Psi}) = \log L_{1c}(\boldsymbol{\pi}) + \log L_{2c}(\boldsymbol{\nu}) + \log L_{3c}(\boldsymbol{\theta}) \qquad (5.10)$$

where

$$\log L_{1c}(\boldsymbol{\pi}) = \sum_{i=1}^{g}\sum_{j=1}^{n} z_{ij} \log \pi_i$$

$$\log L_{2c}(\boldsymbol{\nu}) = \sum_{i=1}^{g}\sum_{j=1}^{n} z_{ij}\{-\log\Gamma(\tfrac{1}{2}\nu_i) + \tfrac{1}{2}\nu_i \log(\tfrac{1}{2}\nu_i) + \tfrac{1}{2}\nu_i(\log u_j - u_j) - \log u_j\}$$

and

$$\log L_{3c}(\boldsymbol{\theta}) = \sum_{i=1}^{g}\sum_{j=1}^{n} z_{ij}\{-\tfrac{1}{2}p\log(2\pi) - \tfrac{1}{2}\log|\boldsymbol{\Sigma}_i| - \tfrac{1}{2}u_j\delta(\boldsymbol{y}_j, \boldsymbol{\mu}_i, ; \boldsymbol{\Sigma}_i)\}$$

where

$$\delta(\boldsymbol{y}_j, \boldsymbol{\mu}_i; \boldsymbol{\Sigma}_i) = (\boldsymbol{y}_j - \boldsymbol{\mu}_i)^T \boldsymbol{\Sigma}_i^{-1}(\boldsymbol{y}_j - \boldsymbol{\mu}_i)$$

3. With reference to the above mixtures of t distributions, show that the E-step on the $(k+1)$th iteration of the EM algorithm involves the calculation of

$$E_{\boldsymbol{\Psi}^{(k)}}(Z_{ij}|\boldsymbol{y}) = \tau_{ij}^{(k)} = \frac{\pi_i^{(k)} f(\boldsymbol{y}_j; \boldsymbol{\mu}_i^{(k)}, \boldsymbol{\Sigma}_i^{(k)}, \nu_i^{(k)})}{f(\boldsymbol{y}_j; \boldsymbol{\Psi}^{(k)})} \tag{5.11}$$

$$E_{\boldsymbol{\Psi}^{(k)}}(U_j|\boldsymbol{y}, z_{ij} = 1) = u_{ij}^{(k)} = \frac{\nu_i^{(k)} + p}{\nu_i^{(k)} + \delta(\boldsymbol{y}_j, \boldsymbol{\mu}_i^{(k)}; \boldsymbol{\Sigma}_i^{(k)})} \tag{5.12}$$

and

$$E_{\boldsymbol{\Psi}^{(k)}}(\log U_j|\boldsymbol{y}, z_{ij} = 1) = \log u_{ij}^{(k)} + \left\{\psi\left(\frac{\nu_i^{(k)} + p}{2}\right) - \log\left(\frac{\nu_i^{(k)} + p}{2}\right)\right\} \tag{5.13}$$

for $i = 1, \ldots, g$; $j = 1, \ldots, n$. In Equation (5.13),

$$\psi(r) = \{\partial\Gamma(r)/\partial r\}/\Gamma(r)$$

is the Digamma function [29]. Hint for Equation (5.12): the gamma distribution is the conjugate prior distribution for U_j; Hint for Equation (5.13): if a random variable S has a gamma(α, β) distribution, then

$$E(\log S) = \psi(\alpha) - \log\beta.$$

Also, it follows from Equation (5.10) that $\boldsymbol{\pi}^{(k+1)}$, $\boldsymbol{\theta}^{(k+1)}$, and $\boldsymbol{\nu}^{(k+1)}$ can be computed on the M-step independently of each other. Show that the updating formulas for the first two are

$$\pi_i^{(k+1)} = \sum_{j=1}^{n} \tau_{ij}^{(k)}/n$$

$$\boldsymbol{\mu}_i^{(k+1)} = \sum_{j=1}^{n} \tau_{ij}^{(k)} u_{ij}^{(k)} \boldsymbol{y}_j \Big/ \sum_{j=1}^{n} \tau_{ij}^{(k)} u_{ij}^{(k)}$$

and

$$\boldsymbol{\Sigma}_i^{(k+1)} = \frac{\sum_{j=1}^n \tau_{ij}^{(k)} u_{ij}^{(k)} (\boldsymbol{y}_j - \boldsymbol{\mu}_i^{(k+1)})(\boldsymbol{y}_j - \boldsymbol{\mu}_i^{(k+1)})^T}{\sum_{j=1}^n \tau_{ij}^{(k)}}$$

The updates $\nu_i^{(k+1)}$ for the degrees of freedom need to be computed iteratively. It follows from Equation (5.10) that $\nu_i^{(k+1)}$ is a solution of the equation

$$\left\{ -\psi\left(\tfrac{1}{2}\nu_i\right) + \log\left(\tfrac{1}{2}\nu_i\right) + 1 + \tfrac{1}{n_i^{(k)}} \sum_{j=1}^n \tau_{ij}^{(k)} \left(\log u_{ij}^{(k)} - u_{ij}^{(k)}\right) + \psi\left(\frac{\nu_i^{(k)} + p}{2}\right) - \log\left(\frac{\nu_i^{(k)} + p}{2}\right) \right\} = 0$$

where $n_i^{(k)} = \sum_{j=1}^n \tau_{ij}^{(k)}$ $(i = 1, \ldots, g)$.

4. The EMMIX program [22] has an option for the fitting of mixtures of multivariate t components. Now fit a mixture of two t components (with unrestricted scale matrices $\boldsymbol{\Sigma}_i$ and unequal degrees of freedom ν_i) to the *Leptograpsus* crab data set of Campbell and Mahon [5]. With the crab data, one species has been split into two new species, previously grouped by color form, orange and blue. Data are available on 50 specimens of each sex of each species. Attention here is focussed on the sample of $n = 100$ five-dimensional measurements on orange crabs (the two components correspond to the males and females). Run the EMMIX program with automatic starting values from 10 random starts (using 100% subsampling of the data), 10 k-means starts, and 6 hierarchical methods (with user-supplied initial values $\nu_1^{(0)} = \nu_2^{(0)} = 13.193$ which is obtained in the case of equal scale matrices and equal degrees of freedom). Verify estimates of $\boldsymbol{\nu}$ are $\hat{\nu}_1 = 12.2$ and $\hat{\nu}_2 = 300.0$ and the numbers assigned to each component are, respectively, 47 and 53 (misclassification rate $= 3\%$).

5. For a mixture of g component distributions of generalized linear models (GLMs) in proportions $\pi_1, \ldots, \pi_g$, the density of the jth response variable Y_j is given by

$$f(y_j; \boldsymbol{\Psi}) = \sum_{i=1}^{g} \pi_i f(y_j; \theta_{ij}, \kappa_i)$$

where the log density for the ith component is given by

$$\log f(y_j; \theta_{ij}, \kappa_i) = \kappa_i^{-1}\{\theta_{ij} y_j - b(\theta_{ij})\} + c(y_j; \kappa_i) \quad (i = 1, \ldots, g)$$

where θ_{ij} is the natural or canonical parameter and κ_i is the dispersion parameter. For the ith component GLM, denote μ_{ij} the conditional mean of Y_j and $\eta_{ij} = h_i(\mu_{ij}) = \boldsymbol{\beta}_i^T \boldsymbol{x}_j$ the linear predictor, where $h_i(\cdot)$ is the link function and $\boldsymbol{x}_j$ is a vector of explanatory variables on the jth response y_j [20]. The vector of unknown parameters is $\boldsymbol{\Psi} = (\pi_1, \ldots, \pi_{g-1}, \kappa_1, \ldots, \kappa_g, \boldsymbol{\beta}_1^T, \ldots, \boldsymbol{\beta}_g^T)^T$. Let z_{ij} denote the component-indicator variables as defined in Section 5.4.1. The E-step is essentially the same as given in Equations (5.5) and (5.6), with the component densities $\phi(\boldsymbol{y}_j; \boldsymbol{\mu}_i, \boldsymbol{\Sigma}_i)$ replaced by $f(y_j; \theta_{ij}, \kappa_i)$. On the M-step, the updating formula for $\pi_i^{(k+1)}$ $(i = 1, \ldots, g-1)$ is

$$\pi_i^{(k+1)} = \sum_{j=1}^{n} \tau_{ij}^{(k)} / n$$

where

$$\tau_{ij}^{(k)} = \pi_i^{(k)} f\left(y_j; \theta_{ij}^{(k)}, \kappa_i^{(k)}\right) \Big/ \sum_{h=1}^{g} \pi_h^{(k)} f\left(y_j; \theta_{hj}^{(k)}, \kappa_h^{(k)}\right)$$

The updates $\kappa_i^{(k+1)}$ and $\boldsymbol{\beta}_i^{(k+1)}$ need to be computed iteratively by solving

$$\begin{aligned} \sum_{j=1}^{n} \tau_{ij}^{(k)} \partial \log f(y_j; \theta_{ij}, \kappa_i)/\partial \kappa &= 0 \\ \sum_{j=1}^{n} \tau_{ij}^{(k)} \partial \log f(y_j; \theta_{ij}, \kappa_i)/\partial \boldsymbol{\beta}_i &= \mathbf{0} \end{aligned} \qquad (5.14)$$

Consider a mixture of gamma distributions, where the gamma density function for the ith component is given by

$$f(y_j; \mu_{ij}, \alpha_i) = \frac{(\frac{\alpha_i}{\mu_{ij}})^{\alpha_i} y_j^{(\alpha_i - 1)} \exp(-\frac{\alpha_i}{\mu_{ij}} y_j)}{\Gamma(\alpha_i)}$$

where $\alpha_i > 0$ is the shape parameter, which does not depend on the explanatory variables. The linear predictor is modelled via a log-link as

$$\eta_{ij} = h_i(\mu_{ij}) = \log \mu_{ij} = \boldsymbol{\beta}_i^T \boldsymbol{x}_j$$

With reference to Equation (5.14), show that the M-step for a mixture of gamma distributions involves solving the nonlinear equations

$$\sum_{j=1}^{n} \tau_{ij}^{(k)} \{1 + \log \alpha_i - \log \mu_{ij} + \log y_j - y_j/\mu_{ij} - \psi(\alpha_i)\} = 0,$$

$$\sum_{j=1}^{n} \tau_{ij}^{(k)} (-1 + y_j/\mu_{ij}) \alpha_i \boldsymbol{x}_j = \mathbf{0}$$

where $\psi(r) = \{\partial \Gamma(r)/\partial r\}/\Gamma(r)$ is the digamma function.

6. With the IEM algorithm described in Section 5.5, let $\boldsymbol{\Psi}^{(k+b/B)}$ denote the value of $\boldsymbol{\Psi}$ after the bth iteration on the $(k+1)$th scan $(b = 1, \ldots, B)$. In the context of g-component normal mixture models (Section 5.4.1), the partial E-step on the $(b+1)$th iteration of the $(k+1)$th scan replaces z_{ij} by $\tau_i(\boldsymbol{y}_j; \boldsymbol{\Psi}^{(k+b/B)})$ for those $\boldsymbol{y}_j$ in the $(b+1)$th block $(b = 0, \ldots, B-1;\ i = 1, \ldots, g)$. With reference to Equation (5.7), let $\boldsymbol{T}_{iq,b+1}^{(k+b/B)}$ denote the conditional expectations of

the sufficient statistics for the $(b+1)$th block $(b = 0, \ldots, B-1;\ q = 1, 2, 3)$. For example,

$$\boldsymbol{T}_{i1,b+1}^{(k+b/B)} = \sum_{j \in S_b} \tau_i(\boldsymbol{y}_j; \boldsymbol{\Psi}^{(k+b/B)}) \qquad (i = 1, \ldots, g)$$

where S_b is a subset of $\{1, \ldots, n\}$ containing the subscripts of those $\boldsymbol{y}_j$ that belong to the $(b+1)$th block $(b = 0, \ldots, B-1)$. From Equations (5.7) and (5.8), show that the M-step on the $(b+1)$th iteration of the $(k+1)$th scan of the IEM algorithm involves the update of the estimates of π_i, $\boldsymbol{\mu}_i$, and $\boldsymbol{\Sigma}_i$ as follows:

$$\begin{aligned}
\pi_i^{(k+(b+1)/B)} &= T_{i1}^{(k+b/B)}/n \\
\boldsymbol{\mu}_i^{(k+(b+1)/B)} &= \boldsymbol{T}_{i2}^{(k+b/B)}/T_{i1}^{(k+b/B)} \\
\boldsymbol{\Sigma}_i^{(k+(b+1)/B)} &= \{\boldsymbol{T}_{i3}^{(k+b/B)} - T_{i1}^{(k+b/B)^{-1}}\boldsymbol{T}_{i2}^{(k+b/B)}\boldsymbol{T}_{i2}^{(k+b/B)^T}\}/T_{i1}^{(k+b/B)}
\end{aligned}$$

for $i = 1, \ldots, g$, where

$$\boldsymbol{T}_{iq}^{(k+b/B)} = \boldsymbol{T}_{iq}^{(k+(b-1)/B)} - \boldsymbol{T}_{iq,b+1}^{(k-1+b/B)} + \boldsymbol{T}_{iq,b+1}^{(k+b/B)} \tag{5.15}$$

for $i = 1, \ldots, g$ and $q = 1, 2, 3$. It is noted that the first and second terms on the right-hand side of Equation (5.15) are already available from the previous iteration and the previous scan, respectively. In practice, the IEM algorithm is implemented by running the standard EM algorithm for the first few scans to avoid the "premature component starvation" problem [26]. In this case, we have

$$\boldsymbol{T}_{iq}^{(k)} = \sum_{b=1}^{B} \boldsymbol{T}_{iq,b}^{(k)} \qquad (i = 1, \ldots, g;\ q = 1, 2, 3)$$

7. With the IEM algorithm, Ng and McLachlan [26] provide a simple guide for choosing the number of blocks B for normal mixtures. In the case of component-covariance matrices specified to be diagonal (such as in Example 5.1), they suggest $B \approx n^{1/3}$. For the *Iris* data in Example 5.1, it implies that $B \approx (150)^{1/3}$. Run an IEM algorithm to the *Iris* data with $B = 5$ and the same initial values of $\boldsymbol{\Psi}$ as in Example 5.1. Verify that (a) the final estimates and the log likelihood value are approximately the same as those using the EM algorithm, and (b) the IEM algorithm converges with fewer scans than the EM algorithm and increases the likelihood at each scan; see the discussion in [27].
8. Ng and McLachlan [28] apply the ECM algorithm for training the mixture of experts (ME) networks [10, 12]. In ME networks, there are several modules, referred to as expert networks. These expert networks approximate the distribution of $\boldsymbol{y}_j$ within each region of the input space. The expert network maps its input $\boldsymbol{x}_j$ to an output $\boldsymbol{y}_j$, with conditional density $f_h(\boldsymbol{y}_j|\boldsymbol{x}_j; \boldsymbol{\theta}_h)$, where $\boldsymbol{\theta}_h$ is a vector of unknown parameters for the hth expert network $(h = 1, \ldots, M)$. The gating network provides a set of scalar coefficients $\pi_h(\boldsymbol{x}_j; \boldsymbol{\alpha})$ that weight the

contributions of the various experts, where $\boldsymbol{\alpha}$ is a vector of unknown parameters in the gating network. The final output of the ME network is a weighted sum of all the output vectors produced by the expert networks,

$$f(\boldsymbol{y}_j|\boldsymbol{x}_j;\boldsymbol{\Psi}) = \sum_{h=1}^{M} \pi_h(\boldsymbol{x}_j;\boldsymbol{\alpha}) f_h(\boldsymbol{y}_j|\boldsymbol{x}_j;\boldsymbol{\theta}_h)$$

Within the incomplete-data framework of the EM algorithm, we introduce the indicator variables Z_{hj}, where z_{hj} is 1 or 0 according to whether $\boldsymbol{y}_j$ belongs or does not belong to the hth expert. Show that the complete-data log likelihood for $\boldsymbol{\Psi}$ is given by

$$\log L_c(\boldsymbol{\Psi}) = \sum_{j=1}^{n}\sum_{h=1}^{M} z_{hj}\{\log \pi_h(\boldsymbol{x}_j;\boldsymbol{\alpha}) + \log f_h(\boldsymbol{y}_j|\boldsymbol{x}_j;\boldsymbol{\theta}_h)\}$$

and the Q-function can be decomposed into two terms with respect to $\boldsymbol{\alpha}$ and $\boldsymbol{\theta}_h$ $(h = 1, \ldots, M)$, respectively, as

$$Q(\boldsymbol{\Psi};\boldsymbol{\Psi}^{(k)}) = Q_{\boldsymbol{\alpha}} + Q_{\boldsymbol{\theta}}$$

where

$$Q_{\boldsymbol{\alpha}} = \sum_{j=1}^{n}\sum_{h=1}^{M} \tau_{hj}^{(k)} \log \pi_h(\boldsymbol{x}_j;\boldsymbol{\alpha})$$

$$Q_{\boldsymbol{\theta}} = \sum_{j=1}^{n}\sum_{h=1}^{M} \tau_{hj}^{(k)} \log f_h(\boldsymbol{y}_j|\boldsymbol{x}_j;\boldsymbol{\theta}_h)$$

and where

$$\tau_{hj}^{(k)} = \pi_h(\boldsymbol{x}_j;\boldsymbol{\alpha}^{(k)}) f_h\left(\boldsymbol{y}_j|\boldsymbol{x}_j;\boldsymbol{\theta}_h^{(k)}\right) \Big/ \sum_{r=1}^{M} \pi_r(\boldsymbol{x}_j;\boldsymbol{\alpha}^{(k)}) f_r\left(\boldsymbol{y}_j|\boldsymbol{x}_j;\boldsymbol{\theta}_r^{(k)}\right)$$

9. With the ME networks above, the output of the gating network is usually modeled by the multinomial logit (or softmax) function as

$$\pi_h(\boldsymbol{x}_j;\boldsymbol{\alpha}) = \frac{\exp(\boldsymbol{v}_h^T\boldsymbol{x}_j)}{1+\sum_{r=1}^{M-1}\exp(\boldsymbol{v}_r^T\boldsymbol{x}_j)} \qquad (h = 1, \ldots, M-1)$$

and $\pi_M(\boldsymbol{x}_j;\boldsymbol{\alpha}) = 1/(1+\sum_{r=1}^{M-1}\exp(\boldsymbol{v}_r^T\boldsymbol{x}_j))$. Here $\boldsymbol{\alpha}$ contains the elements in $\boldsymbol{v}_h$ $(h = 1, \ldots, M-1)$. Show that the updated estimate of $\boldsymbol{\alpha}^{(k+1)}$ on the M-step is obtained by solving

$$\sum_{j=1}^{n}\left(\tau_{hj}^{(k)} - \frac{\exp(\boldsymbol{v}_h^T\boldsymbol{x}_j)}{1+\sum_{r=1}^{M-1}\exp(\boldsymbol{v}_r^T\boldsymbol{x}_j)}\right)\boldsymbol{x}_j = \boldsymbol{0}$$

for $h = 1, \ldots, M-1$, which is a set of nonlinear equations. It is noted that the nonlinear equation for the hth expert depends not only on the parameter vector $\boldsymbol{v}_h$, but also on other parameter vectors in $\boldsymbol{\alpha}$. In other words, each parameter vector $\boldsymbol{v}_h$ cannot be updated independently. With the IRLS algorithm presented in [12], the independence assumption on these parameter vectors was used implicitly. Ng and McLachlan [28] propose an ECM algorithm for which the M-step is replaced by $(M-1)$ computationally simpler CM-steps for $\boldsymbol{v}_h$ $(h = 1, \ldots, M-1)$.

10. McLachlan and Chang [17] consider the mixture model-based approach to the cluster analysis of mixed data, where the observations consist of both continuous and categorical variables. Suppose that p_1 of the p feature variables in $\boldsymbol{Y}_j$ are categorical, where the qth categorical variable takes on m_q distinct values $(q = 1, \ldots, p_1)$. With the location model-based cluster approach [20], the p_1 categorical variables are uniquely transformed to a single multinomial random variable $\boldsymbol{U}$ with S cells, where $S = \prod_{q=1}^{p_1} m_q$ is the number of distinct patterns (locations) of the p_1 categorical variables. We let $(\boldsymbol{u}_j)_s$ be the label for the sth location of the jth entity $(s = 1, \ldots, S;\ j = 1, \ldots, n)$, where $(\boldsymbol{u}_j)_s = 1$ if the realizations of the p_1 categorical variables correspond to the sth pattern, and is zero otherwise. The location model assumes further that conditional on $(\boldsymbol{u}_j)_s = 1$, the conditional distribution of the $p - p_1$ continuous variables is normal with mean $\boldsymbol{\mu}_{is}$ and covariance matrix $\boldsymbol{\Sigma}_i$, which is the same for all S cells. Let p_{is} be the conditional probability that $(\boldsymbol{U}_j)_s = 1$ given its membership of the ith component of the mixture $(s = 1, \ldots, S;\ i = 1, \ldots, g)$. With reference to Section 5.4.1, show that on the $(k+1)$th iteration of the EM algorithm, the updated estimates are given by

$$\pi_i^{(k+1)} = \sum_{s=1}^{S}\sum_{j=1}^{n} \delta_{js}\tau_{ijs}^{(k)} \Big/ n$$

$$p_{is}^{(k+1)} = \sum_{j=1}^{n} \delta_{js}\tau_{ijs}^{(k)} \Big/ \sum_{r=1}^{S}\sum_{j=1}^{n} \delta_{jr}\tau_{ijr}^{(k)}$$

$$\boldsymbol{\mu}_{is}^{(k+1)} = \sum_{j=1}^{n} \delta_{js}\tau_{ijs}^{(k)}\boldsymbol{y}_j^* \Big/ \sum_{j=1}^{n} \delta_{js}\tau_{ijs}^{(k)}$$

and

$$\boldsymbol{\Sigma}_i^{(k+1)} = \sum_{s=1}^{S}\sum_{j=1}^{n} \delta_{js}\tau_{ijs}^{(k)}\left(\boldsymbol{y}_j^* - \boldsymbol{\mu}_{is}^{(k+1)}\right)\left(\boldsymbol{y}_j^* - \boldsymbol{\mu}_{is}^{(k+1)}\right)^T \Big/ \sum_{s=1}^{S}\sum_{j=1}^{n} \delta_{js}\tau_{ijs}^{(k)}$$

where δ_{js} is 1 or 0 according as to whether $(\boldsymbol{u}_j)_s$ equals 1 or 0, $\boldsymbol{y}_j^*$ contains the continuous variables in $\boldsymbol{y}_j$, and

$$\tau_{ijs}^{(k)} = \pi_i^{(k)} p_{is}^{(k)} \phi\left(\boldsymbol{y}_j^*; \boldsymbol{\mu}_{is}^{(k)}, \boldsymbol{\Sigma}_i^{(k)}\right) \Big/ \sum_{h=1}^{g} \pi_h^{(k)} p_{hs}^{(k)} \phi\left(\boldsymbol{y}_j^*; \boldsymbol{\mu}_{hs}^{(k)}, \boldsymbol{\Sigma}_h^{(k)}\right)$$

for $s = 1, \ldots, S;\ i = 1, \ldots, g$.

References

[1] A. Asuncion and D.J. Newman. UCI Machine Learning Repository. University of California, School of Information and Computer Sciences, Irvine, 2007. http://www.ics.uci.edu/ mlearn/MLRepository.html.

[2] L.E. Baum, T. Petrie, G. Soules, and N. Weiss. A maximisation technique occurring in the statistical analysis of probabilistic functions of Markov process. *Annals of Mathematical Statistics*, 41:164–171, 1970.

[3] D. Böhning, P. Schlattmann, and B. Lindsay. Computer-assisted analysis of mixtures (C.A.MAN): Statistical algorithms. *Biometrics*, 48:283–303, 1992.

[4] J.G. Booth and J.P. Hobert. Maximizing generalized linear mixed model likelihoods with an automated Monte Carlo EM algorithm. *Journal of the Royal Statistical Society B*, 61:265–285, 1999.

[5] N.A. Campbell and R.J. Mahon. A multivariate study of variation in two species of rock crab of genus *Leptograpsus*. *Australian Journal of Zoology*, 22:417–425, 1974.

[6] D.R. Cox and D. Hinkley. *Theoretical Statistics*. Chapman & Hall, London, 1974.

[7] H. Cramér. *Mathematical Methods of Statistics*. Princeton University Press, New Jersey, 1946.

[8] A.P. Dempster, N.M. Laird, and D.B. Rubin. Maximum likelihood from incomplete data via the EM algorithm. *Journal of the Royal Statistical Society B*, 39:1–38, 1977.

[9] C. Fraley and A.E. Raftery. Mclust: Software for model-based cluster analysis. *Journal of Classification*, 16:297–306, 1999.

[10] R.A. Jacobs, M.I. Jordan, S.J. Nowlan, and G.E. Hinton. Adaptive mixtures of local experts. *Neural Computation*, 3:79–87, 1991.

[11] M. Jamshidian and R.I. Jennrich. Standard errors for EM estimation. *Journal of the Royal Statistical Society B*, 62:257–270, 2000.

[12] M.I. Jordan and R.A. Jacobs. Hierarchical mixtures of experts and the EM algorithm. *Neural Computation*, 6:181–214, 1994.

[13] E.L. Lehmann and G. Casella. *Theory of Point Estimation*. Springer-Verlag, New York, 2003.

[14] B.G. Leroux and M.L. Puterman. Maximum-penalized-likelihood estimation for independent and Markov-dependent mixture models. *Biometrics*, 48:545–558, 1992.

[15] T.A. Louis. Finding the observed information matrix when using the EM algorithm. *Journal of the Royal Statistical Society B*, 44:226–233, 1982.

[16] G.J. McLachlan and K.E. Basford. *Mixture Models: Inference and Applications to Clustering*. Marcel Dekker, New York, 1988.

[17] G.J. McLachlan and S.U. Chang. Mixture modelling for cluster analysis. *Statistical Methods in Medical Research*, 13:347–361, 2004.

[18] G.J. McLachlan and T. Krishnan. *The EM Algorithm and Extensions (2nd edition)*. Wiley, New Jersey, 2008.

[19] G.J. McLachlan and D. Peel. Robust cluster analysis via mixtures of multivariate t-distributions. In *Lecture Notes in Computer Science*, pages 658–666. Springer-Verlag, Berlin, 1998. Vol. 1451.

[20] G.J. McLachlan and D. Peel. *Finite Mixture Models*. Wiley, New York, 2000.

[21] G.J. McLachlan and D. Peel. Mixtures of factor analyzers. In P. Langley, editor, *Proceedings of the 17th International Conference on Machine Learning*, pages 599–606, San Francisco, 2000. Morgan Kaufmann.

[22] G.J. McLachlan, D. Peel, K.E. Basford, and P. Adams. The emmix software for the fitting of mixtures of normal and t-components. *Journal of Statistical Software*, 4:No. 2, 1999.

[23] X.-L. Meng and D. Rubin. Maximum likelihood estimation via the ECM algorithm: A general framework. *Biometrika*, 80:267–278, 1993.

[24] X.-L. Meng and D.A. van Dyk. The EM algorithm—an old folk song sung to a fast new tune. *Journal of the Royal Statistical Society B*, 59:511–567, 1997.

[25] R.M. Neal and G.E. Hinton. A view of the EM algorithm that justifies incremental, sparse, and other variants. In M.I. Jordan, editor, *Learning in Graphical Models*, pages 355–368. Kluwer, Dordrecht, 1998.

[26] S.K. Ng and G.J. McLachlan. On the choice of the number of blocks with the incremental EM algorithm for the fitting of normal mixtures. *Statistics and Computing*, 13:45–55, 2003.

[27] S.K. Ng and G.J. McLachlan. Speeding up the EM algorithm for mixture model-based segmentation of magnetic resonance images. *Pattern Recognition*, 37:1573–1589, 2004.

[28] S.K. Ng and G.J. McLachlan. Using the EM algorithm to train neural networks: Misconceptions and a new algorithm for multiclass classification. *IEEE Transactions on Neural Networks*, 15:738–749, 2004.

[29] D. Peel and G.J. McLachlan. Robust mixture modelling using the t distribution. *Statistics and Computing*, 10:335–344, 2000.

[30] L.R. Rabiner. A tutorial on hidden Markov models and selected applications in speech recognition. *Proceedings of the IEEE*, 77:257–286, 1989.

[31] C.R. Rao. *Linear Statistical Inference and Its Applications (2nd edition)*. Wiley, New York, 1973.

[32] F.-P. Schelp, P. Vivatanasept, P. Sitaputra, S. Sormani, P. Pongpaew, N. Vudhivai, S. Egormaiphol, and D. Böhning. Relationship of the morbidity of under-fives to anthropometric measurements and community health intervention. *Tropical Medicine and Parasitology*, 41:121–126, 1990.

[33] G.C.G. Wei and M.A. Tanner. A Monte Carlo implementation of the EM algorithm and the poor man's data augmentation algorithms. *Journal of the American Statistical Association*, 85:699–704, 1990.

Chapter 6

PageRank

Bing Liu and Philip S. Yu

Contents

6.1 Introduction

Link-based ranking has contributed significantly to the success of Web search. PageRank [1, 7] is perhaps the best known link-based ranking algorithm, which also powers the Google search engine. Due to the huge business success of Google, PageRank has emerged as the dominant link analysis model on the Web.

The PageRank algorithm was first introduced by Sergey Brin and Larry Page at the *Seventh International World Wide Web Conference* (*WWW7*) in April 1998, with the aim of tackling some major difficulties with the content-based ranking algorithms of early search engines. These early search engines essentially retrieved relevant pages for the user based on content similarities of the user query and the indexed pages of the search engines. The retrieval and ranking algorithms were simply direct implementation of those from information retrieval. However, starting from 1996, it became clear that the content similarity alone was no longer sufficient for search due to two main reasons. First, the number of Web pages grew rapidly during the middle to late 1990s. Given any query, the number of relevant pages can be huge. For example, given the search query "classification technique," the Google search engine estimates that there are about 10 million relevant pages. This abundance of information causes a major problem for ranking, that is, how to choose only 10 to 30 pages and rank them suitably to present to the user. Second, content similarity methods are easily spammed. A page owner can repeat some important words and add many remotely related words in his/her pages to boost the rankings of the pages and/or to make the pages relevant to a large number of possible queries.

From around 1996, researchers in academia and search engine companies began to work on the problem. They resort to hyperlinks. Unlike text documents used in traditional information retrieval, which are often considered independent of one another (i.e., with no explicit relationships or links among them except in citation analysis), Web pages are connected through hyperlinks, which carry important information. Some hyperlinks are used to organize a large amount of information at the same Web site, and thus only point to pages in the same site. Other hyperlinks point to pages in other Web sites. Such outgoing hyperlinks often indicate an implicit conveyance of authority to the pages being pointed to. For example, if your page points to an outside page, you obviously believe that this outside page contains quality and useful information to you. Hence, those pages that are pointed to by many other pages are likely to contain authoritative or quality information. Such linkages should obviously be used in page evaluation and ranking in search engines. PageRank precisely exploits such links to provide a powerful ranking algorithm. In essence, PageRank relies on the democratic nature of the Web by using its vast link structure as an indicator of an individual page's quality. It interprets a hyperlink from page x to page y as a vote, by page x, for page y. Additionally, PageRank looks at more than just the sheer number of votes or links that a page receives. It also analyzes the page that casts the vote. Votes cast by pages that are themselves "important" weigh more heavily and help to make other pages more "important." This is the *rank prestige* idea in social networks [9]. In this chapter, we introduce the PageRank algorithm. Along with it, an extension to the algorithm is also presented, which is called Timed-PageRank. Timed-PageRank adds the temporal dimension to search to deal with the dynamic nature of the Web and the aging of Web pages.

6.2 PageRank Algorithm

PageRank produces a static ranking of Web pages in the sense that a PageRank value is computed for each page off-line, and the value is not dependent on search queries. In other words, the PageRank computation is purely based on the existing links on the Web and has nothing to do with each query issued by users. Before introducing the PageRank formula, let us first state some main concepts.

In-links of page i: These are the hyperlinks that point to page i from other pages. Usually, hyperlinks from the same site are not considered.

Out-links of page i: These are the hyperlinks that point out to other pages from page i. Usually, links to pages of the same site are not considered.

The following ideas based on rank prestige [9] are used to derive the PageRank algorithm.

1. A hyperlink from a page pointing to another page is an implicit conveyance of authority to the target page. Thus, the more in-links that a page i receives, the more prestige the page i has.
2. Pages that point to page i also have their own prestige scores. A page with a higher prestige score pointing to i is more important than a page with a lower prestige score pointing to i. In other words, a page is important if it is pointed to by other important pages.

According to rank prestige in social networks, the importance of page i (i's PageRank score) is determined by summing up the PageRank scores of all pages that point to i. Because a page may point to many other pages, its prestige score should be shared among all the pages to which it points.

To formulate the above ideas, we treat the Web as a directed graph $G = (V, E)$, where V is the set of vertices or nodes, that is, the set of all pages, and E is the set of directed edges in the graph, that is, hyperlinks. Let the total number of pages on the Web be n (i.e., $n = |V|$). The PageRank score of the page i [denoted by $P(i)$] is defined by:

$$P(i) = \sum_{(j,i)\in E} \frac{P(j)}{O_j} \tag{6.1}$$

where O_j is the number of out-links of page j. Mathematically, we have a system of n linear equations [Equation (6.1)] with n unknowns. We can use a matrix to represent all the equations. As a notational convention, we use bold and italic letters to represent matrices. Let $\boldsymbol{P}$ be an n-dimensional column vector of PageRank values, that is,

$$\boldsymbol{P} = (P(1), P(2), \ldots, P(n))^T$$

Let $\boldsymbol{A}$ be the adjacency matrix of our graph with

$$A_{ij} = \begin{cases} \dfrac{1}{O_i} & \text{if } (i, j) \in E \\ 0 & \text{otherwise} \end{cases} \tag{6.2}$$

We can write the system of n equations with

$$\boldsymbol{P} = \boldsymbol{A}^T \boldsymbol{P} \tag{6.3}$$

This is the characteristic equation of the *eigensystem,* where the solution to $\boldsymbol{P}$ is an *eigenvector* with the corresponding *eigenvalue* of 1. Because this is a circular definition, an iterative algorithm is used to solve it. It turns out that if some conditions are satisfied (which will be described shortly), 1 is the largest eigenvalue and the PageRank vector $\boldsymbol{P}$ is the *principal eigenvector*. A well-known mathematical technique called *power iteration* [2] can be used to find $\boldsymbol{P}$.

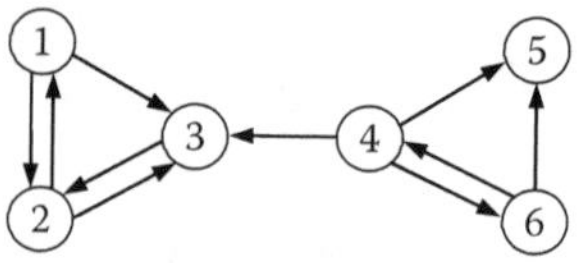

Figure 6.1 An example of a hyperlink graph.

The conditions are that A is a *stochastic matrix* and that it is *irreducible* and *aperiodic*. However, the Web graph does not meet these conditions. In fact, Equation (6.3) can also be derived based on the *Markov chain*. Then some theoretical results from Markov chains can be applied [8], which is where the above three conditions come from.

In the Markov chain model, each Web page or node in the Web graph is regarded as a state. A *hyperlink* is a transition, which leads from one state to another state with a probability. Thus, this framework models Web surfing as a stochastic process. It models a *Web surfer* randomly surfing the Web as a state transition in the Markov chain.

Now let us look at the Web graph and see why all three conditions are not satisfied. First of all, A is not a *stochastic (transition) matrix*. A stochastic matrix is the transition matrix for a finite Markov chain whose entries in each row are nonnegative real numbers and sum to 1. This requires that every Web page must have at least one out-link. This is not true on the Web because many pages have no out-links, which are reflected in transition matrix A by some rows of complete 0's. Such pages are called *dangling pages* (nodes).

Example 6.2.1 Figure 6.1 shows an example of a hyperlink graph.

If we assume that the Web surfer will click the hyperlinks in a page uniformly at random, we have the following transition probability matrix:

$$\boldsymbol{A} = \begin{pmatrix} 0 & 1/2 & 1/2 & 0 & 0 & 0 \\ 1/2 & 0 & 1/2 & 0 & 0 & 0 \\ 0 & 1 & 0 & 0 & 0 & 0 \\ 0 & 0 & 1/3 & 0 & 1/3 & 1/3 \\ 0 & 0 & 0 & 0 & 0 & 0 \\ 0 & 0 & 0 & 1/2 & 1/2 & 0 \end{pmatrix} \tag{6.4}$$

For example, $A_{12} = A_{13} = 1/2$ because node 1 has two out-links. We can see that $\boldsymbol{A}$ is not a stochastic matrix because the fifth row is all 0's, that is, page 5 is a dangling page.

We can fix this problem by adding a complete set of outgoing links from each such page i to all the pages on the Web. Thus, the transition probability of going from i to every page is $1/n$, assuming a uniform probability distribution. That is, we replace each row containing all 0's with $\boldsymbol{e}/n$, where $\boldsymbol{e}$ is n-dimensional vector of all 1's, giving us the following matrix:

$$\bar{A} = \begin{pmatrix} 0 & 1/2 & 1/2 & 0 & 0 & 0 \\ 1/2 & 0 & 1/2 & 0 & 0 & 0 \\ 0 & 1 & 0 & 0 & 0 & 0 \\ 0 & 0 & 1/3 & 0 & 1/3 & 1/3 \\ 1/6 & 1/6 & 1/6 & 1/6 & 1/6 & 1/6 \\ 0 & 0 & 0 & 1/2 & 1/2 & 0 \end{pmatrix} \tag{6.5}$$

Below, we assume that the above is done to make $\boldsymbol{A}$ a stochastic matrix.

Second, $\boldsymbol{A}$ is not *irreducible,* which means that the Web graph G is not strongly connected.

Definition of strongly connected graphs: A directed graph $G = (V, E)$ is *strongly connected* if and only if, for each pair of nodes $u, v \in V$, there is a path from u to v.

The general Web graph represented by $\boldsymbol{A}$ is not irreducible because for some pairs of nodes u and v, there is no path from u to v. For example, in Figure 6.1, there is no directed path from node 3 to node 4. The adjustment in Equation (6.5) is not enough to ensure irreducibility. This problem and the next problem can be dealt with using a single strategy (described below).

Finally, $\boldsymbol{A}$ is not *aperiodic*. A state i in a Markov chain being periodic means that there exists a directed cycle that the chain has to traverse.

Definition of aperiodic graphs: A state i is *periodic* with period $k > 1$ if k is the smallest number such that all paths leading from state i back to state i have a length that is a multiple of k. If a state is not periodic (i.e., $k = 1$), it is aperiodic. A Markov chain is aperiodic if all states are aperiodic.

Example 6.2.2 Figure 6.2 shows a periodic Markov chain with $k = 3$. The transition matrix is given on the left. Each state in this chain has a period of 3. For example, if we start from state 1, the only path to come back to state 1 is 1-2-3-1 for some number of times, say h. Thus, any return to state 1 will take $3h$ transitions. In the Web, there could be many such cases.

$$A = \begin{bmatrix} 0 & 1 & 0 \\ 0 & 0 & 1 \\ 1 & 0 & 0 \end{bmatrix}$$

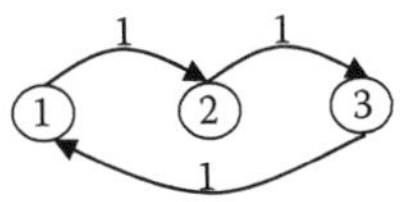

Figure 6.2 A periodic Markov chain with $k = 3$.

It is easy to deal with the above two problems with a single strategy.

- We add a link from each page to every page and give each link a small transition probability controlled by a parameter d.

The augmented transition matrix clearly becomes irreducible and also aperiodic. After this augmentation, we obtain an improved PageRank model:

$$\boldsymbol{P} = \left((1-d)\frac{\boldsymbol{E}}{n} + d\boldsymbol{A}^T\right)\boldsymbol{P} \tag{6.6}$$

where $\boldsymbol{E}$ is $\boldsymbol{e}\boldsymbol{e}^T$ ($\boldsymbol{e}$ is a column vector of all 1's) and thus $\boldsymbol{E}$ is an $n \times n$ square matrix of all 1's. n is the total number of nodes in the Web graph and $1/n$ is the probability of jumping to a random page. Note that Equation (6.6) assumes that $\boldsymbol{A}$ has already been made a stochastic matrix. After scaling, we obtain

$$\boldsymbol{P} = (1-d)\boldsymbol{e} + d\boldsymbol{A}^T\boldsymbol{P} \tag{6.7}$$

This gives us the PageRank formula for each page i:

$$P(i) = (1-d) + d\sum_{j=1}^{n} A_{ji}P(j) \tag{6.8}$$

which is equivalent to the formula given in the original PageRank papers [1, 7]:

$$P(i) = (1-d) + d\sum_{(j,i)\in E} \frac{P(j)}{O_j} \tag{6.9}$$

The parameter d, called the *damping factor,* can be set to a value between 0 and 1. $d = 0.85$ is used in [1, 7].

The computation of PageRank values of the Web pages can be done using the power iteration method [2], which produces the principal eigenvector with an eigenvalue of 1. The algorithm is quite simple (see Figure 6.3). One can start with any initial assignments of PageRank values. The iteration ends when the PageRank values do not change much or converge. In Figure 6.3, the iteration ends after the 1-norm of the residual vector is less than a prespecified threshold ε.

In Web search, we are only interested in the ranking of the pages. Thus, the actual convergence may not be necessary and fewer iterations are needed. In [1], it is reported that on a database of 322 million links the algorithm converges to an acceptable tolerance in roughly 52 iterations.

Since PageRank was presented in [1], researchers have proposed many enhancements to the model, alternative models, and improvements for its computation. The books by Liu [5] and by Langville and Meyer [4] contain in-depth analyses of PageRank and several other link-based algorithms, including HIT [3], which is another well-known algorithm.

PageRank-Iterate(G)

$P_0 \leftarrow e/n$

$k \leftarrow 1$

repeat

$P_k \leftarrow (1-d)e + dA^T P_{k-1}$;

$k \leftarrow k + 1$;

until $||P_k - P_{k-1}||_1 < \varepsilon$

return P_k

Figure 6.3 The power iteration method for PageRank.

6.3 An Extension: Timed-PageRank

One aspect that is not considered by PageRank is the timeliness of search results. The Web is a dynamic environment. It changes constantly. Quality pages in the past may not be quality pages now or in the future. The temporal aspect of search is important as users are often interested in the latest information. Apart from well-established facts and classics which do not change much over time, most contents on the Web change constantly. New pages or contents are added and outdated contents and pages are deleted. However, in practice many outdated pages and links are not deleted. This causes problems for search engines because such outdated pages can still be ranked high due to the fact that they have existed on the Web for a long time and have accumulated a large number of in-links. High-quality new pages with the most up-to-date information will be ranked low because they have few or no in-links, making it difficult for users to find the latest information on the Web.

An algorithm called Timed-PageRank given in [6, 10] adds the temporal dimension to PageRank. The idea of Timed-PageRank is simple. It still follows the random surfer and Markov chain model in PageRank. However, instead of using a constant damping factor d, Timed-PageRank uses a function of time $f(t)$ ($0 \leq f(t) \leq 1$) to "penalize" old links and pages, where t is the difference between the current time and the time when the page was last updated. $f(t)$ returns a probability that the Web surfer will follow an actual link on the page. $1 - f(t)$ returns the probability that the surfer will jump to a random page. Thus, at a particular page i, the Web surfer has two options:

1. With probability $f(t_i)$, he/she randomly chooses an outgoing link to follow.
2. With probability $1 - f(t_i)$, he/she jumps to a random page without a link.

The intuition here is that if the page was last updated (or created) a long time ago, the pages that it points to are even older and are probably out of date. Then the $1 - f(t)$ value for such a page should be large, which means that the surfer will have a high probability of jumping to a random page. If a page is new, then its $1-f(t)$ value should be small, which means that the surfer will have a high probability to follow an out-link of the page and a small probability of jumping to a random page. For a complete new page in a Web site, which does not have any in-links at all, the method given uses the average Timed-PageRank value of the past pages in the Web site. This is reasonable because a quality site in the past usually publishes quality new pages. The Timed-PageRank algorithm has been evaluated based on research publication search and has given promising results. Interested readers, please refer to [6] for additional details.

6.4 Summary

Link-based ranking for search has been instrumental for Web search. PageRank is the best known algorithm for the purpose. It is practically very effective and also well-founded theoretically. This chapter provides introductory material only; further details can be found in [1, 4, 5, 7]. An extension to the PageRank algorithm is also briefly discussed, which adds the temporal dimension to search. Finally, we should note that link-based ranking is not the only strategy used in a search engine. Many other information retrieval and data mining methods and heuristics based on the page content and user clicks are also employed.

6.5 Exercises

1. Given $\boldsymbol{A}$ below, obtain $\boldsymbol{P}$ by solving Equation (6.7) directly.

$$\boldsymbol{A} = \begin{pmatrix} 0 & 1/3 & 1/3 & 1/3 & 0 & 0 \\ 1/2 & 0 & 1/2 & 0 & 0 & 0 \\ 0 & 1 & 0 & 0 & 0 & 0 \\ 0 & 1/4 & 1/4 & 0 & 1/4 & 1/4 \\ 0 & 1/2 & 1/2 & 0 & 0 & 0 \\ 0 & 0 & 0 & 1/2 & 1/2 & 0 \end{pmatrix}$$

2. Given $\boldsymbol{A}$ as in problem 1, use the power iteration method to show the first 10 iterations of $\boldsymbol{P}$.
3. Calculate the squared error on each iteration in problem 2 where the squared error is defined to be the sum of the squared error on each entry of $\boldsymbol{P}$.
4. Plot a curve on the squared errors derived from problem 3 using the number of iterations as the X axis and the squared error as the Y axis. Does the squared error gradually decrease? After how many iterations do the ranking of the pages stabilize?

5. Given the graph G below, what is $\boldsymbol{A}$?

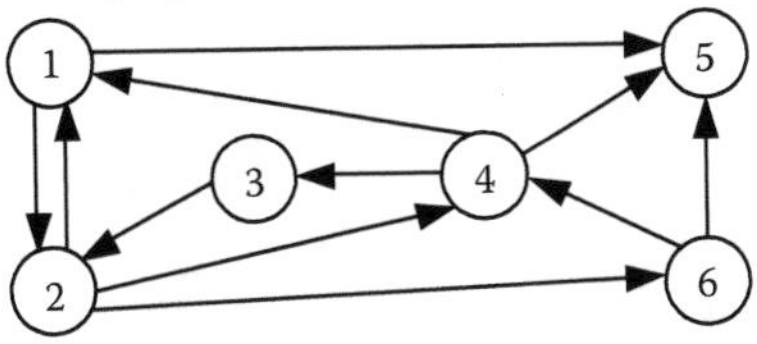

6. For the graph G given in problem 5, what is $\boldsymbol{P}$ after seven iterations based on the power iteration method?
7. Pick a URL, and construct a Web graph containing Web pages within three hops from the starting URL.
8. For the graph derived in problem 7, what is $\boldsymbol{A}$?
9. For the graph derived in problem 7, use the power iteration method to give the first seven iterations of $\boldsymbol{P}$.

References

[1] S. Brin, and L. Page. The anatomy of a large-scale hypertextual Web search engine. *Computer Networks and ISDN Systems*, 30, 1998.

[2] G. H. Golub, and C. F. Van Loan. *Matrix Computations*. The Johns Hopkins University Press, 1983.

[3] J. Kleinberg. Authoritative sources in a hyperlinked environment. *ACM-SIAM Symposium on Discrete Algorithms*, 1998.

[4] A. N. Langville, and C. D. Meyer. *Google's PageRank and Beyond: The Science of Search Engine Rankings*. Princeton University Press, 2006.

[5] B. Liu. *Web Data Mining: Exploring Hyperlinks, Contents and Usage Data*. Springer, 2007.

[6] X. Li, B. Liu, and P. S. Yu. *Time Sensitive Ranking with Application to Publication Search*. Conference on Data Mining 2008.

[7] L. Page, S. Brin, R. Motwami, and T. Winograd. *The PageRank Citation Ranking: Bringing Order to the Web*. Technical Report 1999–0120, Computer Science Department, Stanford University, 1999.

[8] W. Steward. *Introduction to the Numerical Solution of Markov Chains*. Princeton University Press, 1994.

[9] S. Wasserman, and K. Raust. *Social Network Analysis*. Cambridge University Press, 1994.

[10] P. S. Yu, X. Li, and B. Liu. Adding the Temporal Dimension to Search—A Case Study in Publication Search. *WI-2005*.

Chapter 7

AdaBoost

Zhi-Hua Zhou and Yang Yu

Contents

7.1 Introduction

Generalization ability, which characterizes how well the result learned from a given training data set can be applied to unseen new data, is the most central concept in machine learning. Researchers have devoted tremendous efforts to the pursuit of techniques that could lead to a learning system with strong generalization ability. One of the most successful paradigms is *ensemble learning* [32]. In contrast to ordinary machine learning approaches which try to generate *one* learner from training data, ensemble methods try to construct a *set* of *base learners* and combine them. Base learners are usually generated from training data by a *base learning algorithm* which can be a decision tree, a neural network, or other kinds of machine learning algorithms. Just like "many hands make light work," the generalization ability of an ensemble is usually significantly better than that of a single learner. Actually, ensemble methods are appealing mainly because they are able to boost *weak learners*, which are slightly better than random guess, to *strong learners*, which can make very accurate predictions. So, "base learners" are also referred as "weak learners."

AdaBoost [9, 10] is one of the most influential ensemble methods. It took birth from the answer to an interesting question posed by Kearns and Valiant in 1988. That is, whether two complexity classes, *weakly learnable* and *strongly learnable* problems, are equal. If the answer to the question is positive, a weak learner that performs just slightly better than random guess can be "boosted" into an arbitrarily accurate strong learner. Obviously, such a question is of great importance to machine learning. Schapire [21] found that the answer to the question is "yes," and gave a proof by construction, which is the first *boosting* algorithm. An important practical deficiency of this algorithm is the requirement that the error bound of the base learners be known ahead of time, which is usually unknown in practice. Freund and Schapire [9] then proposed an adaptive boosting algorithm, named AdaBoost, which does not require those unavailable information. It is evident that AdaBoost was born with theoretical significance, which has given rise to abundant research on theoretical aspects of ensemble methods in communities of machine learning and statistics. It is worth mentioning that for their AdaBoost paper [9], Schapire and Freund won the Godel Prize, which is one of the most prestigious awards in theoretical computer science, in the year 2003.

AdaBoost and its variants have been applied to diverse domains with great success, owing to their solid theoretical foundation, accurate prediction, and great simplicity (Schapire said it needs only "just 10 lines of code"). For example, Viola and Jones [27] combined AdaBoost with a cascade process for face detection. They regarded rectangular features as weak learners, and by using AdaBoost to weight the weak learners, they got very intuitive features for face detection. In order to get high accuracy as well as high efficiency, they used a cascade process (which is beyond the scope of this chapter). As a result, they reported a very strong face detector: On a 466 MHz machine, face detection on a 384×288 image costs only 0.067 second, which is 15 times faster than state-of-the-art face detectors at that time but with comparable accuracy. This face detector has been recognized as one of the most exciting breakthroughs in computer vision (in particular, face detection) during the past decade. It is not strange that "boosting" has become a buzzword in computer vision and many other application areas.

In the rest of this chapter, we will introduce the algorithm and implementations, and give some illustrations on how the algorithm works. For readers who are eager to know more, we will introduce some theoretical results and extensions as advanced topics.

7.2 The Algorithm

7.2.1 Notations

We first introduce some notations that will be used in the rest of the chapter. Let $\mathcal{X}$ denote the instance space, or in other words, feature space. Let $\mathcal{Y}$ denote the set of labels that express the underlying concepts which are to be learned. For example, we let $\mathcal{Y} = \{-1, +1\}$ for binary classification. A training set D consists of m instances whose associated labels are observed, i.e., $D = \{(\boldsymbol{x}_i, y_i)\}$ $(i \in \{1, \ldots, m\})$, while the label of a test instance is unknown and thus to be predicted. We assume both training and test instances are drawn independently and identically from an underlying distribution $\mathcal{D}$.

After training on a training data set D, a learning algorithm $\mathcal{L}$ will output a hypothesis h, which is a mapping from $\mathcal{X}$ to $\mathcal{Y}$, or called as a *classifier*. The learning process can be regarded as picking the best hypothesis from a hypothesis space, where the word "best" refers to a loss function. For classification, the loss function can naturally be 0/1-loss,

$$loss_{0/1}(h \mid \boldsymbol{x}) = \boldsymbol{I}[h(\boldsymbol{x}) \neq y]$$

where $\boldsymbol{I}[\cdot]$ is the indication function which outputs 1 if the inner expression is true and 0 otherwise, which means that one error is counted if an instance is wrongly classified. In this chapter 0/1-loss is used by default, but it is noteworthy that other kinds of loss functions can also be used in boosting.

7.2.2 A General Boosting Procedure

Boosting is actually a family of algorithms, among which the AdaBoost algorithm is the most influential one. So, it may be easier by starting from a general boosting procedure.

Suppose we are dealing with a binary classification problem, that is, we are trying to classify instances as *positive* and *negative*. Usually we assume that there exists an unknown target concept, which correctly assigns "positive" labels to instances belonging to the concept and "negative" labels to others. This unknown target concept is actually what we want to learn. We call this target concept *ground-truth*. For a binary classification problem, a classifier working by random guess will have 50% 0/1-loss.

Suppose we are unlucky and only have a *weak classifier* at hand, which is only slightly better than random guess on the underlying instance distribution $\mathcal{D}$, say, it has 49% 0/1-loss. Let's denote this weak classifier as h_1. It is obvious that h_1 is not what we want, and we will try to improve it. A natural idea is to correct the mistakes made by h_1.

We can try to derive a new distribution $\mathcal{D}'$ from $\mathcal{D}$, which makes the mistakes of h_1 more evident, for example, it focuses more on the instances wrongly classified by h_1 (we will explain how to generate $\mathcal{D}'$ in the next section). We can train a classifier h_2 from $\mathcal{D}'$. Again, suppose we are unlucky and h_2 is also a weak classifier. Since $\mathcal{D}'$ was derived from $\mathcal{D}$, if $\mathcal{D}'$ satisfies some condition, h_2 will be able to achieve a better performance than h_1 on some places in $\mathcal{D}$ where h_1 does not work well, without scarifying the places where h_1 performs well. Thus, by combining h_1 and h_2 in an appropriate way (we will explain how to combine them in the next section), the combined classifier will be able to achieve less loss than that achieved by h_1. By repeating the above process, we can expect to get a combined classifier which has very small (ideally, zero) 0/1-loss on $\mathcal{D}$.

Input: Instance distribution $\mathcal{D}$;

Base learning algorithm $\mathcal{L}$;

Number of learning rounds T.

Process:

$\mathcal{D}_1 = \mathcal{D}$. % Initialize distribution

for $t = 1, \cdots, T$:

$h_t = \mathcal{L}(\mathcal{D}_t)$; % Train a weak learner from distribution $\mathcal{D}_t$

$\epsilon_t = \Pr_{\boldsymbol{x} \sim \mathcal{D}_t, y} \boldsymbol{I}[h_t(\boldsymbol{x}) \neq y]$; % Measure the error of h_t

$\mathcal{D}_{t+1} = AdjustDistribution(\mathcal{D}_t, \epsilon_t)$

end

Output: $H(\boldsymbol{x}) = CombineOutputs(\{h_t(\boldsymbol{x})\})$

Figure 7.1 A general boosting procedure.

Briefly, boosting works by training a set of classifiers sequentially and combining them for prediction, where the later classifiers focus more on the mistakes of the earlier classifiers. Figure 7.1 summarizes the general boosting procedure.

7.2.3 The AdaBoost Algorithm

Figure 7.1 is not a real algorithm since there are some undecided parts such as *AdjustDistribution* and *CombineOutputs*. The AdaBoost algorithm can be viewed as an instantiation of the general boosting procedure, which is summarized in Figure 7.2.

Input: Data set $D = \{(\boldsymbol{x}_1, y_1), (\boldsymbol{x}_2, y_2), \ldots, (\boldsymbol{x}_m, y_m)\}$;

Base learning algorithm $\mathcal{L}$;

Number of learning rounds T.

Process:

$\mathcal{D}_1(i) = 1/m$. % Initialize the weight distribution

for $t = 1, \cdots, T$:

$h_t = \mathcal{L}(D, \mathcal{D}_t)$; % Train a learner h_t from D using distribution $\mathcal{D}_t$

$\epsilon_t = \Pr_{\boldsymbol{x} \sim \mathcal{D}_t, y} \boldsymbol{I}[h_t(\boldsymbol{x}) \neq y]$; % Measure the error of h_t

if $\epsilon_t > 0.5$ **then break**

$\alpha_t = \frac{1}{2} \ln \left(\frac{1-\epsilon_t}{\epsilon_t} \right)$; % Determine the weight of h_t

$$\mathcal{D}_{t+1}(i) = \frac{\mathcal{D}_t(i)}{Z_t} \times \begin{cases} \exp(-\alpha_t) & \text{if } h_t(\boldsymbol{x}_i) = y_i \\ \exp(\alpha_t) & \text{if } h_t(\boldsymbol{x}_i) \neq y_i \end{cases}$$

$$= \frac{\mathcal{D}_t(i)\exp(-\alpha_t y_i h_t(\boldsymbol{x}_i))}{Z_t}$$ % Update the distribution, where % Z_t is a normalization factor which % enables $\mathcal{D}_{t+1}$ to be distribution

end

Output: $H(\boldsymbol{x}) = \text{sign}\left(\sum_{t=1}^{T} \alpha_t h_t(\boldsymbol{x})\right)$

Figure 7.2 The AdaBoost algorithm.

Now we explain the details.[1] AdaBoost generates a sequence of hypotheses and combines them with weights, which can be regarded as an *additive* weighted combination in the form of

$$H(\boldsymbol{x}) = \sum_{t=1}^{T} \alpha_t h_t(\boldsymbol{x})$$

From this view, AdaBoost actually solves two problems, that is, how to generate the hypotheses h_t's and how to determine the proper weights α_t's.

In order to have a highly efficient error reduction process, we try to minimize an exponential loss

$$loss_{\text{exp}}(h) = \mathbb{E}_{\boldsymbol{x}\sim\mathcal{D},y}[e^{-yh(\boldsymbol{x})}]$$

where $yh(\boldsymbol{x})$ is called as the *classification margin* of the hypothesis.

Let's consider one round in the boosting process. Suppose a set of hypotheses as well as their weights have already been obtained, and let H denote the combined hypothesis. Now, one more hypothesis h will be generated and is to be combined with H to form $H + \alpha h$. The loss after the combination will be

$$loss_{\text{exp}}(H + \alpha h) = \mathbb{E}_{\boldsymbol{x}\sim\mathcal{D},y}[e^{-y(H(\boldsymbol{x})+\alpha h(\boldsymbol{x}))}]$$

The loss can be decomposed to each instance, which is called pointwise loss, as

$$loss_{\text{exp}}(H + \alpha h \mid \boldsymbol{x}) = \mathbb{E}_y[e^{-y(H(\boldsymbol{x})+\alpha h(\boldsymbol{x}))} \mid \boldsymbol{x}]$$

Since y and $h(\boldsymbol{x})$ must be $+1$ or -1, we can expand the expectation as

$$loss_{\text{exp}}(H + \alpha h \mid \boldsymbol{x}) = e^{-yH(\boldsymbol{x})} \left(e^{-\alpha} P(y = h(\boldsymbol{x}) \mid \boldsymbol{x}) + e^{\alpha} P(y \neq h(\boldsymbol{x}) \mid \boldsymbol{x})\right)$$

Suppose we have already generated h, and thus the weight α that minimizes the loss can be found when the derivative of the loss equals zero, that is,

$$\begin{aligned}\frac{\partial loss_{\text{exp}}(H + \alpha h \mid \boldsymbol{x})}{\partial \alpha} &= e^{-yH(\boldsymbol{x})} \left(-e^{-\alpha} P(y = h(\boldsymbol{x}) \mid \boldsymbol{x}) + e^{\alpha} P(y \neq h(\boldsymbol{x}) \mid \boldsymbol{x})\right) \\ &= 0\end{aligned}$$

and the solution is

$$\alpha = \frac{1}{2} \ln \frac{P(y = h(\boldsymbol{x}) \mid \boldsymbol{x})}{P(y \neq h(\boldsymbol{x}) \mid \boldsymbol{x})} = \frac{1}{2} \ln \frac{1 - P(y \neq h(\boldsymbol{x}) \mid \boldsymbol{x})}{P(y \neq h(\boldsymbol{x}) \mid \boldsymbol{x})}$$

By taking an expectation over $\boldsymbol{x}$, that is, solving $\frac{\partial loss_{\text{exp}}(H+\alpha h)}{\partial \alpha} = 0$, and denoting $\epsilon = \mathbb{E}_{\boldsymbol{x}\sim\mathcal{D}}[y \neq h(\boldsymbol{x})]$, we get

$$\alpha = \frac{1}{2} \ln \frac{1-\epsilon}{\epsilon}$$

which is the way of determining α_t in AdaBoost.

[1] Here we explain the AdaBoost algorithm from the view of [11] since it is easier to understand than the original explanation in [9].

Now let's consider how to generate h. Given a base learning algorithm, AdaBoost invokes it to produce a hypothesis from a particular instance distribution. So, we only need to consider what hypothesis is desired for the next round, and then generate an instance distribution to achieve this hypothesis.

We can expand the pointwise loss to second order about $h(\boldsymbol{x}) = 0$, when fixing $\alpha = 1$,

$$\begin{aligned} loss_{\exp}(H + h \mid \boldsymbol{x}) &\approx \mathbb{E}_y[e^{-yH(\boldsymbol{x})}(1 - yh(\boldsymbol{x}) + y^2 h(\boldsymbol{x})^2/2) \mid \boldsymbol{x}] \\ &= \mathbb{E}_y[e^{-yH(\boldsymbol{x})}(1 - yh(\boldsymbol{x}) + 1/2) \mid \boldsymbol{x}] \end{aligned}$$

since $y^2 = 1$ and $h(\boldsymbol{x})^2 = 1$.

Then a perfect hypothesis is

$$\begin{aligned} h^*(\boldsymbol{x}) &= \arg\min_h loss_{\exp}(H + h \mid \boldsymbol{x}) = \arg\max_h \mathbb{E}_y[e^{-yH(\boldsymbol{x})} yh(\boldsymbol{x}) \mid \boldsymbol{x}] \\ &= \arg\max_h e^{-H(\boldsymbol{x})} P(y = 1 \mid \boldsymbol{x}) \cdot 1 \cdot h(\boldsymbol{x}) + e^{H(\boldsymbol{x})} P(y = -1 \mid \boldsymbol{x}) \cdot (-1) \cdot h(\boldsymbol{x}) \end{aligned}$$

Note that $e^{-yH(\boldsymbol{x})}$ is a constant in terms of $h(\boldsymbol{x})$. By normalizing the expectation as

$$h^*(\boldsymbol{x}) = \arg\max_h \frac{e^{-H(\boldsymbol{x})} P(y = 1 \mid \boldsymbol{x}) \cdot 1 \cdot h(\boldsymbol{x}) + e^{H(\boldsymbol{x})} P(y = -1 \mid \boldsymbol{x}) \cdot (-1) \cdot h(\boldsymbol{x})}{e^{-H(\boldsymbol{x})} P(y = 1 \mid \boldsymbol{x}) + e^{H(\boldsymbol{x})} P(y = -1 \mid \boldsymbol{x})}$$

we can rewrite the expectation using a new term $w(\boldsymbol{x}, y)$, which is drawn from $e^{-yH(\boldsymbol{x})} P(y \mid \boldsymbol{x})$, as

$$h^*(\boldsymbol{x}) = \arg\max_h \mathbb{E}_{w(\boldsymbol{x},y) \sim e^{-yH(\boldsymbol{x})} P(y|\boldsymbol{x})}[yh(\boldsymbol{x}) \mid \boldsymbol{x}]$$

Since $h^*(\boldsymbol{x})$ must be $+1$ or -1, the solution to the optimization is that $h^*(\boldsymbol{x})$ holds the same sign with $y|\boldsymbol{x}$, that is,

$$\begin{aligned} h^*(\boldsymbol{x}) &= \mathbb{E}_{w(\boldsymbol{x},y) \sim e^{-yH(\boldsymbol{x})} P(y|\boldsymbol{x})}[y \mid \boldsymbol{x}] \\ &= P_{w(\boldsymbol{x},y) \sim e^{-yH(\boldsymbol{x})} P(y|\boldsymbol{x})}(y = 1 \mid \boldsymbol{x}) - P_{w(\boldsymbol{x},y) \sim e^{-yH(\boldsymbol{x})} P(y|\boldsymbol{x})}(y = -1 \mid \boldsymbol{x}) \end{aligned}$$

As can be seen, h^* simply performs the optimal classification of $\boldsymbol{x}$ under the distribution $e^{-yH(\boldsymbol{x})} P(y \mid \boldsymbol{x})$. Therefore, $e^{-yH(\boldsymbol{x})} P(y \mid \boldsymbol{x})$ is the desired distribution for a hypothesis minimizing 0/1-loss.

So, when the hypothesis $h(\boldsymbol{x})$ has been learned and $\alpha = \frac{1}{2} \ln \frac{1-\epsilon}{\epsilon}$ has been determined in the current round, the distribution for the next round should be

$$\begin{aligned} \mathcal{D}_{t+1}(\boldsymbol{x}) &= e^{-y(H(\boldsymbol{x}) + \alpha h(\boldsymbol{x}))} P(y \mid \boldsymbol{x}) = e^{-yH(\boldsymbol{x})} P(y \mid \boldsymbol{x}) \cdot e^{-\alpha y h(\boldsymbol{x})} \\ &= \mathcal{D}_t(\boldsymbol{x}) \cdot e^{-\alpha y h(\boldsymbol{x})} \end{aligned}$$

which is the way of updating instance distribution in AdaBoost.

But, why optimizing the exponential loss works for minimizing the 0/1-loss? Actually, we can see that

$$h^*(\boldsymbol{x}) = \arg\min_h \mathbb{E}_{\boldsymbol{x} \sim \mathcal{D}, y}[e^{-yh(\boldsymbol{x})} \mid \boldsymbol{x}] = \frac{1}{2} \ln \frac{P(y = 1 \mid \boldsymbol{x})}{P(y = -1 \mid \boldsymbol{x})}$$

and therefore we have

$$sign(h^*(\boldsymbol{x})) = \arg\max_y P(y|\boldsymbol{x})$$

which implies that the optimal solution to the exponential loss achieves the minimum Bayesian error for the classification problem. Moreover, we can see that the function h^* which minimizes the exponential loss is the logistic regression model up to a factor 2. So, by ignoring the factor $1/2$, AdaBoost can also be viewed as fitting an additive logistic regression model.

It is noteworthy that the data distribution is not known in practice, and the AdaBoost algorithm works on a given training set with finite training examples. Therefore, all the expectations in the above derivations are taken on the training examples, and the weights are also imposed on training examples. For base learning algorithms that cannot handle weighted training examples, a resampling mechanism, which samples training examples according to desired weights, can be used instead.

7.3 Illustrative Examples

In this section, we demonstrate how the AdaBoost algorithm works, from an illustration on a toy problem to real data sets.

7.3.1 Solving XOR Problem

We consider an artificial data set in a two-dimensional space, plotted in Figure 7.3(a). There are only four instances, that is,

$$\left\{\begin{array}{l} (\boldsymbol{x}_1 = (0, +1),\ y_1 = +1) \\ (\boldsymbol{x}_2 = (0, -1),\ y_2 = +1) \\ (\boldsymbol{x}_3 = (+1, 0),\ y_3 = -1) \\ (\boldsymbol{x}_4 = (-1, 0),\ y_4 = -1) \end{array}\right\}$$

This is the XOR problem. The two classes cannot be separated by a linear classifier which corresponds to a line on the figure.

Suppose we have a base learning algorithm which tries to select the best of the following eight functions. Note that none of them is perfect. For equally good functions, the base learning algorithm will pick one function from them randomly.

$$h_1(\boldsymbol{x}) = \begin{cases} +1, & \text{if } (x_1 > -0.5) \\ -1, & \text{otherwise} \end{cases} \qquad h_2(\boldsymbol{x}) = \begin{cases} -1, & \text{if } (x_1 > -0.5) \\ +1, & \text{otherwise} \end{cases}$$

$$h_3(\boldsymbol{x}) = \begin{cases} +1, & \text{if } (x_1 > +0.5) \\ -1, & \text{otherwise} \end{cases} \qquad h_4(\boldsymbol{x}) = \begin{cases} -1, & \text{if } (x_1 > +0.5) \\ +1, & \text{otherwise} \end{cases}$$

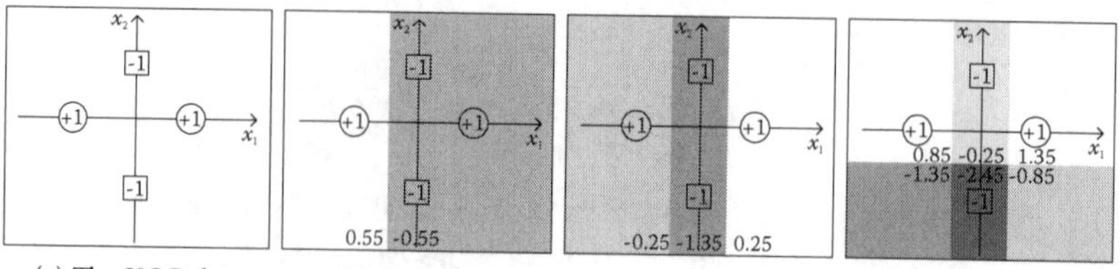

(a) The XOR data (b) 1st round (c) 2nd round (d) 3rd round

Figure 7.3 AdaBoost on the XOR problem.

$$h_5(\boldsymbol{x}) = \begin{cases} +1, & \text{if } (x_2 > -0.5) \\ -1, & \text{otherwise} \end{cases} \quad h_6(\boldsymbol{x}) = \begin{cases} -1, & \text{if } (x_2 > -0.5) \\ +1, & \text{otherwise} \end{cases}$$

$$h_7(\boldsymbol{x}) = \begin{cases} +1, & \text{if } (x_2 > +0.5) \\ -1, & \text{otherwise} \end{cases} \quad h_8(\boldsymbol{x}) = \begin{cases} -1, & \text{if } (x_2 > +0.5) \\ +1, & \text{otherwise} \end{cases}$$

where x_1 and x_2 are the values of $\boldsymbol{x}$ at the first and second dimension, respectively.

Now we track how AdaBoost works:

1. The first step is to invoke the base learning algorithm on the original data. h_2, h_3, h_5, and h_8 all have 0.25 classification errors. Suppose h_2 is picked as the first base learner. One instance, $\boldsymbol{x}_1$, is wrongly classified, so the error is $1/4 = 0.25$. The weight of h_2 is $0.5 \ln 3 \approx 0.55$. Figure 7.3(b) visualizes the classification, where the shadowed area is classified as negative (-1) and the weights of the classification, 0.55 and -0.55, are displayed.
2. The weight of $\boldsymbol{x}_1$ is increased and the base learning algorithm is invoked again. This time h_3, h_5, and h_8 have equal errors. Suppose h_3 is picked, of which the weight is 0.80. Figure 7.3(c) shows the combined classification of h_2 and h_3 with their weights, where different gray levels are used for distinguishing negative areas according to classification weights.
3. The weight of $\boldsymbol{x}_3$ is increased, and this time only h_5 and h_8 equally have the lowest errors. Suppose h_5 is picked, of which the weight is 1.10. Figure 7.3(d) shows the combined classification of h_2, h_3, and h_8. If we look at the sign of classification weights in each area in Figure 7.3(d), all the instances are correctly classified. Thus, by combining the imperfect linear classifiers, AdaBoost has produced a nonlinear classifier which has zero error.

7.3.2 Performance on Real Data

We evaluate the AdaBoost algorithm on 56 data sets from the UCI Machine Learning Repository,[2] which covers a broad range of real-world tasks. We use the Weka (will be introduced in Section 7.6) implementation of AdaBoost.M1 using reweighting with

[2] `http://www.ics.uci.edu/~mlearn/MLRepository.html`

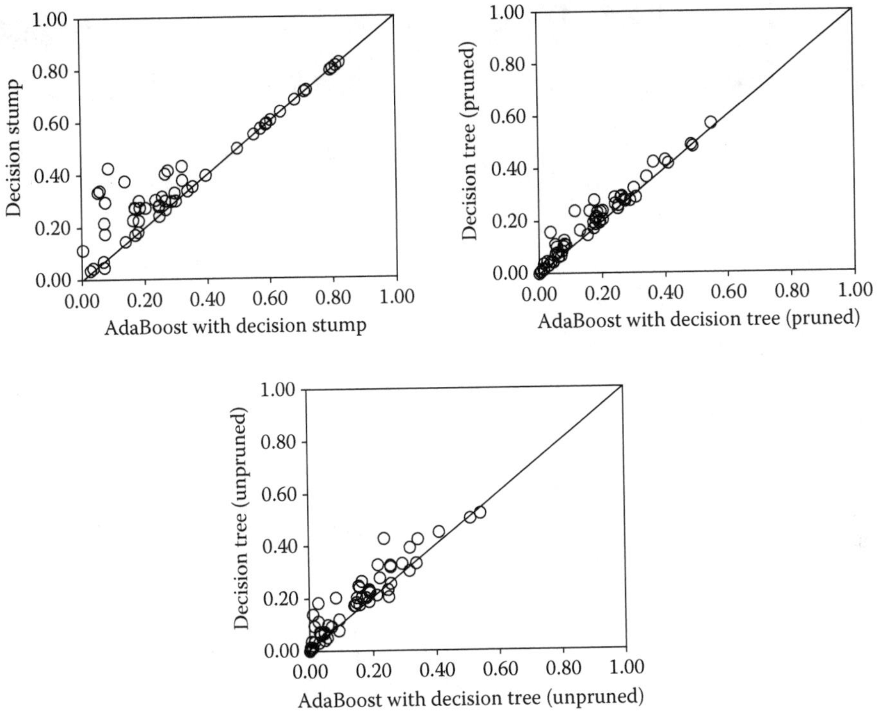

Figure 7.4 Comparison of predictive errors of AdaBoost against decision stump, pruned, and unpruned single decision trees on 56 UCI data sets.

50 base learners. Almost all kinds of learning algorithms can be taken as base learning algorithms, such as decision trees, neural networks, and so on. Here, we have tried three base learning algorithms, including decision stump, pruned, and unpruned J4.8 decision trees (Weka implementation of C4.5).

We plot the comparison results in Figure 7.4, where each circle represents a data set and locates according to the predictive errors of the two compared algorithms. In each plot of Figure 7.4, the diagonal line indicates where the two compared algorithms have identical errors. It can be observed that AdaBoost often outperforms its base learning algorithm, with a few exceptions on which it degenerates the performance.

The famous *bias-variance decomposition* [12] has been employed to empirically study why AdaBoost achieves excellent performance [2,3,34]. This powerful tool breaks the expected error of a learning approach into the sum of three nonnegative quantities, that is, the intrinsic noise, the bias, and the variance. The bias measures how closely the average estimate of the learning approach is able to approximate the target, and the variance measures how much the estimate of the learning approach fluctuates for the different training sets of the same size. It has been observed [2,3,34] that AdaBoost primarily reduces the bias but it is also able to reduce the variance.

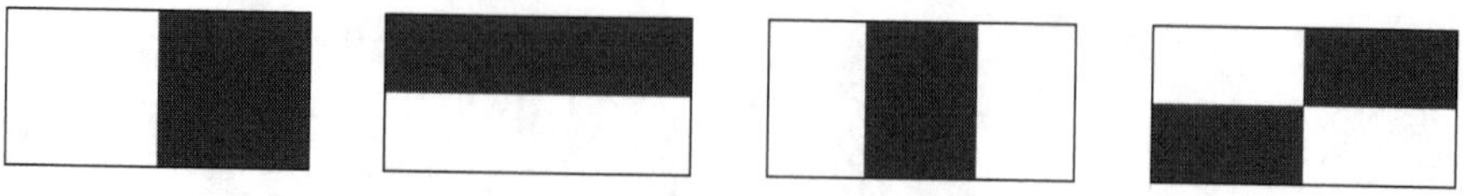

Figure 7.5 Four feature masks to be applied to each rectangle.

7.4 Real Application

Viola and Jones [27] combined AdaBoost with a cascade process for face detection. As the result, they reported that on a 466 MHz machine, face detection on a 384×288 image costs only 0.067 seconds, which is almost 15 times faster than state-of-the-art face detectors at that time but with comparable accuracy. This face detector has been recognized as one of the most exciting breakthroughs in computer vision (in particular, face detection) during the past decade. In this section, we briefly introduce how AdaBoost works in the Viola-Jones face detector.

Here the task is to locate all possible human faces in a given image. An image is first divided into subimages, say 24×24 squares. Each subimage is then represented by a feature vector. To make the computational process efficient, very simple features are used. All possible rectangles in a subimage are examined. On every rectangle, four features are extracted using the masks shown in Figure 7.5. With each mask, the sum of pixels' gray level in white areas is subtracted by the sum of those in dark areas, which is regarded as a feature. Thus, by a 24×24 splitting, there are more than 1 million features, but each of the features can be calculated very fast.

Each feature is regarded as a weak learner, that is,

$$h_{i,p,\theta}(\boldsymbol{x}) = \boldsymbol{I}[px_i \leq p\theta] \quad (p \in \{+1, -1\})$$

where x_i is the value of $\boldsymbol{x}$ at the i-th feature.

The base learning algorithm tries to find the best weak classifier h_{i^*,p^*,θ^*} that minimizes the classification error, that is,

$$(i^*, p^*, \theta^*) = \underset{i,p,\theta}{\arg\min}\, \mathbb{E}_{(\boldsymbol{x},y)}\boldsymbol{I}[h_{i,p,\theta}(\boldsymbol{x}) \neq y]$$

Face rectangles are regarded as positive examples, as shown in Figure 7.6, while rectangles that do not contain any face are regarded as negative examples. Then, the AdaBoost process is applied and it will return a few weak learners, each corresponds to one of the over 1 million features. Actually, the AdaBoost process can be regarded as a feature selection tool here.

Figure 7.7 shows the first two selected features and their position relative to a human face. It is evident that these two features are intuitive, where the first feature measures how the intensity of the eye areas differ from that of the lower areas, while

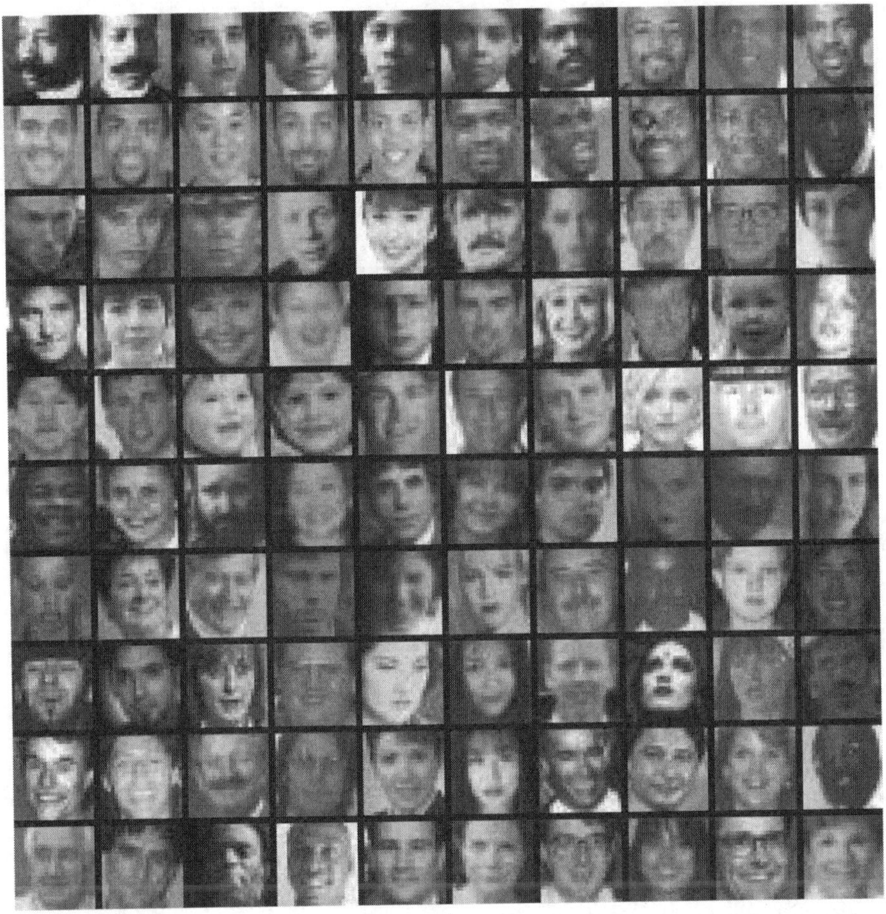

Figure 7.6 Positive training examples [27].

the second feature measures how the intensity of the two eye areas differ from the area between two eyes.

Using the selected features in order, an extremely imbalanced decision tree is built, which is called *cascade* of classifiers, as illustrated in Figure 7.8.

The parameter θ is adjusted in the cascade such that, at each tree node, branching into "not a face" means that the image is really not a face. In other words, the false negative rate is minimized. This design owes to the fact that a nonface image is easier to be recognized, and it is possible to use a few features to filter out a lot of candidate image rectangles, which endows the high efficiency. It was reported [27] that 10 features per subimage are examined in average. Some test results of the Viola-Jones face detector are shown in Figure 7.9.

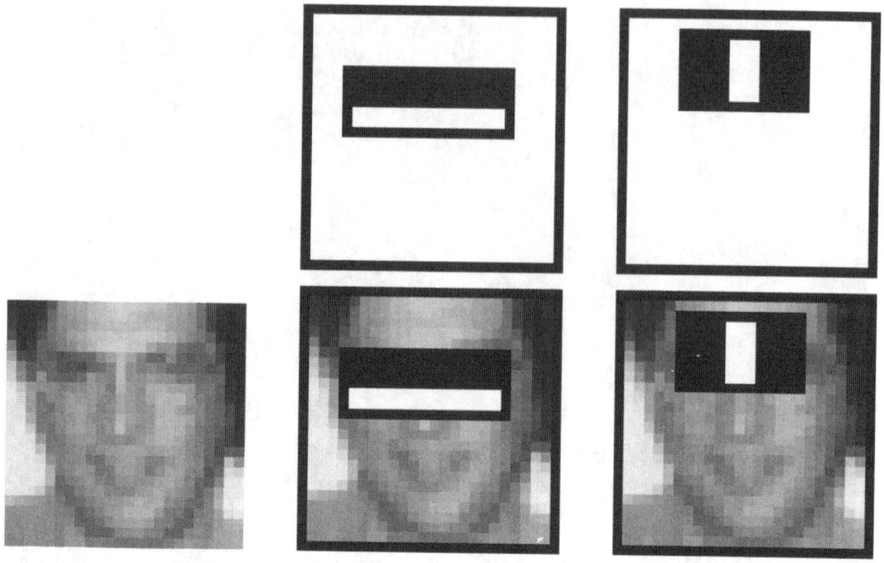

Figure 7.7 Selected features [27].

7.5 Advanced Topics

7.5.1 Theoretical Issues

Computational learning theory studies some fundamental theoretical issues of machine learning. First introduced by Valiant in 1984 [25], the *Probably Approximately Correct* (PAC) framework models learning algorithms in a distribution free manner. Roughly speaking, for binary classification, a problem is *learnable* or *strongly learnable* if there exists an algorithm that outputs a hypothesis h in polynomial time

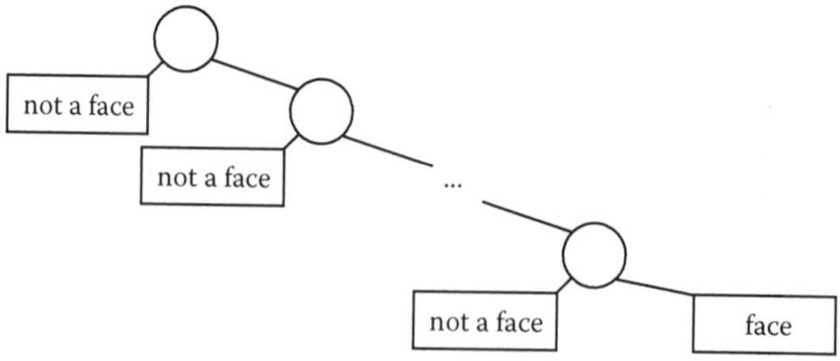

Figure 7.8 A cascade of classifiers.

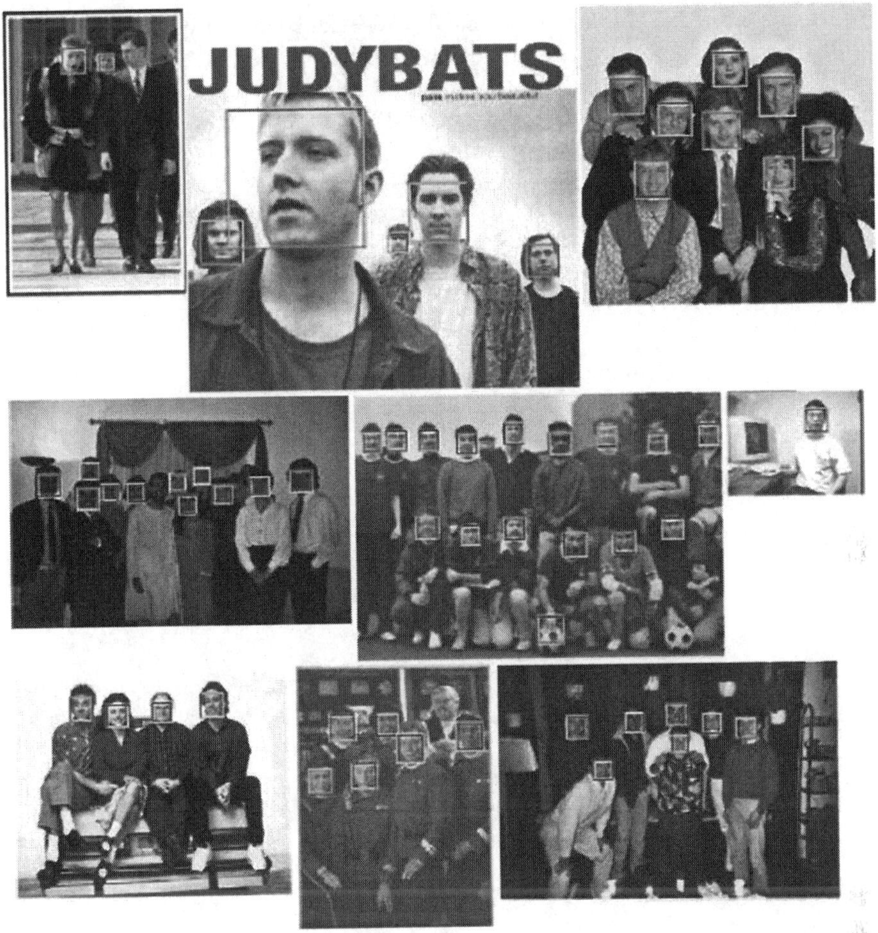

Figure 7.9 Outputs of the Viola-Jones face detector on a number of test images [27].

such that for all $0 < \delta, \epsilon \leq 0.5$,

$$P\left(\mathbb{E}_{\boldsymbol{x}\sim\mathcal{D},y}\left[\boldsymbol{I}\left[h(\boldsymbol{x}) \neq y\right]\right] < \epsilon\right) \geq 1 - \delta$$

and a problem is *weakly learnable* if the above holds for all $0 < \delta \leq 0.5$ but only when ϵ is slightly smaller than 0.5 (or in other words, h is only slightly better than random guess).

In 1988, Kearns and Valiant [15] posed an interesting question, that is, whether the strongly learnable problem class equals the weakly learnable problem class. This question is of fundamental importance, since if the answer is "yes," any weak learner is potentially able to be boosted to a strong learner. In 1989, Schapire [21] proved that the answer is really "yes," and the proof he gave is a construction, which is the first boosting algorithm. One year later, Freund [7] developed a more efficient algorithm. Both algorithms, however, suffered from the practical deficiency that the error bound of the base learners need to be known ahead of time, which is usually unknown in practice. Later, in 1995, Freund and Schapire [9] developed the AdaBoost algorithm, which is effective and efficient in practice.

Freund and Schapire [9] proved that, if the base learners of AdaBoost have errors $\epsilon_1, \epsilon_2, \cdots, \epsilon_T$, the error of the final combined learner, ϵ, is upper bounded as

$$\epsilon = \mathbb{E}_{\boldsymbol{x}\sim\mathcal{D},y}\boldsymbol{I}[H(\boldsymbol{x}) \neq y] \leq 2^T \prod_{t=1}^{T} \sqrt{\epsilon_t(1-\epsilon_t)} \leq e^{-2\sum_{t=1}^{T}\gamma_t^2}$$

where $\gamma_t = 0.5 - \epsilon_t$. It can be seen that AdaBoost reduces the error exponentially fast. Also, it can be derived that, to achieve an error less than ϵ, the round T is upper bounded as

$$T \leq \left\lceil \frac{1}{2\gamma^2} \ln \frac{1}{\epsilon} \right\rceil$$

where it is assumed that $\gamma = \gamma_1 = \gamma_2 = \cdots = \gamma_T$.

In practice, however, all the operations of AdaBoost can only be carried out on training data D, that is,

$$\epsilon_D = \mathbb{E}_{\boldsymbol{x}\sim D,y}\boldsymbol{I}[H(\boldsymbol{x}) \neq y]$$

and thus the errors are training errors, while the generalization error, that is, the error over instance distribution $\mathcal{D}$

$$\epsilon_{\mathcal{D}} = \mathbb{E}_{\boldsymbol{x}\sim\mathcal{D},y}\boldsymbol{I}[H(\boldsymbol{x}) \neq y]$$

is of more interest.

The initial analysis [9] showed that the generalization error of AdaBoost is upper bounded as

$$\epsilon_{\mathcal{D}} \leq \epsilon_D + \tilde{O}\left(\sqrt{\frac{dT}{m}}\right)$$

with probability at least $1-\delta$, where d is the VC-dimension of base learners, m is the number of training instances, and $\tilde{O}(\cdot)$ is used instead of $O(\cdot)$ to hide logarithmic terms and constant factors.

The above bound suggests that in order to achieve a good generalization ability, it is necessary to constrain the complexity of base learners as well as the number of learning rounds; otherwise AdaBoost will overfit. However, empirical studies show that AdaBoost often does not overfit, that is, its test error often tends to decrease even after the training error reaches zero, even after a large number of rounds, such as 1000.

For example, Schapire et al. [22] plotted the performance of AdaBoost on the *letter* data set from UCI Machine Learning Repository, as shown in Figure 7.10 (left), where the higher curve is test error while the lower one is training error. It can be observed that AdaBoost achieves zero training error in less than 10 rounds but the generalization error keeps on reducing. This phenomenon seems to counter Occam's

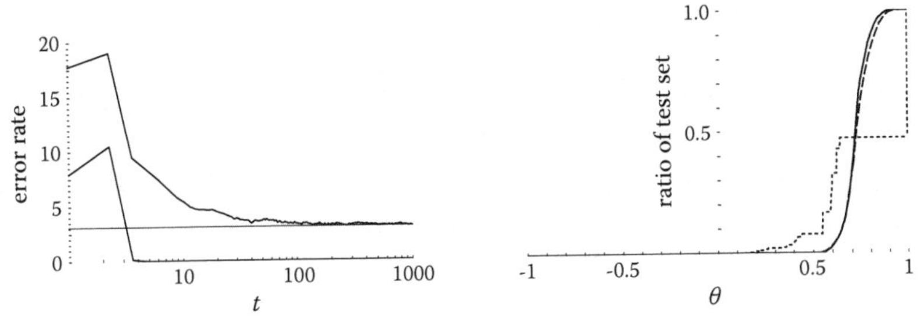

Figure 7.10 Training and test error (left) and margin distribution (right) of AdaBoost on the *letter* data set [22].

Razor, that is, nothing more than necessary should be done, which is one of the basic principles in machine learning.

Many researchers have studied this phenomena, and several theoretical explanations have been given, for example, [11]. Schapire et al. [22] introduced the *margin-based* explanation. They argued that AdaBoost is able to increase the margin even after the training error reaches zero, and thus it does not overfit even after a large number of rounds. The classification margin of h on $\boldsymbol{x}$ is defined as $yh(\boldsymbol{x})$, and that of $H(\boldsymbol{x}) = \sum_{t=1}^{T} \alpha_t h_t(\boldsymbol{x})$ is defined as

$$yH(\boldsymbol{x}) = \frac{\sum_{t=1}^{T} \alpha_t y h_t(\boldsymbol{x})}{\sum_{t=1}^{T} \alpha_t}$$

Figure 7.10 (right) plots the distribution of $yH(\boldsymbol{x}) \leq \theta$ for different values of θ. It was proved in [22] that the generalization error is upper bounded as

$$\begin{aligned} \epsilon_{\mathcal{D}} &\leq P_{\boldsymbol{x}\sim D,y}(yH(\boldsymbol{x}) \leq \theta) + \tilde{O}\left(\sqrt{\frac{d}{m\theta^2} + \ln\frac{1}{\delta}}\right) \\ &\leq 2^T \prod_{t=1}^{T} \sqrt{\epsilon_t^{1-\theta}(1-\epsilon)^{1+\theta}} + \tilde{O}\left(\sqrt{\frac{d}{m\theta^2} + \ln\frac{1}{\delta}}\right) \end{aligned}$$

with probability at least $1 - \delta$. This bound qualitatively explains that when other variables in the bound are fixed, the larger the margin, the smaller the generalization error.

However, this margin-based explanation was challenged by Brieman [4]. Using *minimum margin* ϱ,

$$\varrho = \min_{\boldsymbol{x}\in D} yH(\boldsymbol{x})$$

Breiman proved a generalization error bound is tighter than the above one using minimum margin. Motivated by the tighter bound, the arc-gv algorithm, which is a variant of AdaBoost, was proposed to maximize the minimum margin directly, by updating α_t according to

$$\alpha_t = \frac{1}{2}\ln\left(\frac{1+\gamma_t}{1-\gamma_t}\right) - \frac{1}{2}\ln\left(\frac{1+\varrho_t}{1-\varrho_t}\right)$$

Interestingly, the minimum margin of arc-gv is uniformly better than that of AdaBoost, but the test error of arc-gv increases drastically on all tested data sets [4]. Thus, the margin theory for AdaBoost was almost sentenced to death.

In 2006, Reyzin and Schapire [20] reported an interesting finding. It is well-known that the bound of the generalization error is associated with margin, the number of rounds, and the complexity of base learners. When comparing arc-gv with AdaBoost, Breiman [4] tried to control the complexity of base learners by using decision trees with the same number of leaves, but Reyzin and Schapire found that these are trees with very different shapes. The trees generated by arc-gv tend to have larger depth, while those generated by AdaBoost tend to have larger width. Figure 7.11 (top) shows the difference of depth of the trees generated by the two algorithms on the *breast cancer* data set from UCI Machine Learning Repository. Although the trees have the same number of leaves, it seems that a deeper tree makes more attribute tests than a wider tree, and therefore they are unlikely to have equal complexity. So, Reyzin and Schapire repeated Breiman's experiments by using decision stump, which has only one leaf and therefore is with a fixed complexity, and found that the margin distribution of AdaBoost is actually better than that of arc-gv, as illustrated in Figure 7.11 (bottom).

Recently, Wang et al. [28] introduced *equilibrium margin* and proved a new bound tighter than that obtained by using minimum margin, which suggests that the minimum margin may not be crucial for the generalization error of AdaBoost. It will be interesting to develop an algorithm that maximizes equilibrium margin directly, and to see whether the test error of such an algorithm is smaller than that of AdaBoost, which remains an open problem.

7.5.2 Multiclass AdaBoost

In the previous sections we focused on AdaBoost for binary classification, that is, $\mathcal{Y} = \{+1, -1\}$. In many classification tasks, however, an instance belongs to one of many instead of two classes. For example, a handwritten number belongs to 1 of 10 classes, that is, $\mathcal{Y} = \{0, \ldots, 9\}$. There is more than one way to deal with a multiclass classification problem.

AdaBoost.M1 [9] is a very direct extension, which is as same as the algorithm shown in Figure 7.2, except that now the base learners are multiclass learners instead of binary classifiers. This algorithm could not use binary base classifiers, and requires every base learner have less than 1/2 multiclass 0/1-loss, which is an overstrong constraint.

SAMME [35] is an improvement over AdaBoost.M1, which replaces Line 5 of AdaBoost.M1 in Figure 7.2 by

$$\alpha_t = \frac{1}{2}\ln\left(\frac{1-\epsilon_t}{\epsilon_t}\right) + \ln(|\mathcal{Y}| - 1)$$

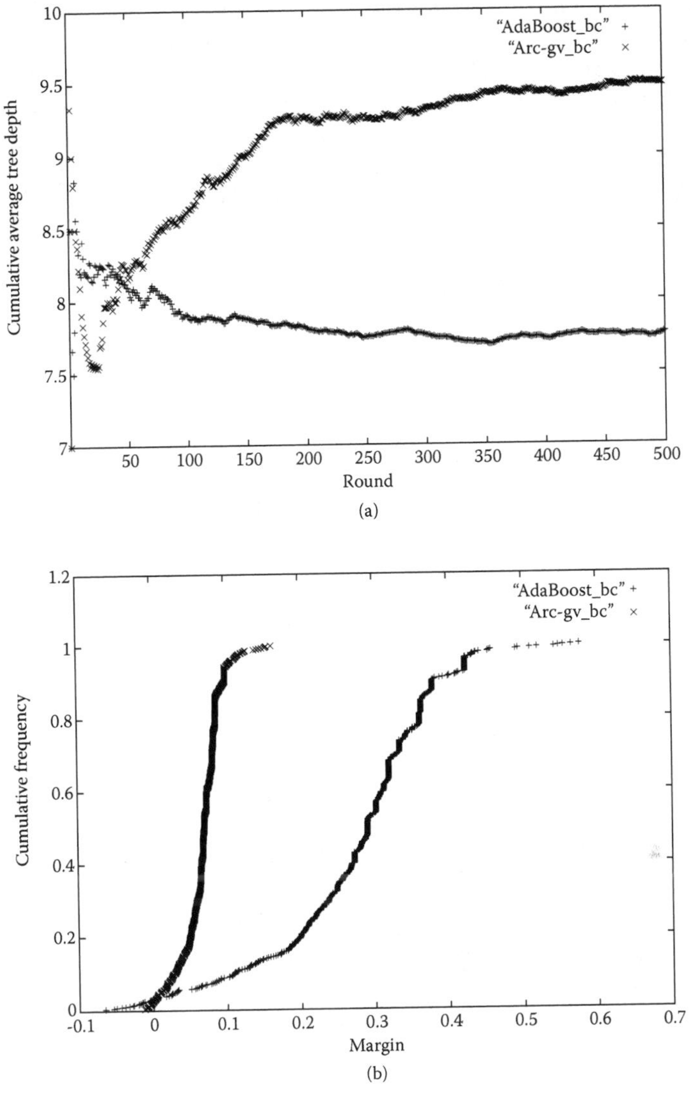

Figure 7.11 Tree depth (top) and margin distribution (bottom) of AdaBoost against arc-gv on the breast cancer data set [20].

This modification is derived from the minimization of multiclass exponential loss. It was proved that, similar to the case of binary classification, optimizing the multiclass exponential loss approaches to the optimal Bayesian error, that is,

$$sign[h^*(\boldsymbol{x})] = \arg\max_{y \in \mathcal{Y}} P(y|\boldsymbol{x})$$

where h^* is the optimal solution to the multiclass exponential loss.

A popular solution to multiclass classification problem is to decompose the task into multiple binary classification problems. Direct and popular decompositions include *one-vs-rest* and *one-vs-one*. One-vs-rest decomposes a multiclass task of $|\mathcal{Y}|$ classes into $|\mathcal{Y}|$ binary classification tasks, where the i-th task is to classify whether an instance belongs to the i-th class or not. One-vs-one decomposes a multiclass task of $|\mathcal{Y}|$ classes into $\frac{|\mathcal{Y}|(|\mathcal{Y}|-1)}{2}$ binary classification tasks, where each task is to classify whether an instance belongs to, say, the i-th class or the j-th class.

AdaBoost.MH [23] follows the one-vs-rest approach. After training $|\mathcal{Y}|$ number of (binary) AdaBoost classifiers, the real-value output $H(\boldsymbol{x}) = \sum_{t=1}^{T} \alpha_t h_t(\boldsymbol{x})$ of each AdaBoost is used instead of the crisp classification to find the most probable class, that is,

$$H(\boldsymbol{x}) = \arg\max_{y \in \mathcal{Y}} H_y(\boldsymbol{x})$$

where H_y is the AdaBoost classifier that classifies the y-th class from the rest.

AdaBoost.M2 [9] follows the one-vs-one approach, which minimizes a pseudo-loss. This algorithm is later generalized as AdaBoost.MR [23] which minimizes a ranking loss motivated by the fact that the highest ranked class is more likely to be the correct class. Binary classifiers obtained by one-vs-one decomposition can also be aggregated by voting or pairwise coupling [13].

Error correcting output codes (ECOCs) [6] can also be used to decompose a multiclass classification problem into a series of binary classification problems. For example, Figure 7.12a shows output codes for four classes using five classifiers. Each classifier is trained to discriminate the $+1$ and -1 classes in the corresponding column. For a test instance, by concatenating the classifications output by the five classifiers, a code vector of predictions is obtained. This vector will be compared with the code vector of the classes (every row in Figure 7.12(a) using Hamming distance, and the class with the shortest distance is deemed the final prediction. According to information theory, when the binary classifiers are independent, the larger the minimum Hamming distance within the code vectors, the smaller the 0/1-loss. Later, a unified framework was proposed for multiclass decomposition approaches [1]. Figure 7.12(b) shows the output codes for one-vs-rest decomposition and Figure 7.12(c) shows the output codes for one-vs-one decomposition, where zeros mean that the classifiers should ignore the instances of those classes.

	H_1 ↓	H_2 ↓	H_3 ↓	H_4 ↓	H_5 ↓
$y_1 =$	+1	−1	+1	−1	+1
$y_2 =$	+1	+1	−1	−1	−1
$y_3 =$	−1	−1	+1	−1	−1
$y_4 =$	−1	+1	−1	+1	+1

(a) Original code

	H_1 ↓	H_2 ↓	H_3 ↓	H_4 ↓
$y_1 =$	+1	−1	−1	−1
$y_2 =$	−1	+1	−1	−1
$y_3 =$	−1	−1	+1	−1
$y_4 =$	−1	−1	−1	+1

(b) One-vs-rest code

	H_1 ↓	H_2 ↓	H_3 ↓	H_4 ↓	H_5 ↓	H_6 ↓
$y_1 =$	+1	+1	+1	0	0	0
$y_2 =$	−1	0	0	+1	+1	0
$y_3 =$	0	−1	0	−1	0	+1
$y_4 =$	0	0	−1	0	−1	−1

(c) One-vs-one code

Figure 7.12 ECOC output codes.

7.5.3 Other Advanced Topics

Comprehensibility, that is, understandability of the learned model to user, is desired in many real applications. Similar to other ensemble methods, a serious deficiency of AdaBoost and its variants is the lack of comprehensibility. Even when the base learners are comprehensible models such as small decision trees, the combination of them will lead to a black-box model. Improving the comprehensibility of ensemble methods is an important yet largely understudied direction [33].

In most ensemble methods, all the generated base learners are used in the ensemble. However, it has been proved that stronger ensembles with smaller sizes can be obtained through *selective ensemble*, that is, ensembling some instead of all the available base learners [34]. This finding is different from previous results which suggest that ensemble pruning may sacrifice the generalization ability [17,24], and therefore provides support for better selective ensemble or ensemble pruning methods [18,31].

In many applications, training examples of one class are far more than other classes. Learning algorithms that do not consider class imbalance tend to be overwhelmed by the majority class; however, the primary interest is often on the minority class. Many variants of AdaBoost have been developed for class-imbalance learning [5,14,19,26]. Moreover, a recent study [16] suggests that the performance of AdaBoost could be used as a clue to judge whether a task suffers from class imbalance or not, based on which new powerful algorithms may be designed.

As mentioned before, in addition to the 0/1-loss, boosting can also work with other kinds of loss functions. For example, by considering the ranking loss, RankBoost [8] and AdaRank [30] have been developed for information retrieval tasks.

7.6 Software Implementations

As an off-the-shelf machine learning technique, AdaBoost and its variants have easily accessible codes in Java, MATLAB®, R, and C++.

Java implementations can be found in Weka,[3] one of the most famous open-source packages for machine learning and data mining. Weka includes AdaBoost.M1 algorithm [9], which provides options to choose the base learning algorithms, set the number of base learners, and switch between reweighting and resampling mechanisms. Weka also includes other boosting algorithms, such as LogitBoost [11], MultiBoosting [29], and so on.

MATLAB implementation can be found in Spider.[4] R implementation can be found in R-Project.[5] C++ implementation can be found in Sourceforge.[6] There are also many other implementations that can be found on the Internet.

[3] `http://www.cs.waikato.ac.nz/ml/weka/.`
[4] `http://www.kyb.mpg.de/bs/people/spider/.`
[5] `http://cran.r-project.org/web/packages/.`
[6] `http://sourceforge.net/projects/multiboost.`

7.7 Exercises

1. What is the basic idea of Boosting?
2. In Figure 7.2, why should it break when $\epsilon_t \geq 0.5$?
3. Given a training set

$$\left\{ \begin{array}{c} (\boldsymbol{x}_1 = (+1, 0), y_1 = +1) \\ (\boldsymbol{x}_2 = (0, +1), y_2 = +1) \\ (\boldsymbol{x}_3 = (-1, 0), y_3 = +1) \\ (\boldsymbol{x}_4 = (0, -1), y_4 = +1) \\ (\boldsymbol{x}_5 = (0, 0), y_5 = -1) \end{array} \right\}$$

is there any linear classifier that can reach zero training error? Why/why not?

4. Given the above training set, show that AdaBoost can reach zero training error by using five linear base classifiers from the following pool.

$$\begin{array}{ll} h_1(\boldsymbol{x}) = 2\boldsymbol{I}[x_1 > 0.5] - 1 & h_2(\boldsymbol{x}) = 2\boldsymbol{I}[x_1 < 0.5] - 1 \\ h_3(\boldsymbol{x}) = 2\boldsymbol{I}[x_1 > -0.5] - 1 & h_4(\boldsymbol{x}) = 2\boldsymbol{I}[x_1 < -0.5] - 1 \\ h_5(\boldsymbol{x}) = 2\boldsymbol{I}[x_2 > 0.5] - 1 & h_6(\boldsymbol{x}) = 2\boldsymbol{I}[x_2 < 0.5] - 1 \\ h_7(\boldsymbol{x}) = 2\boldsymbol{I}[x_2 > -0.5] - 1 & h_8(\boldsymbol{x}) = 2\boldsymbol{I}[x_2 < -0.5] - 1 \\ h_9(\boldsymbol{x}) = +1 & h_{10}(\boldsymbol{x}) = -1 \end{array}$$

5. In the above exercise, will AdaBoost reach nonzero training error for any $T \geq 5$? T is the number of base classifiers.
6. The *nearest neighbor classifier* classifies an instance by assigning it with the label of its nearest training example. Can AdaBoost boost the performance of such classifier? Why/why not?
7. Plot the following functions in a graph within range $z \in [-2, 2]$, and observe their difference.

$$l_1(z) = \begin{cases} 0, & z \geq 0 \\ 1, & z < 0 \end{cases} \qquad l_2(z) = \begin{cases} 0, & z \geq 1 \\ 1 - z, & z < 1 \end{cases}$$

$$l_3(z) = (z - 1)^2 \qquad l_4(z) = e^{-z}$$

Note that, when $z = yf(\boldsymbol{x})$, l_1, l_2, l_3, and l_4 are functions of 0/1-loss, hinge loss (used by support vector machines), square loss (used by least square regression), and exponential loss (the loss function used by AdaBoost), respectively.

8. Show that the l_2, l_3, and l_4 functions in the above exercise are all convex (l is convex if $\forall z_1, z_2 : l(z_1 + z_2) \geq (l(z_1) + l(z_2))$). Considering a binary classification task $z = yf(\boldsymbol{x})$ where $y = \{-1, +1\}$, find that function to which the optimal solution is the Bayesian optimal solution.
9. Can AdaBoost be extended to solve regression problems? If your answer is yes, how? If your answer is no, why?

10. Run experiments to compare AdaBoost using reweighting and AdaBoost using resampling. You can use Weka implementation and data sets from UCI Machine Learning Repository.

References

[1] E. L. Allwein, R. E. Schapire, and Y. Singer. Reducing multiclass to binary: A unifying approach for margin classifiers. *Journal of Machine Learning Research*, 1:113–141, 2000.

[2] E. Bauer and R. Kohavi. An empirical comparison of voting classification algorithms: Bagging, boosting, and variants. *Machine Learning*, 36(1-2):105–139, 1999.

[3] L. Breiman. Bias, variance, and arcing classifiers. Technical Report 460, Statistics Department, University of California, Berkeley, 1996.

[4] L. Breiman. Prediction games and arcing algorithms. *Neural Computation*, 11(7):1493–1517, 1999.

[5] N. V. Chawla, A. Lazarevic, L. O. Hall, and K. W. Bowyer. SMOTEBoost: Improving prediction of the minority class in boosting. In *Proceedings of the 7th European Conference on Principles and Practice of Knowledge Discovery in Databases*, pages 107–119, Cavtat-Dubrovnik, Croatia, 2003.

[6] T. G. Dietterich and G. Bakiri. Solving multiclass learning problems via error-correcting output codes. *Journal of Artificial Intelligence Research*, 2:263–286, 1995.

[7] Y. Freund. Boosting a weak learning algorithm by majority. *Information and Computation*, 121(2):256–285, 1995.

[8] Y. Freund, R. Iyer, R. E. Schapire, and Y. Singer. An efficient boosting algorithm for combining preferences. *Journal of Machine Learning Research*, 4:933–963, 2003.

[9] Y. Freund and R. E. Schapire. A decision-theoretic generalization of on-line learning and an application to boosting. *Journal of Computer and System Sciences*, 55(1):119–139, 1997.

[10] Y. Freund and R. E. Schapire. A short introduction to boosting. *Journal of Japanese Society for Artificial Intelligence*, 14(5):771–780, 1999.

[11] J. Friedman, T. Hastie, and R. Tibshirani. Additive logistic regression: A statistical view of boosting (with discussions). *The Annals of Statistics*, 28(2):337–407, 2000.

[12] S. German, E. Bienenstock, and R. Doursat. Neural networks and the bias/variance dilemma. *Neural Computation*, 4(1):1–58, 1992.

[13] T. Hastie and R. Tibshirani. Classification by pairwise coupling. *The Annals of Statistics*, 26(2):451–471, 1998.

[14] M. V. Joshi, R. C. Agarwal, and V. Kumar. Predicting rare classes: Can boosting make any weak learner strong? In *Proceedings of the 8th ACM SIGKDD International Conference on Knowledge Discovery and Data Mining*, pages 297–306, Edmonton, Canada, 2002.

[15] M. Kearns and L. G. Valiant. Cryptographic limitations on learning Boolean formulae and finite automata. In *Proceedings of the 21st Annual ACM Symposium on Theory of Computing*, pages 433–444, Seattle, WA, 1989.

[16] X.-Y. Liu, J.-X. Wu, and Z.-H. Zhou. Exploratory under-sampling for class-imbalance learning. *IEEE Transactions on Systems, Man and Cybernetics—Part B*, 2009.

[17] D. Margineantu and T. G. Dietterich. Pruning adaptive boosting. In *Proceedings of the 14th International Conference on Machine Learning*, pages 211–218, Nashville, TN, 1997.

[18] G. Martínez-Muñoz and A. Suárez. Pruning in ordered bagging ensembles. In *Proceedings of the 23rd International Conference on Machine Learning*, pages 609–616, Pittsburgh, PA, 2006.

[19] H. Masnadi-Shirazi and N. Vasconcelos. Asymmetric boosting. In *Proceedings of the 24th International Conference on Machine Learning*, pages 609–619, Corvallis, OR, 2007.

[20] L. Reyzin and R. E. Schapire. How boosting the margin can also boost classifier complexity. In *Proceedings of the 23rd International Conference on Machine Learning*, pages 753–760, Pittsburgh, PA, 2006.

[21] R. E. Schapire. The strength of weak learnability. *Machine Learning*, 5(2):197–227, 1990.

[22] R. E. Schapire, Y. Freund, P. Bartlett, and W. S. Lee. Boosting the margin: A new explanation for the effectiveness of voting methods. *The Annals of Statistics*, 26(5):1651–1686, 1998.

[23] R. E. Schapire and Y. Singer. Improved boosting algorithms using confidence-rated predictions. *Machine Learning*, 37(3):297–336, 1999.

[24] C. Tamon and J. Xiang. On the boosting pruning problem. In *Proceedings of the 11th European Conference on Machine Learning*, pages 404–412, Barcelona, Spain, 2000.

[25] L. G. Valiant. A theory of the learnable. *Communications of the ACM*, 27(11):1134–1142, 1984.

[26] P. Viola and M. Jones. Fast and robust classification using asymmetric AdaBoost and a detector cascade. In T. G. Dietterich, S. Becker, and Z. Ghahramani, editors, *Advances in Neural Information Processing Systems 14*, pages 1311–1318. MIT Press, Cambridge, MA, 2002.

[27] P. Viola and M. Jones. Robust real-time object detection. *International Journal of Computer Vision*, 57(2):137–154, 2004.

[28] L. Wang, M. Sugiyama, C. Yang, Z.-H. Zhou, and J. Feng. On the margin explanation of boosting algorithm. In *Proceedings of the 21st Annual Conference on Learning Theory*, pages 479–490, Helsinki, Finland, 2008.

[29] G. I. Webb. MultiBoosting: A technique for combining boosting and wagging. *Machine Learning*, 40(2):159–196, 2000.

[30] J. Xu and H. Li. AdaRank: A boosting algorithm for information retrieval. In *Proceedings of the 30th Annual International ACM SIGIR Conference on Research and Development in Information Retrieval*, pages 391–398, Amsterdam, The Netherlands, 2007.

[31] Y. Zhang, S. Burer, and W. N. Street. Ensemble pruning via semi-definite programming. *Journal of Machine Learning Research*, 7:1315–1338, 2006.

[32] Z.-H. Zhou. Ensemble learning. In S. Z. Li, editor, *Encyclopedia of Biometrics*. Springer, Berlin, 2008.

[33] Z.-H. Zhou, Y. Jiang, and S.-F. Chen. Extracting symbolic rules from trained neural network ensembles. *AI Communications*, 16(1):3–15, 2003.

[34] Z.-H. Zhou, J. Wu, and W. Tang. Ensembling neural networks: Many could be better than all. *Artificial Intelligence*, 137(1-2):239–263, 2002.

[35] J. Zhu, S. Rosset, H. Zou, and T. Hastie. Multi-class AdaBoost. Technical report, Department of Statistics, University of Michigan, Ann Arbor, 2006.

Chapter 8

kNN: k-Nearest Neighbors

Michael Steinbach and Pang-Ning Tan

Contents

8.1 Introduction

One of the simplest and rather trivial classifiers is the Rote classifier, which memorizes the entire training data and performs classification only if the attributes of the test object exactly match the attributes of one of the training objects. An obvious problem with this approach is that many test records will not be classified because they do not exactly match any of the training records. Another issue arises when two or more training records have the same attributes but different class labels.

A more sophisticated approach, k-nearest neighbor (kNN) classification [10,11,21], finds a group of k objects in the training set that are closest to the test object, and bases the assignment of a label on the predominance of a particular class in this neighborhood. This addresses the issue that, in many data sets, it is unlikely that one object will exactly match another, as well as the fact that conflicting information about the class of an object may be provided by the objects closest to it. There are several key elements of this approach: (i) the set of labeled objects to be used for evaluating a test object's class,[1] (ii) a distance or similarity metric that can be used to compute

[1]This need not be the entire training set.

the closeness of objects, (iii) the value of k, the number of nearest neighbors, and (iv) the method used to determine the class of the target object based on the classes and distances of the k nearest neighbors. In its simplest form, kNN can involve assigning an object the class of its nearest neighbor or of the majority of its nearest neighbors, but a variety of enhancements are possible and are discussed below.

More generally, kNN is a special case of instance-based learning [1]. This includes case-based reasoning [3], which deals with symbolic data. The kNN approach is also an example of a lazy learning technique, that is, a technique that waits until the query arrives to generalize beyond the training data.

Although kNN classification is a classification technique that is easy to understand and implement, it performs well in many situations. In particular, a well-known result by Cover and Hart [6] shows that the classification error[2] of the nearest neighbor rule is bounded above by twice the optimal Bayes error[3] under certain reasonable assumptions. Furthermore, the error of the general kNN method asymptotically approaches that of the Bayes error and can be used to approximate it.

Also, because of its simplicity, kNN is easy to modify for more complicated classification problems. For instance, kNN is particularly well-suited for multimodal classes[4] as well as applications in which an object can have many class labels. To illustrate the last point, for the assignment of functions to genes based on microarray expression profiles, some researchers found that kNN outperformed a support vector machine (SVM) approach, which is a much more sophisticated classification scheme [17].

The remainder of this chapter describes the basic kNN algorithm, including various issues that affect both classification and computational performance. Pointers are given to implementations of kNN, and examples of using the Weka machine learning package to perform nearest neighbor classification are also provided. Advanced techniques are discussed briefly and this chapter concludes with a few exercises.

8.2 Description of the Algorithm

8.2.1 High-Level Description

Algorithm 8.1 provides a high-level summary of the nearest-neighbor classification method. Given a training set D and a test object $\mathbf{z}$, which is a vector of attribute values and has an unknown class label, the algorithm computes the distance (or similarity)

[2]The classification error of a classifier is the percentage of instances it incorrectly classifies.

[3]The Bayes error is the classification error of a Bayes classifier, that is, a classifier that knows the underlying probability distribution of the data with respect to class, and assigns each data point to the class with the highest probability density for that point. For more detail, see [9].

[4]With multimodal classes, objects of a particular class label are concentrated in several distinct areas of the data space, not just one. In statistical terms, the probability density function for the class does not have a single "bump" like a Gaussian, but rather, has a number of peaks.

Algorithm 8.1 Basic *k*NN Algorithm

Input : D, the set of training objects, the test object, $\mathbf{z}$, which is a vector of attribute values, and L, the set of classes used to label the objects

Output : $c_z \in L$, the class of z

foreach object $\mathbf{y} \in D$ **do**

| Compute $d(\mathbf{z}, \mathbf{y})$, the distance between $\mathbf{z}$ and $\mathbf{y}$;

end

Select $N \subseteq D$, the set (neighborhood) of k closest training objects for z;

$c_z = \underset{v \in L}{\text{argmax}} \sum_{y \in N} I(v = class(c_y))$;

where $I(\cdot)$ is an indicator function that returns the value 1 if its argument is true and 0 otherwise.

---

between $\mathbf{z}$ and all the training objects to determine its nearest-neighbor list. It then assigns a class to $\mathbf{z}$ by taking the class of the majority of neighboring objects. Ties are broken in an unspecified manner, for example, randomly or by taking the most frequent class in the training set.

The storage complexity of the algorithm is $O(n)$, where n is the number of training objects. The time complexity is also $O(n)$, since the distance needs to be computed between the target and each training object. However, there is no time taken for the construction of the classification model, for example, a decision tree or separating hyperplane. Thus, *k*NN is different from most other classification techniques which have moderately to quite expensive model-building stages, but very inexpensive $O(constant)$ classification steps.

8.2.2 Issues

There are several key issues that affect the performance of *k*NN. One is the choice of k. This is illustrated in Figure 8.1, which shows an unlabeled test object, $\mathbf{x}$, and training objects that belong to either a "+" or "−" class. If k is too small, then the result can be sensitive to noise points. On the other hand, if k is too large, then the neighborhood may include too many points from other classes. An estimate of the best value for k can be obtained by cross-validation. However, it is important to point out that $k = 1$ may be able to perform other values of k, particularly for small data sets, including those typically used in research or for class exercises. However, given enough samples, larger values of k are more resistant to noise.

Another issue is the approach to combining the class labels. The simplest method is to take a majority vote, but this can be a problem if the nearest neighbors vary widely in their distance and the closer neighbors more reliably indicate the class of the object. A more sophisticated approach, which is usually much less sensitive to the choice of k, weights each object's vote by its distance. Various choices are possible; for example, the weight factor is often taken to be the reciprocal of the squared distance: $w_i = 1/d(\mathbf{y}, \mathbf{z})^2$. This amounts to replacing the last step of Algorithm 8.1 with the

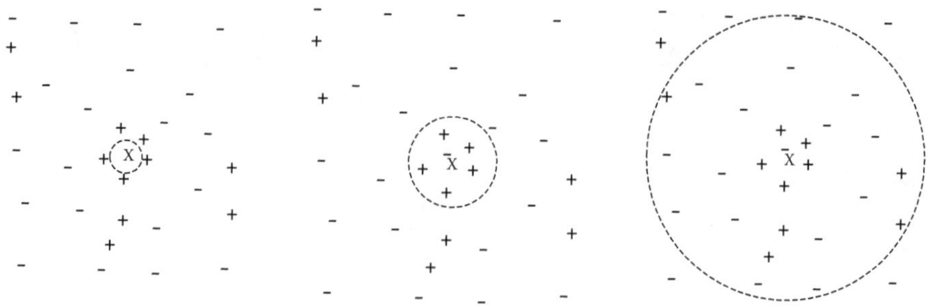

(a) Neighborhood too small.

(b) Neighborhood just right.

(c) Neighborhood too large.

Figure 8.1 k-nearest neighbor classification with small, medium, and large k.

following:

$$\text{Distance-Weighted Voting: } c_z = \underset{v \in L}{\operatorname{argmax}} \sum_{y \in N} w_i \times I(v = class(c_y)) \tag{8.1}$$

The choice of the distance measure is another important consideration. Commonly, Euclidean or Manhattan distance measures are used [21]. For two points, **x** and **y**, with n attributes, these distances are given by the following formulas:

$$d(\mathbf{x}, \mathbf{y}) = \sqrt{\sum_{k=1}^{n} (x_k - y_k)^2} \quad \text{Euclidean distance} \tag{8.2}$$

$$d(\mathbf{x}, \mathbf{y}) = \sqrt{\sum_{k=1}^{n} |x_k - y_k|} \quad \text{Manhattan distance} \tag{8.3}$$

where x_k and y_k are the kth attributes (components) of x and y, respectively.

Although these and various other measures can be used to compute the distance between two points, conceptually, the most desirable distance measure is one for which a smaller distance between two objects implies a greater likelihood of having the same class. Thus, for example, if kNN is being applied to classify documents, then it may be better to use the cosine measure rather than Euclidean distance. Note that kNN can also be used for data with categorical or mixed categorical and numerical attributes as long as a suitable distance measure can be defined [21].

Some distance measures can also be affected by the high dimensionality of the data. In particular, it is well known that the Euclidean distance measure becomes less discriminating as the number of attributes increases. Also, attributes may have to be scaled to prevent distance measures from being dominated by one of the attributes. For example, consider a data set where the height of a person varies from 1.5 to 1.8 m, the weight of a person varies from 90 to 300 lb, and the income of a person varies from $10,000 to $1,000,000. If a distance measure is used without scaling, the income attribute will dominate the computation of distance, and thus the assignment of class labels.

8.2.3 Software Implementations

Algorithm 8.1 is easy to implement in almost any programming language. However, this section contains a short guide to some readily available implementations of this algorithm and its variants for those who would rather use an existing implementation. One of the most readily available *k*NN implementations can be found in Weka [26]. The main function of interest is IBk, which is basically Algorithm 8.1. However, IBk also allows you to specify a couple of choices of distance weighting and the option to determine a value of *k* by using cross-validation.

Another popular nearest neighbor implementation is PEBLS (Parallel Exemplar-Based Learning System) [5,19] from the CMU Artificial Intelligence repository [20]. According to the site, "PEBLS (Parallel Exemplar-Based Learning System) is a nearest-neighbor learning system designed for applications where the instances have symbolic feature values."

8.3 Examples

In this section we provide a couple of examples of the use of *k*NN. For these examples, we will use the Weka package described in the previous section. Specifically, we used Weka 3.5.6.

To begin, we applied *k*NN to the Iris data set that is available from the UCI Machine Learning Repository [2] and is also available as a sample data file with Weka. This data set consists of 150 flowers split equally among three Iris species: Setosa, Versicolor, and Virginica. Each flower is characterized by four measurements: petal length, petal width, sepal length, and sepal width.

The Iris data set was classified using the IB1 algorithm, which corresponds to the IBk algorithm with $k = 1$. In other words, the algorithm looks at the closest neighbor, as computed using Euclidean distance from Equation 8.2. The results are quite good, as the reader can see by examining the confusion matrix[5] given in Table 8.1.

However, further investigation shows that this is a quite easy data set to classify since the different species are relatively well separated in the data space. To illustrate, we show a plot of the data with respect to petal length and petal width in Figure 8.2. There is some mixing between the Versicolor and Virginica species with respect to

[5] A confusion matrix tabulates how the actual classes of various data instances (rows) compare to their predicted classes (columns).

TABLE 8.1 Confusion Matrix for Weka *k*NN Classifier IB1 on the Iris Data Set

Actual/Predicted	Setosa	Versicolor	Virginica
Setosa	50	0	0
Versicolor	0	47	3
Virginica	0	4	46

their petal lengths and widths, but otherwise the species are well separated. Since the other two variables, sepal width and sepal length, add little if any discriminating information, the performance seen with basic *k*NN approach is about the best that can be achieved with a *k*NN approach or, indeed, any other approach.

The second example uses the ionosphere data set from UCI. The data objects in this data set are radar signals sent into the ionosphere and the class value indicates whether or not the signal returned information on the structure of the ionosphere. There are 34 attributes that describe the signal and 1 class attribute. The IB1 algorithm applied on the original data set gives an accuracy of 86.3% evaluated via tenfold cross-validation, while the same algorithm applied to the first nine attributes gives an accuracy of 89.4%. In other words, using fewer attributes gives better results. The confusion matrices are given below. Using cross-validation to select the number of nearest neighbors gives an accuracy of 90.8% with two nearest neighbors. The confusion matrices for these cases are given below in Tables 8.2, 8.3, and 8.4, respectively. Adding weighting for nearest neighbors actually results in a modest drop in accuracy. The biggest improvement is due to reducing the number of attributes.

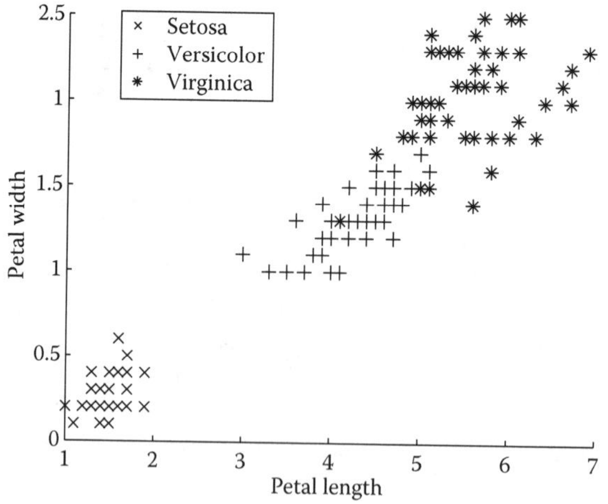

Figure 8.2 Plot of Iris data using petal length and width.

TABLE 8.2 Confusion Matrix for Weka *k*NN Classifier IB1 on the Ionosphere Data Set Using All Attributes

Actual/Predicted	Good Signal	Bad Signal
Good Signal	85	41
Bad Signal	7	218

8.4 Advanced Topics

To address issues related to the distance function, a number of schemes have been developed that try to compute the weights of each individual attribute or in some other way determine a more effective distance metric based upon a training set [13, 15]. In addition, weights can be assigned to the training objects themselves. This can give more weight to highly reliable training objects, while reducing the impact of unreliable objects. The PEBLS system by Cost and Salzberg [5] is a well-known example of such an approach.

As mentioned, *k*NN classifiers are lazy learners, that is, models are not built explicitly unlike eager learners (e.g., decision trees, SVM, etc.). Thus, building the model is cheap, but classifying unknown objects is relatively expensive since it requires the computation of the *k*-nearest neighbors of the object to be labeled. This, in general, requires computing the distance of the unlabeled object to all the objects in the labeled set, which can be expensive particularly for large training sets. A number of techniques, e.g., multidimensional access methods [12] or fast approximate similarity search [16], have been developed for efficient computation of *k*-nearest neighbor distance that make use of the structure in the data to avoid having to compute distance to all objects in the training set. These techniques, which are particularly applicable for low dimensional data, can help reduce the computational cost without affecting classification accuracy. The Weka package provides a choice of some of the multidimensional access methods in its IBk routine. (See Exercise 4.)

Although the basic *k*NN algorithm and some of its variations, such as weighted *k*NN and assigning weights to objects, are relatively well known, some of the more advanced techniques for *k*NN are much less known. For example, it is typically possible to eliminate many of the stored data objects, but still retain the classification accuracy of the *k*NN classifier. This is known as "condensing" and can greatly speed up the classification of new objects [14]. In addition, data objects can be removed to

TABLE 8.3 Confusion Matrix for Weka *k*NN Classifier IB1 on the Ionosphere Data Set Using the First Nine Attributes

Actual/Predicted	Good Signal	Bad Signal
Good Signal	100	26
Bad Signal	11	214

TABLE 8.4 Confusion Matrix for Weka kNN Classifier IBk on the Ionosphere Data Set Using the First Nine Attributes with $k = 2$

Actual/Predicted	Good Signal	Bad Signal
Good Signal	103	9
Bad Signal	23	216

improve classification accuracy, a process known as "editing" [25]. There has also been a considerable amount of work on the application of proximity graphs (nearest neighbor graphs, minimum spanning trees, relative neighborhood graphs, Delaunay triangulations, and Gabriel graphs) to the kNN problem. Recent papers by Toussaint [22–24], which emphasize a proximity graph viewpoint, provide an overview of work addressing these three areas and indicate some remaining open problems.

Other important resources include the collection of papers by Dasarathy [7] and the book by Devroye, Gyorfi, and Lugosi [8]. Also, a fuzzy approach to kNN can be found in the work of Bezdek [4]. Finally, an extensive bibliography on this subject is also available online as part of the Annotated Computer Vision Bibliography [18].

8.5 Exercises

1. Download the Weka machine learning package from the Weka project homepage and the Iris and ionosphere data sets from the UCI Machine Learning Repository. Repeat the analyses performed in this chapter.
2. Prove that the error of the nearest neighbor rule is bounded above by twice the Bayes error under certain reasonable assumptions.
3. Prove that the error of the general kNN method asymptotically approaches that of the Bayes error and can be used to approximate it.
4. Various spatial or multidimensional access methods can be used to speed up the nearest neighbor computation. For the k-d tree, which is one such method, estimate how much the saving would be. Comment: The IBk Weka classification algorithm allows you to specify the method of finding nearest neighbors. Try this on one of the larger UCI data sets, for example, predicting sex on the abalone data set.
5. Consider the one-dimensional data set shown in Table 8.5.

TABLE 8.5 Data Set for Exercise 5

x	1.5	2.5	3.5	4.5	5.0	5.5	5.75	6.5	7.5	10.5
y	+	+	−	−	−	+	+	−	+	+

(a) Given the data points listed in Table 8.5, compute the class of $x = 5.5$ according to its 1-, 3-, 6-, and 9-nearest neighbors (using majority vote).

(b) Repeat the previous exercise, but use the weighted version of *k*NN given in Equation (8.1).

6. Comment on the use of *k*NN when documents are compared with the cosine measure, which is a measure of similarity, not distance.
7. Discuss kernel density estimation and its relationship to *k*NN.
8. Given an end user who desires not only a classification of unknown cases, but also an understanding of why cases were classified the way they were, which classification method would you prefer: decision tree or *k*NN?
9. Sampling can be used to reduce the number of data points in many kinds of data analysis. Comment on the use of sampling for *k*NN.
10. Discuss how *k*NN could be used to perform classification when each class can have multiple labels and/or classes are organized in a hierarchy.

Acknowledgments

This work was supported by NSF Grant CNS-0551551, NSF ITR Grant ACI-0325949, NSF Grant IIS-0308264, and NSF Grant IIS-0713227. Access to computing facilities was provided by the University of Minnesota Digital Technology Center and Supercomputing Institute.

References

[1] D. W. Aha, D. Kibler, and M. K. Albert. Instance-based learning algorithms. *Mach. Learn.*, 6(1):37–66, January 1991.

[2] A. Asuncion and D. Newman. UCI Machine Learning Repository, 2007.

[3] B. Bartsch-Spörl, M. Lenz, and A. Hübner. Case-based reasoning—survey and future directions. In F. Puppe, editor, *XPS-99: Knowledge-Based Systems—Survey and Future Directions, 5th Biannual German Conference on Knowledge-Based Systems*, volume 1570 of *Lecture Notes in Computer Science*, Würzburg, Germany, March 3-5 1999. Springer.

[4] J. C. Bezdek, S. K. Chuah, and D. Leep. Generalized k-nearest neighbor rules. *Fuzzy Sets Syst.*, 18(3):237–256, 1986.

[5] S. Cost and S. Salzberg. A weighted nearest neighbor algorithm for learning with symbolic features. *Mach. Learn.*, 10(1):57–78, 1993.

[6] T. Cover and P. Hart. Nearest neighbor pattern classification. *IEEE Transactions on Information Theory*, 13(1):21–27, January 1967.

[7] B. Dasarathy. *Nearest Neighbor (NN) Norms: NN Pattern Classification Techniques*. Computer Society Press, 1991.

[8] L. Devroye, L. Gyorfi, and G. Lugosi. *A Probabilistic Theory of Pattern Recognition*. Springer-Verlag, 1996.

[9] R. O. Duda, P. E. Hart, and D. G. Stork. *Pattern Classification (2nd Edition)*. Wiley-Interscience, November 2000.

[10] E. Fix and J. J. Hodges. Discriminatory analysis: Non-parametric discrimination: Consistency properties. Technical report, USAF School of Aviation Medicine, 1951.

[11] E. Fix and J. J. Hodges. Discriminatory analysis: Non-parametric discrimination: Small sample performance. Technical report, USAF School of Aviation Medicine, 1952.

[12] V. Gaede and O. Günther. Multidimensional access methods. *ACM Comput. Surv.*, 30(2):170–231, 1998.

[13] E.-H. Han, G. Karypis, and V. Kumar. Text categorization using weight adjusted k-nearest neighbor classification. In *PAKDD '01: Proceedings of the 5th Pacific-Asia Conference on Knowledge Discovery and Data Mining*, pages 53–65, London, UK, 2001. Springer-Verlag.

[14] P. Hart. The condensed nearest neighbor rule. *IEEE Trans. Inform.*, 14(5):515–516, May 1968.

[15] T. Hastie and R. Tibshirani. Discriminant adaptive nearest neighbor classification. *IEEE Trans. Pattern Anal. Mach. Intell.*, 18(6):607–616, 1996.

[16] M. E. Houle and J. Sakuma. Fast approximate similarity search in extremely high-dimensional data sets. In *ICDE '05: Proceedings of the 21st International Conference on Data Engineering*, pages 619–630, Washington, DC, 2005. IEEE Computer Society.

[17] M. Kuramochi and G. Karypis. Gene classification using expression profiles: A feasibility study. In *BIBE '01: Proceedings of the 2nd IEEE International Symposium on Bioinformatics and Bioengineering*, page 191, Washington, DC, 2001. IEEE Computer Society.

[18] K. Price. Nearest neighbor classification bibliography. http://www.visionbib.com/bibliography/pattern621.html, 2008. Part of the Annotated Computer Vision Bibliography.

[19] J. Rachlin, S. Kasif, S. Salzberg, and D. W. Aha. Towards a better understanding of memory-based reasoning systems. In *International Conference on Machine Learning*, pages 242–250, 1994.

[20] S. Salzberg. PEBLS: Parallel exemplar-based learning system. http://www.cs.cmu.edu/afs/cs/project/ai-repository/ai/areas/learning/systems/pebls/0.html, 1994.

[21] P.-N. Tan, M. Steinbach, and V. Kumar. *Introduction to Data Minining*. Pearson Addison-Wesley, 2006.

[22] G. T. Toussaint. Proximity graphs for nearest neighbor decision rules: Recent progress. In *Interface-2002, 34th Symposium on Computing and Statistics*, Montreal, Canada, April 17–20, 2002.

[23] G. T. Toussaint. Open problems in geometric methods for instance-based learning. In *Discrete and Computational Geometry*, volume 2866 of *Lecture Notes in Computer Science*, pages 273–283, December 6–9, 2003.

[24] G. T. Toussaint. Geometric proximity graphs for improving nearest neighbor methods in instance-based learning and data mining. *Int. J. Comput. Geometry Appl.*, 15(2):101–150, 2005.

[25] D. Wilson. Asymptotic properties of nearest neighbor rules using edited data. *IEEE Trans. Syst., Man, and Cybernetics*, 2:408–421, 1972.

[26] I. H. Witten and E. Frank. *Data Mining: Practical Machine Learning Tools and Techniques, Second Edition (Morgan Kaufmann Series in Data Management Systems)*. Morgan Kaufmann, June 2005.

Chapter 9

Naïve Bayes

David J. Hand

Contents

9.1 Introduction

Given a set of objects, each of which belongs to a known class, and each of which has a known vector of variables, our aim is to construct a rule which will allow us to assign future objects to a class, given only the vectors of variables describing the future objects. Problems of this kind, called problems of *supervised classification*, are ubiquitous, and many methods for constructing such rules have been developed. One very important method is the *naïve Bayes* method—also called *idiot's Bayes, simple Bayes*, and *independence Bayes*. This method is important for several reasons, including the following. It is very easy to construct, not needing any complicated iterative parameter estimation schemes. This means it may be readily applied to huge data sets. It is easy to interpret, so users unskilled in classifier technology can understand why it is making the classification it makes. And, particularly important, it often does surprisingly well: It may not be the best possible classifier in any given application, but it can usually be relied on to be robust and to do quite well. For example, in an early classic study comparing supervised classification methods, Titterington et al. (1981) found that the independence model yielded the best overall result, while Mani et al. (1997) found that the model was most effective in predicting breast cancer recurrence. Many further examples showing the surprising effectiveness of the naïve Bayes method are listed in Hand and Yu (2001) and further empirical comparisons, with the same result, are given in Domingos and Pazzani (1997). Of course, there are also some other studies which show poorer relative performance from this method: For a comparative assessment of such studies, see Jamain and Hand (2008).

For convenience, most of this chapter will describe the case in which there are just two classes. This is, in fact, the most important special case as many situations naturally form two classes (right/wrong, yes/no, good/bad, present/absent, and so on). However, the simplicity of the naïve Bayes method is such that it permits ready generalization to more than two classes.

Labeling the classes by $i = 0, 1$, our aim is to use the initial set of objects which have known class memberships (known as the training set) to construct a score such that larger scores are associated with class 1 objects (say) and smaller scores with class 0 objects. New objects are then classified by comparing their score with a "classification threshold." New objects with a score larger than the threshold will be classified into class 1, and new objects with a score less than the threshold will be classified into class 0.

There are two broad perspectives on supervised classification, termed the *diagnostic paradigm* and the *sampling paradigm*. The diagnostic paradigm focuses attention on the differences between the classes—on *discriminating* between the classes—while the sampling paradigm focuses attention on the individual distributions of the classes, comparing these to indirectly produce a comparison between the classes. As we show below, the naïve Bayes method can be viewed from either perspective.

9.2 Algorithm Description

Beginning with the sampling paradigm, define $P(i|x)$ to be the probability that an object with measurement vector $x = (x_1, \ldots, x_p)$ belongs to class i, $f(x|i)$ to be the conditional distribution of x for class i objects, $P(i)$ to be the probability that an object will belong to class i if we know nothing further about it (the "prior" probability of class i), and $f(x)$ to be the overall mixture distribution of the two classes:

$$f(x) = f(x|0)P(0) + f(x|1)P(1)$$

Clearly, an estimate of $P(i|x)$ itself would form a suitable score for use in a classification rule. We would need to choose some suitable threshold probability to act as the classification threshold to yield a classification. For example, it is very common to use a threshold of 1/2, so that each new object is assigned to the class it is estimated as most likely to have come from. More sophisticated approaches take into account the relative severities of different kinds of misclassifications when choosing the threshold.

A simple application of Bayes theorem yields $P(i|x) = f(x|i)P(i)/f(x)$, and to obtain an estimate of $P(i|x)$ from this, we need to estimate each of the $P(i)$ and each of the $f(x|i)$.

If the training set is a simple random sample drawn from the overall population distribution $f(x)$, the $P(i)$ can be estimated directly from the proportion of class i objects in the training set. Sometimes, however, the training set is obtained by more complicated means. For example, in many problems the classes are *unbalanced*, with one being much larger than the other (e.g., in credit card fraud detection, where only 1 in 1,000 transactions may be fraudulent; in rare disease detection, where the ratio may be even more extreme; and so on). In such cases, the larger of the two classes is often subsampled. For example, perhaps only 1 in 10 or 1 in 100 of the larger class will be used in the training set. If this is the case, then it is necessary to reweight the simple observed proportion in the training set to yield an estimate of $P(i)$. In general, if the observations are not drawn as a simple random sample from the training set, some thought will need to go into how best to estimate the $P(i)$.

The core of the naïve Bayes method lies in the method for estimating the $f(x|i)$. The naïve Bayes method assumes that the components of x are independent within each class, so that $f(x|i) = \prod_{j=1}^{p} f(x_j|i)$—hence the alternative name of "independence Bayes." Each of the univariate marginal distributions, $f(x_j|i)$, $j = 1, \ldots, p$; $i = 0, 1$, is then estimated separately. By this means, the p dimensional multivariate problem is reduced to p univariate estimation problem. Univariate estimation is familiar and simple, and requires smaller training set sizes to obtain accurate estimates than does the estimation of multivariate distributions.

If the marginal distributions $f(x_j|i)$ are discrete, with x_j taking only a few values, one can estimate each of the $f(x_j|i)$ by simple multinomial histogram-type estimators. Because this is so straightforward, this is a very common approach to the naïve Bayes estimator, and many implementations adopt this approach. Indeed, it is so straightforward that many implementations partition any continuous variables (age, weight, income, and so on) into cells so that a multinomial histogram-type estimator can be constructed for all of the variables. At first glance, this strategy might seem to be a weak one. After all, it means that any notion of continuity between neighboring cells of the histogram has been sacrificed. It also requires the cells to be wide enough to contain sufficient data points that accurate probability estimates can be obtained. On the other hand, it can be regarded as providing a very general nonparametric estimate of the univariate distribution, so avoiding any distributional assumptions. In particular, it is a nonlinear transformation, so that, for example, the relationship between estimates of $f(x_j|i)$ does not need to be monotonic in x_j.

At a cost of more computational expense (in particular, at the cost of losing the simple counting procedure which underlies histogram-type estimates), one can fit more elaborate models to the univariate marginals. For example, one can assume particular parametric forms for the distributions (e.g., normal, lognormal, and so on) and estimate their parameters by standard and very familiar estimators, or one can adopt more sophisticated nonparametric estimators, such as kernel density estimation. While these do sacrifice the speed of the histogram approach, this is less important in the modern world in which all the calculations will be done by machine. Having said that, there is another reason why one might prefer to use the histogram approach based on forcing all the variables to be discrete—that of interpreting the results. We discuss this below.

The assumption of independence at the core of the naïve Bayes method is clearly a strong one. It is unlikely to be true for most real problems. (How often does a diagonal covariance matrix arise from real data in practice?) A priori, then, one might expect the method to perform poorly precisely because of this improbable assumption lying at its core. However, the fact is that it often does surprisingly well in real practical applications. Reasons for this counterintuitive result are discussed below.

So far we have approached the naïve Bayes method from the sampling paradigm, describing it as being based on estimating the separate class conditional distributions using the simplifying assumption that the variables in each of these distributions were independent. However, the elegance of the naïve Bayes method only really becomes apparent when we note that we can obtain classifications equivalent to the above if we use any strictly monotonic transformation of $P(i|x)$, transforming the classification threshold in a similar way. To see this, note that if T is a strictly monotonic increasing transformation then

$$P(i|x) > P(i|y) \Leftrightarrow T(P(i|x)) > T(P(i|y))$$

and, in particular, $P(i|x) > t \Leftrightarrow T(P(i|x)) > T(t)$. This means that if t is the classification threshold with which $P(i|x)$ is compared, then comparing $T(P(i|x))$ with $T(t)$ will yield the same classification results. (We will assume only monotonic increasing transformations, though the extension to monotonic decreasing transformations is trivial.)

One such monotonic transformation is the ratio

$$P(1|x)/(1 - P(1|x)) = P(1|x)/P(0|x) \tag{9.1}$$

Using the naïve Bayes assumption that the variables within each class are independent, so that the distribution for class i has the form $f(x|i) = \prod_{j=1}^{p} f(x_j|i)$, the ratio $P(1|x)/(1 - P(1|x))$ can be rewritten:

$$\frac{P(1|x)}{1 - P(1|x)} = \frac{P(1)\prod_{j=1}^{p} f(x_j|1)}{P(0)\prod_{j=1}^{p} f(x_j|0)} = \frac{P(1)}{P(0)}\prod_{j=1}^{p}\frac{f(x_j|1)}{f(x_j|0)} \tag{9.2}$$

The log transformation is also monotonic (and combination of monotonic functions yields monotonic functions) so that another alternative score is given by

$$\ln\frac{P(1|x)}{1 - P(1|x)} = \ln\frac{P(1)}{P(0)} + \sum_{j=1}^{p}\ln\frac{f(x_j|1)}{f(x_j|0)} \tag{9.3}$$

If we define $w_j(x_j) = \ln(f(x_j|1)/f(x_j|0))$ and $k = \ln\{P(1)/(P(0))\}$ we see that Equation (9.3) takes the form of a simple sum

$$\ln\frac{P(1|x)}{1 - P(1|x)} = k + \sum_{j=1}^{p} w_j(x_j) \tag{9.4}$$

of contributions from the separate variables. Since the score $S = k + \sum_{j=1}^{p} w_j(x_j)$ is a direct estimate of (a monotonic transformation of) $P(1|x)$, it is based on the diagnostic paradigm. The ease of interpretation now becomes apparent: The naïve Bayes model is simply a sum of transformed values of the raw x_j values.

In cases when each variable is discrete, or is made to be discrete by partitioning it into cells, Equation (9.4) takes a particularly simple form. Suppose that variable x_j takes a value in the k_jth cell of the variable, denoted $x_j^{(k_j)}$. Then $w_j(x_j^{(k_j)})$ is simply a logarithm of a ratio of proportions: the proportion of class 1 points which fall into the k_jth cell of variable x_j divided by the proportion of class 0 points which fall into the k_jth cell of variable x_j. These $w_j(x_j^{(k_j)})$ are called *weights of evidence* in some applications: $w_j(x_j^{(k_j)})$ shows the contribution the jth variable makes toward the total score, or the evidence in favor of the object belonging to class 1 that is provided by the jth variable. Such weights of evidence are useful in identifying which variables are important in assigning any particular object to a class. (This is vital in some applications, such as credit scoring in personal banking, where the law requires that reasons must be given if an application for a loan is declined.)

9.3 Power Despite Independence

The assumption of independence of the x_j within each class implicit in the naïve Bayes model might seem unduly restrictive. After all, as noted above, variables are rarely independent in real problems. In fact, however, various factors may come into play which means that the assumption is not as detrimental as it might seem (Hand and Yu, 2001).

Firstly, the complexity of p-univariate marginal distributions is far lower than that of a single p-variate multivariate distribution. This means that far fewer data points are needed to obtain a given accuracy under the independence model than are needed without this assumption. Put another way, the available sample will lead to an estimator with smaller variance if one is prepared to restrict the model form by assuming independence of the variables within classes. Of course, if the assumption is not true, then there is a risk of bias. This is a manifestation of the classic bias/variance trade-off, which applies to all data analysis modeling, and is not specific to the naïve Bayes model.

To decrease the risk of bias arising from the assumption of independence, a simple modification of the basic naïve Bayes model has been proposed. To understand the reasoning behind this modification, consider the special case in which the marginal distributions of all the variables are the same, and the extreme in which the variables are perfectly correlated. This means that, for any given class, the probability that the x_jth variable takes a value r is the same for all variables. In this perfectly correlated case, the naïve Bayes estimator is

$$\frac{P(1|x)}{P(0|x)} = \frac{P(1)}{P(0)}\left[\frac{f(x_k|1)}{f(x_k|0)}\right]^p$$

while the true odds ratio is

$$\frac{P(1|x)}{P(0|x)} = \frac{P(1)}{P(0)}\frac{f(x_k|1)}{f(x_k|0)}$$

for any $k \in \{1, \ldots, p\}$. We can see from this that if $f(x_k|1)/f(x_k|0)$ is larger than 1, the presence of correlation will mean that the naïve Bayes estimator tends to overestimate $P(1|x)/P(0|x)$, and if $f(x_k|1)/f(x_k|0)$ is less than 1, the presence of correlation will mean that the naïve Bayes estimator tends to underestimate $P(1|x)/P(0|x)$. This phenomenon immediately suggests modifying the naïve Bayes estimator by raising the $f(x_k|1)/f(x_k|0)$ ratios by some power less than 1, to shrink the overall estimator toward the true odds. In general, this yields the improved naïve Bayes estimator

$$\frac{P(1|x)}{P(0|x)} = \frac{f(x|1)P(1)}{f(x|0)P(0)} = \frac{P(1)}{P(0)}\prod_{j=1}^{p}\left[\frac{f(x_j|1)}{f(x_j|0)}\right]^\beta$$

with $\beta < 1$. β is typically chosen by searching over possible values and choosing that which gives best predictive results by means of a method such as cross-validation. We can also see that this leads to a shrinkage factor appearing as a coefficient of the $w_j(x_j)$ terms in Equation (9.4).

A second reason why the assumption of independence is not as unreasonable as might at first seem is that often data might have undergone an initial variable selection procedure in which highly correlated variables have been eliminated on the grounds that they are likely to contribute in a similar way to the separation between classes. Think of variable selection methods in linear regression, for example. This means that the relationships between the remaining variables might well be approximated by independence.

A third reason why the independence assumption may not be too detrimental is that only the decision surface matters. While the assumption might lead to poor estimates of probability or of the ratio $P(1|x)/P(0|x)$, this does not necessarily imply that the decision surface is far from (or even different from) the true decision surface. Consider, for example, a situation in which the two classes have multivariate normal distributions with the same (nondiagonal) covariance matrix, and with the vector of differences between the means lying parallel to the first principal axis of the covariance matrix. The optimal decision surface is linear and is the same with the true covariance matrices and under the independence assumption.

Finally, of course, the decision surface produced by the naïve Bayes model can in fact have a complicated nonlinear shape: The surface is linear in the $w_j(x_j)$ but highly nonlinear in the original variables x_j, so that it can fit quite elaborate surfaces.

9.4 Extensions of the Model

We have seen that the naïve Bayes model is often surprisingly effective. It also has the singular merit of being very easy to compute, especially if the discrete variable version is used. Coupled with the ease of understanding and interpretation of the model, perhaps especially in terms of the simple points-scoring perspective in Equation (9.4), these factors explain why it is so widely used. However, its very simplicity, along with the fact that its core assumption often appears unrealistic, has led many researchers to propose extensions of it in an attempt to improve its predictive accuracy.

We have already seen one of these above, to ease the independence assumption by shrinking the probability estimates. Shrinking has also been proposed to improve the simplistic multinomial estimate of the proportions of objects falling into each category in the case of discrete predictor variables. So, if the jth discrete predictor variable, x_j, has c_r categories, and if n_{jr} of the total of n objects fall into the rth category of this variable, the usual multinomial estimator of the probability that a future object will fall into this category, n_{jr}/n, is replaced by $(n_{jr} + c_r^{-1})/(n + 1)$. This shrinkage, which is also sometimes called the *Laplacian correction*, also has a direct Bayesian interpretation. It can be useful if the sample size and cell widths are such that there may not be very many objects in a cell.

Perhaps the most obvious way of easing the independence assumption is by introducing extra terms in the models of the distributions of x in each class, to allow for interactions. This has been attempted in a large number of ways, but all of them necessarily introduce complications, and so sacrifice the basic simplicity and elegance of the naïve Bayes model. In particular, if an interaction between two of the variables in x is to be included in the model, then the estimate cannot be based merely on the univariate marginals.

Within the ith class, the joint distribution of x is

$$f(x|i) = f(x_1|i)f(x_2|x_1, i)f(x_3|x_1, x_2, i)\dots f(x_p|x_1, x_2, \dots, x_{p-1}, i) \quad (9.5)$$

and this can be approximated by simplifying the conditional probabilities. The extreme arises with $f(x_j|x_1, \dots, x_{j-1}, i) = f(x_j|i)$ for all j, and this is the naïve Bayes method. Obviously, however, models between these two extremes can be used. If the variables are discrete, one can estimate appropriate models, with arbitrary degrees of interaction included, by using log-linear models. For continuous variables, graphical models and the literature on conditional independence graphs are appropriate. An example which is appropriate in some circumstances is the Markov model

$$f(x|i) = f(x_1|i)f(x_2|x_1, i)f(x_3|x_2, i), \dots, f(x_p|x_{p-1}, i) \quad (9.6)$$

This is equivalent to using a subset of two-way marginal distributions instead of merely the univariate marginal distributions in the naïve Bayes model.

Yet other extensions combine naïve Bayes models with tree methods (e.g., Langley, 1993), for example splitting the overall population into subsets on the basis of the values the objects take on some of the variables and then fitting naïve Bayes models to each subset. Such models are popular in some applications, where they are known as *segmented scorecards*. The segmentation is a way to allow for interactions which would cause difficulties if a single overall independence model was fitted.

Another way of embedding naïve Bayes models in higher-level approaches is by means of multiple classifier systems, for example, in a random forest or via boosting.

There is a very close relationship between the naïve Bayes model and another very important model for supervised classification: the logistic regression model. This was originally developed within the statistical community, and is very widely used in medicine, banking, marketing, and other areas. It is more powerful than the naïve Bayes model, but this extra power comes at the cost of necessarily requiring a more complicated estimation scheme. In particular, as we will see, although it has the same attractively simply basic form as the naïve Bayes model, the parameters (e.g., the $w_j(x_j^{(k_j)})$) cannot be estimated simply by determining proportions, but require an iterative algorithm.

In examining the naïve Bayes model above, we obtained the decomposition Equation (9.2) by adopting the independence assumption. However, exactly the same structure for the ratio results if we model $f(x|1)$ by $g(x)\prod_{j=1}^{p} h_1(x_j)$ and $f(x|0)$ by $g(x)\prod_{j=1}^{p} h_0(x_j)$, where the function $g(x)$ is the same in each model. If $g(x)$ does not factorize into a product of components, one for each of the raw x_j, we are not assuming independence of the x_j. The dependence structure implicit in $g(x)$ can be as complicated as we like—the only restriction being that it is the same in the two classes; that is, that $g(x)$ is common in the factorizations of $f(x|1)$ and $f(x|0)$. With these factorizations of the $f(x|i)$, we obtain

$$\frac{P(1|x)}{1-P(1|x)} = \frac{P(1)g(x)\prod_{j=1}^{p} h_1(x_j)}{P(0)g(x)\prod_{j=1}^{p} h_0(x_j)} = \frac{P(1)}{P(0)}\cdot\frac{\prod_{j=1}^{p} h_1(x_j)}{\prod_{j=1}^{p} h_0(x_j)} \tag{9.7}$$

Since the $g(x)$ terms cancel, we are left with a structure identical to Equation (9.2), although the $h_i(x_j)$ are not the same as the $f(x_j|i)$ (unless $g(x) \equiv 1$). Note that in this factorization it is not even necessary that the $h_i(x_j)$ be probability density functions. All that is needed is that the overall products $g(x)\prod_{j=1}^{p} h_i(x_j)$ are densities.

The model in Equation (9.7) is just as simple as the naïve Bayes model, and takes exactly the same form. In particular, by taking logs we end up with a points-scoring model as in Equation (9.4). But the model in Equation (9.7) is more flexible than the naïve Bayes model because it does not assume independence of the x_j in each class. Of course, this considerable extra flexibility of the logistic regression model is not obtained without cost. Although the resulting model form is identical to the naïve Bayes model form (with different parameter values, of course), it cannot be estimated by looking at the univariate marginals separately: An iterative procedure must be used. Standard statistical texts (e.g., Collett, 1991) give algorithms for estimating the parameters of logistic regression models. Often an iterative proportional weighted least squares method is used to find the parameters which maximize the likelihood.

The version of the naïve Bayes model based on the discretization transformation of the raw x_j can be generalized to yield other extensions. In particular, the more general class of *generalized additive models* (Hastie and Tibshirani, 1990) take exactly the form of additive combinations of transformations of the x_j.

The naïve Bayes model is tremendously appealing because of its simplicity, elegance, robustness, as well as the speed with which such a model can be constructed, and the speed with which it can be applied to produce a classification. It is one of the oldest formal classification algorithms, and yet even in its simplest form it is often surprisingly effective. A large number of modifications have been introduced, by the statistical, data mining, machine learning, and pattern recognition communities, in an attempt to make it more flexible, but one has to recognize that such modifications are necessarily complications, which detract from its basic simplicity.

9.5 Software Implementations

The simplicity of the naïve Bayes algorithm means that, in its basic form, it has been very widely implemented, and many free versions are available on the Web. The open-source Weka implementation (http://www.cs.waikato.ac.nz/ml/weka/) allows the individual variables to be modeled by normal distributions, by kernel estimates, or by splitting them into discrete categories.

Perhaps it is worthwhile making a cautionary comment. The term *Bayesian* has several different interpretations, and its now common use in the phrase "naïve Bayes classifier" can mislead the unwary. In particular, "Bayesian networks" are more general classes of models, which include the naïve Bayes model as a special case, but which generally also allow various interactions to be included in the model. An example of the sorts of confusion this can lead to is described in Jamain and Hand (2005).

9.6 Examples

9.6.1 Example 1

To illustrate the principles of the naïve Bayes method, consider the artificial data set shown in Table 9.1. The aim is to use these data as a training set to construct a rule which will allow prediction of variable D for future customers, where D is default on a bank loan (the last column, labeled 1 for default and 0 for nondefault). The variables which will be used for the prediction are columns 1 to 3: time with current employer, T, in years; size of loan requested, S, in dollars; and H, whether the applicant is a homeowner (1), rental tenant (2), or "other" (3). In fact, the naïve Bayes method is a common approach to credit default problems of this kind, although typically in such applications the training set will contain hundreds of thousands of accounts and will use many more variables, and the naïve Bayes method will be used as leaves in a segmented scorecard of the kind described above.

TABLE 9.1 Data for Example 1

Time with Emp, T	Size of Loan, S	Homeowner, H	Default, D
5	10,000	1	0
20	10,000	1	0
1	25,000	1	0
1	15,000	3	0
15	2,000	2	0
6	12,000	1	0
1	5,000	2	1
12	8,000	2	1
3	10,000	1	1
1	5,000	3	1

Time with employer is a continuous variable. For each of the two classes separately, we could estimate the distribution $f(T|i)$, $i = 0, 1$ using a kernel method or some assumed parametric form (lognormal would probably be a sensible choice for such a variable), or we could use the naïve Bayes approach in which the variable is split into cells, estimating the probability of falling in each cell by the proportion of cases from class i which fall in that cell. We shall take this third approach and, to keep things as simple as possible, will split T into only two cells, whether or not the customer has been with the employer for 10 or more years. This yields probability estimates

$$\hat{f}(T < 10|D = 0) = 4/6, \quad \hat{f}(T \geq 10|D = 0) = 2/6$$
$$\hat{f}(T < 10|D = 1) = 3/4, \quad \hat{f}(T \geq 10|D = 1) = 1/4$$

Similarly, we shall do the same sort of thing with size of loan, splitting it into just two cells (purely for convenience of explanation) according to the intervals $\leq$ 10,000 and $>$ 10,000. This yields probability estimates

$$\hat{f}(S \leq 10000|D = 0) = 3/6, \quad \hat{f}(S > 10000|D = 0) = 3/6$$
$$\hat{f}(S \leq 10000|D = 1) = 3/4, \quad \hat{f}(S > 10000|D = 1) = 1/4$$

For the nondefaulter class, the homeowner column yields three estimated probabilities:

$$\hat{f}(H = 1|D = 0) = 4/6, \quad \hat{f}(H = 2|D = 0) = 1/6, \quad \hat{f}(H = 3|D = 0) = 1/6$$

For the defaulter class, the respective probabilities are

$$\hat{f}(H = 1|D = 1) = 1/4, \quad \hat{f}(H = 2|D = 1) = 2/4, \quad \hat{f}(H = 3|D = 1) = 1/4$$

Suppose now that a new application form is received, from an applicant who has been with his or her (this phrasing is chosen deliberately: It is illegal to use sex as a predictor for making loan decisions such as this.) employer for less than 10 years

($T < 10$), is seeking a loan of \$10,000 ($S \leq 10000$), and is a homeowner ($H = 1$). This leads to an estimated value of the ratio $\hat{P}(1|x)/\hat{P}(0|x)$ of

$$\frac{P(1|x)}{P(0|x)} = \frac{P(1)}{P(0)} \prod_{j=1}^{p} \frac{\hat{f}(x_j|1)}{\hat{f}(x_j|0)} = \frac{P(1)}{P(0)} \times \frac{\hat{f}(T|1)\hat{f}(S|1)\hat{f}(H|1)}{\hat{f}(T|0)\hat{f}(S|0)\hat{f}(H|0)}$$

$$= \frac{4/10}{6/10} \times \frac{3/4 \times 3/4 \times 1/4}{4/6 \times 4/6 \times 3/6 \times 4/6} = 0.422$$

Since $P(1|x) = 1 - P(0|x)$, this is equivalent to $P(1|x) = 0.296$ and $P(0|x) = 0.703$. If the classification threshold is 0.5 [i.e., if we decide to classify a customer with vector x to class 1 if $P(1|x) > 0.5$ and to class 0 otherwise], then this customer will be classified as likely to belong to class 0—the nondefaulter class. This customer would be a good bet for making a loan to.

9.6.2 Example 2

An important and relatively new application domain for the naïve Bayes method is spam filtering. *Spams* are unsolicited and typically unwanted emails, often direct marketing of some kind and frequently offering dubious financial or other opportunities. Some of them are so-called *phishing* exercises. The principle behind them is that even a low response rate is profitable if (a) the cost of mailing the emails is negligible and (b) enough are sent. Since they are sent out automatically to millions of email addresses, one may receive many hundreds of these daily. With this number, even to move the cursor and physically hit the delete button would consume significant amounts of time. For this reason researchers have developed classification rules called *spam filters*, which examine incoming emails, and assign them to spam or not-spam classes. Those assigned to the spam class can be deleted automatically, or sent to a holding file for later examination, or treated in any other way deemed appropriate.

Naïve Bayes models are very popular for use as spam filters, going back to the early seminal work by Sahami et al. (1998). In their simplest form, the variables in the model are binary variables corresponding to the presence or absence, in the email, of each word. However, the naïve Bayes model also permits the ready addition of other binary variables corresponding to the presence or absence of other syntactic features such as punctuation marks, currency units (\$, £, €, and so on), combinations of words, whether the source of the email was an individual or a list, and so on. In addition, other nonbinary variables are useful as further predictors, for example, the type of domain of the source, the percentage of nonalphanumeric characters in the subject heading, and so on. It will be clear from the above that the potential number of variables is very large. Because of this, a feature selection step is typically undertaken (recall the discussion of why the naïve Bayes model may do well, despite its underlying independence assumption).

One important aspect of spam filtering is the imbalance in the severity of the misclassification costs. Misclassifying a legitimate email as spam is much more serious than the reverse. Both this and the relative size of the two classes play roles in determining the classification threshold. In their experiments, Sahami et al. (1998) chose a threshold of 0.999 with which to compare $P(\text{spam} \mid x)$.

One strength of the naïve Bayes model is that it can just as easily be applied to count variables as to binary variables. The multivariate binary spam filter described above is easy to extend to more elaborate models for the distributions of the values of the variables. We have already referred to the use of multinomial models earlier, in which continuous variables are partitioned into more than two cells (and the homeowner variable in the artificial data of Example 1 was a case of a trinomial variable). Experiments suggest that, at least for spam filtering, the multinomial approach using frequencies of word appearances in the emails is superior to using mere presence/absence variables. Metsis et al. (2006) carried out a comparative analysis of different versions of the naïve Bayes model, in which the marginal variables are treated in different ways, applying the methods to some real email data sets.

9.7 Advanced Topics

The chief attraction of the naïve Bayes model is its extreme simplicity, permitting easy (univariate) estimation and straightforward interpretation via the weights of evidence. The first of these properties is also associated with robustness, provided the estimates of the marginal distributions are robust. In particular, if the marginal distributions are categorical, then each cell needs to contain sufficient data points to yield accurate estimates. With this in mind, researchers have explored optimal partitioning of each variable. The approach, most in tune with the straightforward naïve Bayes estimator, is to examine each variable separately—perhaps splitting into equal quantiles (this is generally superior to splitting into equal length cells). A more sophisticated approach will choose the cells based on the relative number from each class in each cell. This can also be done by considering each variable separately. Finally, one can partition each cell taking into account the overall fit to the distribution in each (or both) classes, but this moves away from the simple marginal approach. Investigations of some of these issues are described in Hand and Adams (2000).

Missing data are a potential problem in all data analysis. Classification methods which cannot handle incomplete data are at a disadvantage. When the data are missing completely at random, then the naïve Bayes model copes without any difficulty: Valid estimates are obtained by simply estimating the marginal distributions from the observed data. If the data are informatively missing, however, then more complex procedures are needed. This is an area meriting further research.

More and more problems involve dynamic data, and data sets which sequentially accrue. The naïve Bayes method can be adapted very readily to such problems, by virtue of its straightforward estimation.

So-called "small n, large p" problems have become important in certain areas, such as bioinformatics, genomics, and proteomics, especially in the analysis of microarray data. These are problems characterized by the fact that the number of variables is much larger than the sample size. Such problems pose difficulties; for example, the covariance matrix will be singular, leading to overfitting. To tackle such problems, it is necessary to make some kinds of assumptions or (equivalently) to shrink the estimators in some way. One approach to such problems in the context of supervised classification is to use the naïve Bayes method. This has its in-built assumption of independence, which acts to protect against overfitting. More elaborate versions of this idea combine naïve Bayes models with more sophisticated classifiers, trying to strike the best balance.

9.8 Exercises

1. Using a package such as the open-source package R, generate samples of size 100 from each of the two classes. Class 1 is bivariate normal, with zero means and identity covariance matrix. Class 2 is bivariate normal, with mean vector (0, 2) and diagonal covariance matrix with leading diagonal (1, 2). Fit a naïve Bayes model to these data, based on assuming (correctly) that the marginal distributions are normal. Plot the decision surface to see that it is not linear.
2. The tables below show the bivariate distributions from samples for two classes, where the variables each have three categories. Show that the two variables are independent in each of the two classes. Taking the classification threshold as 1/2, calculate the decision surface for a naïve Bayes classifier and show that it is nonlinear.

144	144	144
144	144	144
144	144	144

9	90	9
90	900	90
9	90	9

3. For the data from Exercise 2, calculate the weights of evidence for the categories of each variable, so that the naïve Bayes classifier can be expressed as a weighted sum.
4. The tables below show the bivariate distributions from samples for two classes, where the variables each have three categories. Show that the two variables are *not* independent in each of the two classes. Taking the classification threshold as 1/2, fit a naïve Bayes classifier to these data and show that nevertheless its decision surface is optimal.

27	30	27
30	2700	30
27	30	27

432	48	432
48	432	48
432	48	432

5. Using data simulated from multivariate normal distributions, compare the relative performance of a naïve Bayes classifier and a simple linear discriminant classification rule as the (assumed common) correlation between the variables increases.
6. Using a suitable data set from the UCI Machine Learning Repository, with continuous variables which are partitioned into discrete cells, investigate the effect of changing the number and width of the cells in each variable.
7. Using the same data set as in Exercise 6, compare the models produced by the naïve Bayes classifier and logistic regression.
8. A common way to extend the naïve Bayes classifier in some applications is to partition the data into segments, with separate naïve Bayes classifiers constructed for each segment. Clearly such partitioning will be most effective if its splits allow for interactions which the naïve Bayes classifier would not pick up. Develop guidelines to assist people in making such splits.
9. The idea of modeling the distribution of each class by assuming independence extends immediately to more than two classes. For more than two classes write down appropriate classification models in the weights of evidence format.
10. One of the particular attractions of the naïve Bayes classifier is that it permits very simple estimation. Develop updating rules which allow the classifier to be sequentially updated as new data arrive.

References

Collett D. (1991) *Modelling Binary Data.* London: Chapman and Hall.

Domingos P. and Pazzani M. (1997) On the optimality of the simple Bayesian classifier under zero-one loss. *Machine Learning*, **29**, 103–130.

Hand D.J. and Adams N.M. (2000) Defining attributes for scorecard construction. *Journal of Applied Statistics*, **27**, 527–540.

Hand D.J. and Yu K. (2001) Idiot's Bayes—not so stupid after all? *International Statistical Review*, **69**, 385–398.

Hastie T.J. and Tibshirani R.J. (1990) *Generalized Additive Models*. London: Chapman and Hall.

Jamain A. and Hand D.J. (2005) The naïve Bayes mystery: A statistical detective story. *Pattern Recognition Letters*, **26**, 1752–1760.

Jamain A. and Hand D.J. (2008) Mining supervised classification performance studies: A meta-analytic investigation. *Journal of Classification*, **25**, 87–112.

Langley P. (1993) Induction of recursive Bayesian classifiers. *Proceedings of the Eighth European Conference on Machine Learning*, Vienna, Austria: Springer-Verlag, 153–164.

Mani S., Pazzani M.J., and West J. (1997) Knowledge discovery from a breast cancer database. *Lecture Notes in Artificial Intelligence*, **1211**, 130–133.

Metsis V., Androutsopoulos I., and Paliouras G. (2006) Spam filtering with naïve Bayes—which naïve Bayes? *CEAS 2006—Third Conference on Email and Anti-Spam*, Mountain View, California.

Sahami M., Dumains S., Heckerman D., and Horvitz E. (1998) A Bayesian approach to filtering junk e-mail. In *Learning for Text Categorization—Papers from the AAAI Workshop*, Madison, Wisconsin, pp. 55–62.

Titterington D.M., Murray G.D., Murray L.S., Spiegelhalter D.J., Skene A.M., Habbema J.D.F., and Gelpke G.J. (1981) Comparison of discrimination techniques applied to a complex data set of head injured patients. *Journal of the Royal Statistical Society, Series A*, **144**, 145–175.

Chapter 10

CART: Classification and Regression Trees

Dan Steinberg

Contents

The 1984 monograph, "CART: Classification and Regression Trees," coauthored by Leo Breiman, Jerome Friedman, Richard Olshen, and Charles Stone (BFOS), represents a major milestone in the evolution of artificial intelligence, machine learning, nonparametric statistics, and data mining. The work is important for the comprehensiveness of its study of decision trees, the technical innovations it introduces, its sophisticated examples of tree-structured data analysis, and its authoritative treatment of large sample theory for trees. Since its publication the CART monograph has been cited some 3000 times according to the science and social science citation indexes; Google Scholar reports about 8,450 citations. CART citations can be found in almost any domain, with many appearing in fields such as credit risk, targeted marketing, financial markets modeling, electrical engineering, quality control, biology, chemistry, and clinical medical research. CART has also strongly influenced image compression via tree-structured vector quantization. This brief account is intended to introduce CART basics, touching on the major themes treated in the CART monograph, and to encourage readers to return to the rich original source for technical details, discussions revealing the thought processes of the authors, and examples of their analytical style.

10.1 Antecedents

CART was not the first decision tree to be introduced to machine learning, although it is the first to be described with analytical rigor and supported by sophisticated statistics and probability theory. CART explicitly traces its ancestry to the automatic interaction detection (AID) tree of Morgan and Sonquist (1963), an automated recursive method for exploring relationships in data intended to mimic the iterative drill-downs typical of practicing survey data analysts. AID was introduced as a potentially useful tool without any theoretical foundation. This 1960s-era work on trees was greeted with profound skepticism amidst evidence that AID could radically overfit the training data and encourage profoundly misleading conclusions (Einhorn, 1972; Doyle, 1973), especially in smaller samples. By 1973 well-read statisticians were convinced that trees were a dead end; the conventional wisdom held that trees were dangerous and unreliable tools particularly because of their lack of a theoretical foundation. Other researchers, however, were not yet prepared to abandon the tree line of thinking. The work of Cover and Hart (1967) on the large sample properties of nearest neighbor (NN) classifiers was instrumental in persuading Richard Olshen and Jerome Friedman that trees had sufficient theoretical merit to be worth pursuing. Olshen reasoned that if NN classifiers could reach the Cover and Hart bound on misclassification error, then a similar result should be derivable for a suitably constructed tree because the terminal nodes of trees could be viewed as dynamically constructed NN classifiers. Thus, the Cover and Hart NN research was the immediate stimulus that persuaded Olshen to investigate the asymptotic properties of trees. Coincidentally, Friedman's algorithmic work on fast identification of nearest neighbors via trees (Friedman, Bentley, and Finkel, 1977) used a recursive partitioning mechanism that evolved into CART. One predecessor of CART appears in the 1975 Stanford Linear Accelerator Center (SLAC) discussion paper (Friedman,1975), subsequently published in a shorter form by Friedman (1977). While Friedman was working out key elements of CART at SLAC, with Olshen conducting mathematical research in the same lab, similar independent research was under way in Los Angeles by Leo Breiman and Charles Stone (Breiman and Stone, 1978). The two separate strands of research (Friedman and Olshen at Stanford, Breiman and Stone in Los Angeles) were brought together in 1978 when the four CART authors formally began the process of merging their work and preparing to write the CART monograph.

10.2 Overview

The CART decision tree is a binary recursive partitioning procedure capable of processing continuous and nominal attributes as targets and predictors. Data are handled in their raw form; no binning is required or recommended. Beginning in the root node, the data are split into two children, and each of the children is in turn split into grandchildren. Trees are grown to a maximal size without the use of a stopping rule; essentially the tree-growing process stops when no further splits are possible due to lack of data. The maximal-sized tree is then pruned back to the root (essentially split by split) via the novel method of cost-complexity pruning. The next split to be pruned is the one contributing least to the overall performance of the tree on training data (and more than one split may be removed at a time). The CART mechanism is intended to produce not one tree, but a sequence of nested pruned trees, each of which is a candidate to be the optimal tree. The "right sized" or "honest" tree is identified by evaluating the predictive performance of every tree in the pruning sequence on independent test data. Unlike C4.5, CART does not use an internal (training-data-based) performance measure for tree selection. Instead, tree performance is always measured on independent test data (or via cross-validation) and tree selection proceeds only after test-data-based evaluation. If testing or cross-validation has not been performed, CART remains agnostic regarding which tree in the sequence is best. This is in sharp contrast to methods such as C4.5 or classical statistics that generate preferred models on the basis of training data measures.

The CART mechanism includes (optional) automatic class balancing and automatic missing value handling, and allows for cost-sensitive learning, dynamic feature construction, and probability tree estimation. The final reports include a novel attribute importance ranking. The CART authors also broke new ground in showing how cross-validation can be used to assess performance for every tree in the pruning sequence, given that trees in different cross-validation folds may not align on the number of terminal nodes. It is useful to keep in mind that although BFOS addressed all these topics in the 1970s, in some cases the BFOS treatment remains the state-of-the-art. The literature of the 1990s contains a number of articles that rediscover core insights first introduced in the 1984 CART monograph. Each of these major features is discussed separately below.

10.3 A Running Example

To help make the details of CART concrete we illustrate some of our points using an easy-to-understand real-world example. (The data have been altered to mask some of the original specifics.) In the early 1990s the author assisted a telecommunications company in understanding the market for mobile phones. Because the mobile phone

TABLE 10.1 Example Data Summary Statistics

Attribute	N	N Missing	% Missing	N Distinct	Mean	Min	Max
AGE	813	18	2.2	9	5.059	1	9
CITY	830	0	0	5	1.769	1	5
HANDPRIC	830	0	0	4	145.3	60	235
MARITAL	822	9	1.1	3	1.9015	1	3
PAGER	825	6	0.72	2	0.076364	0	1
RENTHOUS	830	0	0	3	1.7906	1	3
RESPONSE	830	0	0	2	0.1518	0	1
SEX	819	12	1.4	2	1.4432	1	2
TELEBILC	768	63	7.6	6	54.199	8	116
TRAVTIME	651	180	22	5	2.318	1	5
USEPRICE	830	0	0	4	11.151	10	30

MARITAL = Marital Status (Never Married, Married, Divorced/Widowed)
TRAVTIME = estimated commute time to major center of employment
AGE is recorded as an integer ranging from 1 to 9

was a new technology at that time, we needed to identify the major drivers of adoption of this then-new technology and to identify demographics that might be related to price sensitivity. The data consisted of a household's response (yes/no) to a market test offer of a mobile phone package; all prospects were offered an identical package of a handset and service features, with one exception that the pricing for the package was varied randomly according to an experimental design. The only choice open to the households was to accept or reject the offer.

A total of 830 households were approached and 126 of the households agreed to subscribe to the mobile phone service plan. One of our objectives was to learn as much as possible about the differences between subscribers and nonsubscribers. A set of summary statistics for select attributes appear in Table 10.1. HANDPRIC is the price quoted for the mobile handset, USEPRIC is the quoted per-minute charge, and the other attributes are provided with common names.

A CART classification tree was grown on these data to predict the RESPONSE attribute using all the other attributes as predictors. MARITAL and CITY are categorical (nominal) attributes. A decision tree is grown by recursively partitioning the training data using a splitting rule to identify the split to use at each node. Figure 10.1 illustrates this process beginning with the root node splitter at the top of the tree.

The root node at the top of the diagram contains all our training data, including 704 nonsubscribers (labeled with a 0) and 126 subscribers (labeled 1). Each of the 830 instances contains data on the 10 predictor attributes, although there are some missing values. CART begins by searching the data for the best splitter available, testing each predictor attribute-value pair for its goodness-of-split. In Figure 10.1 we see the results of this search: HANDPRIC has been determined to be the best splitter using a threshold of 130 to partition the data. All instances presented with a HANDPRIC less than or equal to 130 are sent to the left child node and all other instances are sent to the right. The resulting split yields two subsets of the data with substantially different

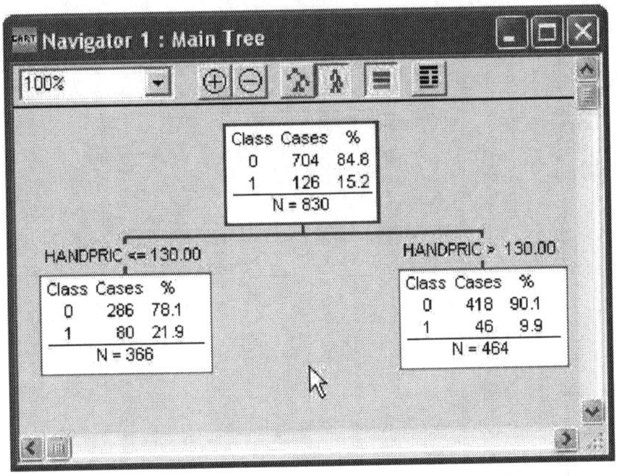

Figure 10.1 Root node split.

response rates: 21.9% for those quoted lower prices and 9.9% for those quoted the higher prices. Clearly both the root node splitter and the magnitude of the difference between the two child nodes are plausible. Observe that the split always results in two nodes: CART uses only binary splitting.

To generate a complete tree CART simply repeats the splitting process just described in each of the two child nodes to produce grandchildren of the root. Grandchildren are split to obtain great-grandchildren and so on until further splitting is impossible due to a lack of data. In our example, this growing process results in a "maximal tree" consisting of 81 terminal nodes: nodes at the bottom of the tree that are not split further.

10.4 The Algorithm Briefly Stated

A complete statement of the CART algorithm, including all relevant technical details, is lengthy and complex; there are multiple splitting rules available for both classification and regression, separate handling of continuous and categorical splitters, special handling for categorical splitters with many levels, and provision for missing value handling. Following the tree-growing procedure there is another complex procedure for pruning the tree, and finally, there is tree selection. In Figure 10.2 a simplified algorithm for tree growing is sketched out. Formal statements of the algorithm are provided in the CART monograph. Here we offer an informal statement that is highly simplified.

Observe that this simplified algorithm sketch makes no reference to missing values, class assignments, or other core details of CART. The algorithm sketches a mechanism for growing the largest possible (maximal) tree.

```
BEGIN:  Assign all training data to the root node
        Define the root node as a terminal node

SPLIT:
New_splits=0
FOR every terminal node in the tree:
   If the terminal node sample size is too small or all instances in the
   node belong to the same target class goto GETNEXT
   Find the attribute that best separates the node into two child nodes
   using an allowable splitting rule
   New_splits+1
GETNEXT:
NEXT
```

Figure 10.2 Simplified tree-growing algorithm sketch.

Having grown the tree, CART next generates the nested sequence of pruned subtrees. A simplified algorithm sketch for pruning follows that ignores priors and costs. This is different from the actual CART pruning algorithm and is included here for the sake of brevity and ease of reading. The procedure begins by taking the largest tree grown ($T_{\max}$) and removing all splits, generating two terminal nodes that do not improve the accuracy of the tree on training data. This is the starting point for CART pruning. Pruning proceeds further by a natural notion of iteratively removing the weakest links in the tree, the splits that contribute the least to performance of the tree on test data. In the algorithm presented in Figure 10.3 the pruning action is restricted to parents of two terminal nodes.

```
DEFINE:  r(t)= training data misclassification rate in node t
         p(t)= fraction of the training data in node t
         R(t)= r(t)*p(t)
         t_left=left child of node t
         t_right=right child of node t
         |T| = number of terminal nodes in tree T

BEGIN:   Tmax=largest tree grown
         Current_Tree=Tmax
         For all parents t of two terminal nodes
           Remove all splits for which R(t)=R(t_left) + R(t_right)
         Current_tree=Tmax after pruning

PRUNE:   If |Current_tree|=1 then goto DONE
         For all parents t of two terminal nodes
         Remove node(s) t for which R(t)-R(t_left) - R(t_right)
             is minimum
Current_tree=Current_Tree after pruning
```

Figure 10.3 Simplified pruning algorithm.

The CART pruning algorithm differs from the above in employing a penalty on nodes mechanism that can remove an entire subtree in a single pruning action. The monograph offers a clear and extended statement of the procedure. We now discuss major aspects of CART in greater detail.

10.5 Splitting Rules

CART splitting rules are always couched in the form

> An instance goes left if CONDITION, and goes right otherwise

where the CONDITION is expressed as "attribute $X\_i <= C\_$" for continuous attributes. For categorical or nominal attributes the CONDITION is expressed as membership in a list of values. For example, a split on a variable like CITY might be expressed as

> An instance goes left if CITY is in {Chicago, Detroit, Nashville) and goes right otherwise

The splitter and the split point are both found automatically by CART with the optimal split selected via one of the splitting rules defined below. Observe that because CART works with unbinned data the optimal splits are always invariant with respect to order-preserving transforms of the attributes (such as log, square root, power transforms, and so on). The CART authors argue that binary splits are to be preferred to multiway splits because (1) they fragment the data more slowly than multiway splits and (2) repeated splits on the same attribute are allowed and, if selected, will eventually generate as many partitions for an attribute as required. Any loss of ease in reading the tree is expected to be offset by improved predictive performance.

The CART authors discuss examples using four splitting rules for classification trees (Gini, twoing, ordered twoing, symmetric gini), but the monograph focuses most of its discussion on the Gini, which is similar to the better known entropy (information-gain) criterion. For a binary (0/1) target the "Gini measure of impurity" of a node t is

$$G(t) = 1 - p(t)^2 - (1 - p(t))^2$$

where $p(t)$ is the (possibly weighted) relative frequency of class 1 in the node. Specifying $G(t) = -p(t) \ln p(t) - (1 - p(t)) \ln(1 - p(t))$ instead yields the entropy rule. The improvement (gain) generated by a split of the parent node P into left and right children L and R is

$$I(P) = G(P) - qG(L) - (1 - q)G(R)$$

Here, q is the (possibly weighted) fraction of instances going left. The CART authors favored the Gini over entropy because it can be computed more rapidly, can be readily extended to include symmetrized costs (see below), and is less likely to generate "end cut" splits—splits with one very small (and relatively pure) child and another much larger child. (Later versions of CART have added entropy as an optional splitting rule.) The twoing rule is based on a direct comparison of the target attribute distribution in two child nodes:

$$I(\text{split}) = \left\{ .25(q(1-q))^u \sum_k |p_L(k) - p_R(k)| \right\}^2$$

where k indexes the target classes, $pL()$ and $pR()$ are the probability distributions of the target in the left and right child nodes, respectively. (This splitter is a modified version of Messenger and Mandell, 1972.) The twoing "improvement" measures the difference between the left and right child probability vectors, and the leading $[.25(q(1-q)]$ term, which has its maximum value at $q = .5$, implicitly penalizes splits that generate unequal left and right node sizes. The power term u is user-controllable, allowing a continuum of increasingly heavy penalties on unequal splits; setting $u = 10$, for example, is similar to enforcing all splits at the median value of the split attribute. In our practical experience the twoing criterion is a superior performer on multiclass targets as well as on inherently difficult-to-predict (e.g., noisy) binary targets. BFOS also introduce a variant of the twoing split criterion that treats the classes of the target as ordered. Called the *ordered twoing* splitting rule, it is a classification rule with characteristics of a regression rule as it attempts to separate low-ranked from high-ranked target classes at each split.

For regression (continuous targets), CART offers a choice of least squares (LS, sum of squared prediction errors) and least absolute deviation (LAD, sum of absolute prediction errors) criteria as the basis for measuring the improvement of a split. As with classification trees the best split yields the largest improvement. Three other splitting rules for cost-sensitive learning and probability trees are discussed separately below.

In our mobile phone example the Gini measure of impurity in the root node is 1 − (.84819)^2 − (.15181)^2; calculating the Gini for each child and then subtracting their sample share weighted average from the parent Gini yields an improvement score of .00703 (results may vary slightly depending on the precision used for the calculations and the inputs). CART produces a table listing the best split available using each of the other attributes available. (We show the five top competitors and their improvement scores in Table 10.2.)

TABLE 10.2 Main Splitter Improvement = 0.007033646

	Competitor	Split	Improvement
1	TELEBILC	50	0.006883
2	USEPRICE	9.85	0.005961
3	CITY	1,4,5	0.002259
4	TRAVTIME	3.5	0.001114
5	AGE	7.5	0.000948

10.6 Prior Probabilities and Class Balancing

Balancing classes in machine learning is a major issue for practitioners as many data mining methods do not perform well when the training data are highly unbalanced. For example, for most prime lenders, default rates are generally below 5% of all accounts, in credit card transactions fraud is normally well below 1%, and in Internet advertising "click through" rates occur typically for far fewer than 1% of all ads displayed (impressions). Many practitioners routinely confine themselves to training data sets in which the target classes have been sampled to yield approximately equal sample sizes. Clearly, if the class of interest is quite small such sample balancing could leave the analyst with very small overall training samples. For example, in an insurance fraud study the company identified about 70 cases of documented claims fraud. Confining the analysis to a balanced sample would limit the analyst to a total sample of just 140 instances (70 fraud, 70 not fraud).

It is interesting to note that the CART authors addressed this issue explicitly in 1984 and devised a way to free the modeler from any concerns regarding sample balance. Regardless of how extremely unbalanced the training data may be, CART will automatically adjust to the imbalance, requiring no action, preparation, sampling, or weighting by the modeler. The data can be modeled as they are found without any preprocessing.

To provide this flexibility CART makes use of a "priors" mechanism. Priors are akin to target class weights but they are invisible in that they do not affect any counts reported by CART in the tree. Instead, priors are embedded in the calculations undertaken to determine the goodness of splits. In its default classification mode CART always calculates class frequencies in any node relative to the class frequencies in the root. This is equivalent to automatically reweighting the data to balance the classes, and ensures that the tree selected as optimal minimizes balanced class error. The reweighting is implicit in the calculation of all probabilities and improvements and requires no user intervention; the reported sample counts in each node thus reflect the unweighted data. For a binary (0/1) target any node is classified as class 1 if, and only if,

$$\frac{N_1(node)}{N_1(root)} > \frac{N_0(node)}{N_0(root)}$$

Observe that this ensures that each class is assigned a working probability of $1/K$ in the root node when there are K target classes, regardless of the actual distribution of the classes in the data. This default mode is referred to as "priors equal" in the monograph. It has allowed CART users to work readily with any unbalanced data, requiring no special data preparation to achieve class rebalancing or the introduction of manually constructed weights. To work effectively with unbalanced data it is sufficient to run CART using its default settings. Implicit reweighting can be turned off by selecting the "priors data" option. The modeler can also elect to specify an arbitrary set of priors to reflect costs, or potential differences between training data and future data target class distributions.

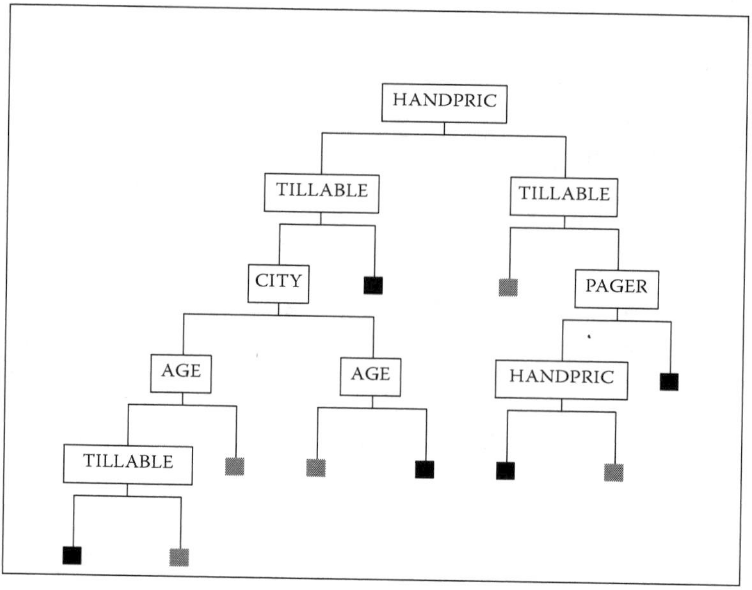

Figure 10.4 Red Terminal Node = Above Average Response. Instances with a value of the splitter greater than a threshold move to the right.

Note: The priors settings are unlike weights in that they do not affect the reported counts in a node or the reported fractions of the sample in each target class. Priors do affect the class any node is assigned to as well as the selection of the splitters in the tree-growing process.

(Being able to rely on priors does not mean that the analyst should ignore the topic of sampling at different rates from different target classes; rather, it gives the analyst a broad range of flexibility regarding when and how to sample.)

We used the "priors equal" settings to generate a CART tree for the mobile phone data to better adapt to the relatively low probability of response and obtained the tree schematic shown in Figure 10.4.

By convention, splits on continuous variables send instances with larger values of the splitter to the right, and splits on nominal variables are defined by the lists of values going left or right. In the diagram the terminal nodes are color coded to reflect the relative probability of response. A red node is above average in response probability and a blue node is below average. Although this schematic displays only a small fraction of the detailed reports available it is sufficient to tell this fascinating story: Even though they are quoted a high price for the new technology, households with higher landline telephone bills who use a pager (beeper) service are more likely to subscribe to the new service. The schematic also reveals how CART can reuse an attribute multiple times. Again, looking at the right side of the tree, and considering households with larger landline telephone bills but without a pager service, we see that the HANDPRIC attribute reappears, informing us that this customer segment is willing to pay a somewhat higher price but will resist the highest prices. (The second split on HANDPRIC is at 200.)

10.7 Missing Value Handling

Missing values appear frequently in the real world, especially in business-related databases, and the need to deal with them is a vexing challenge for all modelers. One of the major contributions of CART was to include a fully automated and effective mechanism for handling missing values. Decision trees require a missing value-handling mechanism at three levels: (a) during splitter evaluation, (b) when moving the training data through a node, and (c) when moving test data through a node for final class assignment. (See Quinlan, 1989 for a clear discussion of these points.) Regarding (a), the first version of CART evaluated each splitter strictly on its performance on the subset of data for which the splitter is not missing. Later versions of CART offer a family of penalties that reduce the improvement measure to reflect the degree of missingness. (For example, if a variable is missing in 20% of the records in a node then its improvement score for that node might be reduced by 20%, or alternatively by half of 20%, and so on.) For (b) and (c), the CART mechanism discovers "surrogate" or substitute splitters for every node of the tree, whether missing values occur in the training data or not. The surrogates are thus available, should a tree trained on complete data be applied to new data that includes missing values. This is in sharp contrast to machines that cannot tolerate missing values in the training data or that can only learn about missing value handling from training data that include missing values. Friedman (1975) suggests moving instances with missing splitter attributes into both left and right child nodes and making a final class assignment by taking a weighted average of all nodes in which an instance appears. Quinlan opts for a variant of Friedman's approach in his study of alternative missing value-handling methods. Our own assessments of the effectiveness of CART surrogate performance in the presence of missing data are decidedly favorable, while Quinlan remains agnostic on the basis of the approximate surrogates he implements for test purposes (Quinlan). In Friedman, Kohavi, and Yun (1996), Friedman notes that 50% of the CART code was devoted to missing value handling; it is thus unlikely that Quinlan's experimental version replicated the CART surrogate mechanism.

In CART the missing value handling mechanism is fully automatic and locally adaptive at every node. At each node in the tree the chosen splitter induces a binary partition of the data (e.g., $X1 <= c1$ and $X1 > c1$). A surrogate splitter is a single attribute Z that can predict this partition where the surrogate itself is in the form of a binary splitter (e.g., $Z <= d$ and $Z > d$). In other words, every splitter becomes a new target which is to be predicted with a single split binary tree. Surrogates are

TABLE 10.3 Surrogate Splitter Report Main Splitter TELEBILC Improvement = 0.023722

	Surrogate	Split	Association	Improvement
1	MARITAL	1	0.14	0.001864
2	TRAVTIME	2.5	0.11	0.006068
3	AGE	3.5	0.09	0.000412
4	CITY	2,3,5	0.07	0.004229

ranked by an association score that measures the advantage of the surrogate over the default rule, predicting that all cases go to the larger child node (after adjustments for priors). To qualify as a surrogate, the variable must outperform this default rule (and thus it may not always be possible to find surrogates). When a missing value is encountered in a CART tree the instance is moved to the left or the right according to the top-ranked surrogate. If this surrogate is also missing then the second-ranked surrogate is used instead (and so on). If all surrogates are missing the default rule assigns the instance to the larger child node (after adjusting for priors). Ties are broken by moving an instance to the left.

Returning to the mobile phone example, consider the right child of the root node, which is split on TELEBILC, the landline telephone bill. If the telephone bill data are unavailable (e.g., the household is a new one and has limited history with the company), CART searches for the attributes that can best predict whether the instance belongs to the left or the right side of the split.

In this case (Table 10.3) we see that of all the attributes available the best predictor of whether the landline telephone is high (greater than 50) is marital status (never-married people spend less), followed by the travel time to work, age, and, finally, city of residence. Surrogates can also be seen as akin to synonyms in that they help to interpret a splitter. Here we see that those with lower telephone bills tend to be never married, live closer to the city center, be younger, and be concentrated in three of the five cities studied.

10.8 Attribute Importance

The importance of an attribute is based on the sum of the improvements in all nodes in which the attribute appears as a splitter (weighted by the fraction of the training data in each node split). Surrogates are also included in the importance calculations, which means that even a variable that never splits a node may be assigned a large importance score. This allows the variable importance rankings to reveal variable masking and nonlinear correlation among the attributes. Importance scores may optionally be confined to splitters; comparing the splitters-only and the full (splitters and surrogates) importance rankings is a useful diagnostic.

TABLE 10.4 Variable Importance (Including Surrogates)

Attribute	Score
TELEBILC	100.00
HANDPRIC	68.88
AGE	55.63
CITY	39.93
SEX	37.75
PAGER	34.35
TRAVTIME	33.15
USEPRICE	17.89
RENTHOUS	11.31
MARITAL	6.98

TABLE 10.5 Variable Importance (Excluding Surrogates)

Variable	Score
TELEBILC	100.00
HANDPRIC	77.92
AGE	51.75
PAGER	22.50
CITY	18.09

Observe that the attributes MARITAL, RENTHOUS, TRAVTIME, and SEX in Table 10.4 do not appear as splitters but still appear to have a role in the tree. These attributes have nonzero importance strictly because they appear as surrogates to the other splitting variables. CART will also report importance scores ignoring the surrogates on request. That version of the attribute importance ranking for the same tree is shown in Table 10.5.

10.9 Dynamic Feature Construction

Friedman (1975) discusses the automatic construction of new features within each node and, for the binary target, suggests adding the single feature

$$x \times w$$

where x is the subset of continuous predictor attributes vector and w is a scaled difference of means vector across the two classes (the direction of the Fisher linear discriminant). This is similar to running a logistic regression on all continuous attributes in the node and using the estimated logit as a predictor. In the CART monograph, the authors discuss the automatic construction of linear combinations that include feature selection; this capability has been available from the first release of the CART software. BFOS also present a method for constructing Boolean combinations of splitters within each node, a capability that has not been included in the released software. While there are situations in which linear combination splitters are the best way to uncover structure in data (see Olshen's work in Huang et al., 2004), for the most part we have found that such splitters increase the risk of overfitting due to the large amount of learning they represent in each node, thus leading to inferior models.

10.10 Cost-Sensitive Learning

Costs are central to statistical decision theory but cost-sensitive learning received only modest attention before Domingos (1999). Since then, several conferences have been devoted exclusively to this topic and a large number of research papers have appeared in the subsequent scientific literature. It is therefore useful to note that the CART monograph introduced two strategies for cost-sensitive learning and the entire mathematical machinery describing CART is cast in terms of the costs of misclassification. The cost of misclassifying an instance of class i as class j is $C(i, j)$ and is assumed to be equal to 1 unless specified otherwise; $C(i, i) = 0$ for all i. The complete set of costs is represented in the matrix C containing a row and a column for each target class. Any classification tree can have a total cost computed for its terminal node assignments by summing costs over all misclassifications. The issue in cost-sensitive learning is to induce a tree that takes the costs into account during its growing and pruning phases.

The first and most straightforward method for handling costs makes use of weighting: Instances belonging to classes that are costly to misclassify are weighted upward, with a common weight applying to all instances of a given class, a method recently rediscovered by Ting (2002). As implemented in CART, weighting is accomplished transparently so that all node counts are reported in their raw unweighted form. For multiclass problems BFOS suggested that the entries in the misclassification cost matrix be summed across each row to obtain relative class weights that approximately reflect costs. This technique ignores the detail within the matrix but has now been widely adopted due to its simplicity. For the Gini splitting rule, the CART authors show that it is possible to embed the entire cost matrix into the splitting rule, but only after it has been symmetrized. The "symGini" splitting rule generates trees sensitive to the difference in costs $C(i, j)$ and $C(i, k)$, and is most useful when the symmetrized cost matrix is an acceptable representation of the decision maker's problem. By contrast, the instance weighting approach assigns a single cost to all misclassifications of objects of class i. BFOS observe that pruning the tree using the full cost matrix is essential to successful cost-sensitive learning.

10.11 Stopping Rules, Pruning, Tree Sequences, and Tree Selection

The earliest work on decision trees did not allow for pruning. Instead, trees were grown until they encountered some stopping condition and the resulting tree was considered final. In the CART monograph the authors argued that no rule intended to stop tree growth can guarantee that it will not miss important data structure (e.g., consider the two-dimensional XOR problem). They therefore elected to grow trees without stopping. The resulting overly large tree provides the raw material from which a final optimal model is extracted.

The pruning mechanism is based strictly on the training data and begins with a cost-complexity measure defined as

$$Ra(T) = R(T) + a|T|$$

where $R(T)$ is the training sample cost of the tree, $|T|$ is the number of terminal nodes in the tree and a is a penalty imposed on each node. If $a = 0$, then the minimum cost-complexity tree is clearly the largest possible. If a is allowed to progressively increase, the minimum cost-complexity tree will become smaller because the splits at the bottom of the tree that reduce $R(T)$ the least will be cut away. The parameter a is progressively increased in small steps from 0 to a value sufficient to prune away all splits. BFOS prove that any tree of size Q extracted in this way will exhibit a cost $R(Q)$ that is minimum within the class of all trees with Q terminal nodes. This is practically important because it radically reduces the number of trees that must be tested in the search for the optimal tree. Suppose a maximal tree has $|T|$ terminal nodes. Pruning involves removing the split generating two terminal nodes and absorbing the two children into their parent, thereby replacing the two terminal nodes with one. The number of possible subtrees extractable from the maximal tree by such pruning will depend on the specific topology of the tree in question but will sometimes be greater than $.5|T|!$ But given cost-complexity pruning we need to examine a much smaller number of trees. In our example we grew a tree with 81 terminal nodes and cost-complexity pruning extracts a sequence of 28 subtrees, but if we had to look at all possible subtrees we might have to examine on the order of $25! = 15{,}511{,}210{,}043{,}330{,}985{,}984{,}000{,}000$ trees.

The *optimal tree* is defined as that tree in the pruned sequence that achieves minimum cost on test data. Because test misclassification cost measurement is subject to sampling error, uncertainty always remains regarding which tree in the pruning sequence is optimal. Indeed, an interesting characteristic of the error curve (misclassification error rate as a function of tree size) is that it is often flat around its minimum for large training data sets. BFOS recommend selecting the "1 SE" tree that is the smallest tree with an estimated cost within 1 standard error of the minimum cost (or "0 SE") tree. Their argument for the 1 SE rule is that in simulation studies it yields a stable tree size across replications whereas the 0 SE tree size can vary substantially across replications.

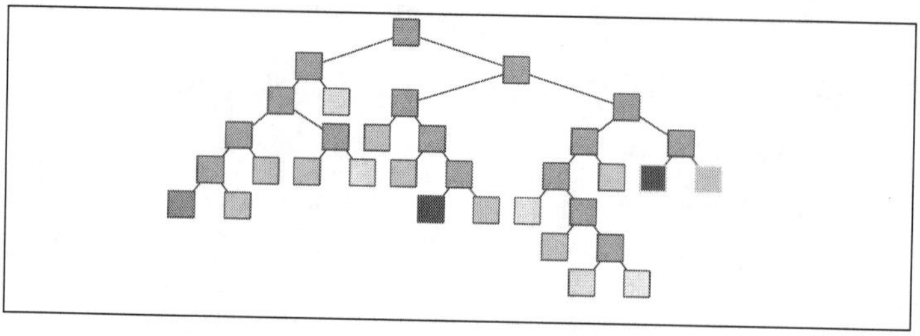

Figure 10.5 One stage in the CART pruning process: the 17-terminal-node subtree. Highlighted nodes are to be pruned next.

Figure 10.5 shows a CART tree along with highlighting of the split that is to be removed next via cost-complexity pruning.

Table 10.6 contains one row for every pruned subtree obtained starting with the maximal 81-terminal-node tree grown. The pruning sequence continues all the way back to the root because we must allow for the possibility that our tree will demonstrate no predictive power on test data. The best performing subtree on test data is the SE 0 tree with 40 nodes, and the smallest tree within a standard error of the SE 0 tree is the SE 1 tree (with 35 terminal nodes). For simplicity we displayed details of the suboptimal 10-terminal-node tree in the earlier dicussion.

10.12 Probability Trees

Probability trees have been recently discussed in a series of insightful articles elucidating their properties and seeking to improve their performance (see Provost and Domingos, 2000). The CART monograph includes what appears to be the first detailed discussion of probability trees and the CART software offers a dedicated splitting rule for the growing of "class probability trees." A key difference between classification trees and probability trees is that the latter want to keep splits that generate two terminal node children assigned to the same class as their parent whereas the former will not. (Such a split accomplishes nothing so far as classification accuracy is concerned.) A probability tree will also be pruned differently from its counterpart classification tree. Therefore, building both a classification and a probability tree on the same data in CART will yield two trees whose final structure can be somewhat different (although the differences are usually modest). The primary drawback of probability trees is that the probability estimates based on training data in the terminal nodes tend to be biased (e.g., toward 0 or 1 in the case of the binary target) with the bias increasing with the depth of the node. In the recent ML literature the use of the Laplace adjustment has been recommended to reduce this bias (Provost and Domingos, 2002). The CART monograph offers a somewhat more complex method to adjust the terminal node

TABLE 10.6 Complete Tree Sequence for CART Model: All Nested Subtrees Reported

Tree	Nodes	Test Cost			Train Cost	Complexity
1	81	0.635461	+/-	0.046451	0.197939	0
2	78	0.646239	+/-	0.046608	0.200442	0.000438
3	71	0.640309	+/-	0.046406	0.210385	0.00072
4	67	0.638889	+/-	0.046395	0.217487	0.000898
5	66	0.632373	+/-	0.046249	0.219494	0.001013
6	61	0.635214	+/-	0.046271	0.23194	0.001255
7	57	0.643151	+/-	0.046427	0.242131	0.001284
8	50	0.639475	+/-	0.046303	0.262017	0.00143
9	42	0.592442	+/-	0.044947	0.289254	0.001709
10	40	0.584506	+/-	0.044696	0.296356	0.001786
11	35	0.611156	+/-	0.045432	0.317663	0.002141
12	32	0.633049	+/-	0.045407	0.331868	0.002377
13	31	0.635891	+/-	0.045425	0.336963	0.002558
14	30	0.638731	+/-	0.045442	0.342307	0.002682
15	29	0.674738	+/-	0.046296	0.347989	0.002851
16	25	0.677918	+/-	0.045841	0.374143	0.003279
17	24	0.659204	+/-	0.045366	0.381245	0.003561
18	17	0.648764	+/-	0.044401	0.431548	0.003603
19	16	0.692798	+/-	0.044574	0.442911	0.005692
20	15	0.725379	+/-	0.04585	0.455695	0.006402
21	13	0.756539	+/-	0.046819	0.486269	0.007653
22	10	0.785534	+/-	0.046752	0.53975	0.008924
23	9	0.784542	+/-	0.045015	0.563898	0.012084
24	7	0.784542	+/-	0.045015	0.620536	0.014169
25	6	0.784542	+/-	0.045015	0.650253	0.014868
26	4	0.784542	+/-	0.045015	0.71043	0.015054
27	2	0.907265	+/-	0.047939	0.771329	0.015235
28	1	1	+/-	0	1	0.114345

estimates that has rarely been discussed in the literature. Dubbed the "Breiman adjustment," it adjusts the estimated misclassification rate $r \times (t)$ of any terminal node upward by

$$r \times (t) = r(t) + e/(q(t) + S)$$

where $r(t)$ is the training sample estimate within the node, $q(t)$ is the fraction of the training sample in the node, and S and e are parameters that are solved for as a function of the difference between the train and test error rates for a given tree. In contrast to the Laplace method, the Breiman adjustment does not depend on the raw predicted probability in the node and the adjustment can be very small if the test data show that the tree is not overfit. Bloch, Olshen, and Walker (2002) discuss this topic in detail and report very good performance for the Breiman adjustment in a series of empirical experiments.

10.13 Theoretical Foundations

The earliest work on decision trees was entirely atheoretical. Trees were proposed as methods that appeared to be useful and conclusions regarding their properties were based on observing tree performance on empirical examples. While this approach remains popular in machine learning, the recent tendency in the discipline has been to reach for stronger theoretical foundations. The CART monograph tackles theory with sophistication, offering important technical insights and proofs for key results. For example, the authors derive the expected misclassification rate for the maximal (largest possible) tree, showing that it is bounded from above by twice the Bayes rate. The authors also discuss the bias variance trade-off in trees and show how the bias is affected by the number of attributes. Based largely on the prior work of CART coauthors Richard Olshen and Charles Stone, the final three chapters of the monograph relate CART to theoretical work on nearest neighbors and show that as the sample size tends to infinity the following hold: (1) the estimates of the regression function converge to the true function and (2) the risks of the terminal nodes converge to the risks of the corresponding Bayes rules. In other words, speaking informally, with large enough samples the CART tree will converge to the true function relating the target to its predictors and achieve the smallest cost possible (the Bayes rate). Practically speaking, such results may only be realized with sample sizes far larger than in common use today.

10.14 Post-CART Related Research

Research in decision trees has continued energetically since the 1984 publication of the CART monograph, as shown in part by the several thousand citations to the monograph found in the scientific literature. For the sake of brevity we confine ourselves here to selected research conducted by the four CART coauthors themselves after 1984. In 1985 Breiman and Friedman offered ACE (alternating conditional expectations), a purely data-based driven methodology for suggesting variable transformations in regression; this work strongly influenced Hastie and Tibshirani's generalized additive models (GAM, 1986). Stone (1985) developed a rigorous theory for the style of nonparametric additive regression proposed with ACE. This was soon followed by Friedman's recursive partitioning approach to spline regression (multivariate adaptive regression splines, MARS). The first version of the MARS program in our archives is labeled Version 2.5 and dated October 1989; the first published paper appeared as a lead article with discussion in the *Annals of Statistics* in 1991. The MARS algorithm leans heavily on ideas developed in the CART monograph but produces models that are readily recognized as regressions on recursively partitioned (and selected) predictors. Stone, with collaborators, extended the spline regression approach to hazard modeling (Kooperberg, Stone, and Truong, 1995) and polychotomous regression (1997).

Breiman was active in searching for ways to improve the accuracy, scope of applicability, and compute speed of the CART tree. In 1992 Breiman was the first to introduce the multivariate decision tree (vector dependent variable) in software but did not write any papers on the topic. In 1995, Spector and Breiman implemented a strategy for parallelizing CART across a network of computers using the C-Linda parallel programming environment. In this study the authors observed that the gains from parallelization were primarily achieved for larger data sets using only a few of the available processors. By 1994 Breiman had hit upon "bootstrap aggregation": creating predictive ensembles by growing a large number of CART trees on bootstrap samples drawn from a fixed training data set. In 1998 Breiman applied the idea of ensembles to online learning and the development of classifiers for very large databases. He then extended the notion of randomly sampling rows in the training data to random sampling columns in each node of the tree to arrive at the idea of the random forest. Breiman devoted the last years of his life to extending random forests with his coauthor Adele Cutler, introducing new methods for missing value imputation, outlier detection, cluster discovery, and innovative ways to visualize data using random forests outputs in a series of papers and Web postings from 2000 to 2004.

Richard Olshen has focused primarily on biomedical applications of decision trees. He developed the first tree-based approach to survival analysis (Gordon and Olshen, 1984), contributed to research on image compression (Cosman et al., 1993), and has recently introduced new linear combination splitters for the analysis of very high dimensional data (the genetics of complex disease).

Friedman introduced stochastic gradient boosting in several papers beginning in 1999 (commercialized as TreeNet software) which appears to be a substantial advance over conventional boosting. Friedman's approach combines the generation of very small trees, random sampling from the training data at every training cycle, slow learning via very small model updates at each training cycle, selective rejection of training data based on model residuals, and allowing for a variety of objective functions, to arrive at a system that has performed remarkably well in a range of real-world applications. Friedman followed this work with a technique for compressing tree ensembles into models containing considerably fewer trees using novel methods for regularized regression. Friedman showed that postprocessing of tree ensembles to compress them may actually improve their performance on holdout data. Taking this line of research one step further, Friedman then introduced methods for reexpressing tree ensemble models as collections of "rules" that can also radically compress the models and sometimes improve their predictive accuracy.

Further pointers to the literature, including a library of applications of CART, can be found at the Salford Systems Web site: http://www.salford-systems.com.

10.15 Software Availability

CART software is available from Salford Systems, at http://www.salford-systems.com; no-cost evaluation versions may be downloaded on request. Executables for Windows operating systems as well as Linux and UNIX may be obtained in both 32-bit and 64-bit versions. Academic licenses for professors automatically grant no-cost licenses to their registered students. CART source code, written by Jerome Friedman, has remained a trade secret and is available only in compiled binaries from Salford Systems. While popular open-source systems (and other commercial proprietary systems) offer decision trees inspired by the work of Breiman, Friedman, Olshen, and Stone, these systems generate trees that are demonstrably different from those of true CART when applied to real-world complex data sets. CART has been used by Salford Systems to win a number of international data mining competitions; details are available on the company's Web site.

10.16 Exercises

1. (a) To the decision tree novice the most important variable in a CART tree should be the root node splitter, yet it is not uncommon to see a different variable listed as most important in the CART summary output. How can this be? (b) If you run a CART model for the purpose of ranking the predictor variables in your data set and then you rerun the model excluding all the 0-importance variables, will you get the same tree in the second run? (c) What if you rerun the tree keeping as predictors only variables that appeared as splitters in the first run? Are there conditions that would guarantee that you obtain the same tree?
2. Every internal node in a CART tree contains a primary splitter, competitor splits, and surrogate splits. In some trees the same variable will appear as both a competitor and a surrogate but using different split points. For example, as a competitor the variable might split the node with $xj <= c$, while as a surrogate the variable might split the node as $xj <= d$. Explain why this might occur.
3. Among its six different splitting rules CART offers the Gini and twoing splitting rules for growing a tree. Explain why an analyst might prefer the results of the twoing rule even if it yielded a lower accuracy.
4. For a binary target if two CART trees are grown on the same data, the first using the Gini splitting rule and the second using the class probability rule, which one is likely to contain more nodes? Will the two trees exhibit the same accuracy? Will the smaller tree be contained within the larger one? Explain the differences between the two trees.
5. Suppose you have a data set for a binary target coded 0/1 in which 80% of the records have a target value of 0 and you grow a CART tree using the default

PRIORS EQUAL setting. How will the results change if you rerun the model using a WEIGHT variable w with $w = 1$ when the target is 0 and $w = 4$ when the target is 1?

6. When growing CART trees on larger data sets containing tens of thousands of records or more, one often finds that tree accuracy declines only slightly as the tree is grown much larger than its optimal size. In other words, on large data sets a too-large CART tree appears to overfit only slightly. Why is this the case?
7. A CART model is not just a single tree but a collection of nested trees, each of which has its own performance characteristics (accuracy, area under the ROC curve). Why do the CART authors suggest that the best tree is not necessarily the most accurate tree but could well be the smallest tree in the tree sequence within some tolerance interval of the most accurate tree? How is the tolerance interval calculated?
8. For cost-sensitive learning, when different mistakes are associated with different costs, the CART authors adjust the priors to reflect costs, which is essentially a form of reweighting the data. When do adjusted priors perfectly reflect costs and when do they only approximate the costs? How does the symmetric gini splitting rule help to reflect costs of misclassification?
9. The CART authors decided on a grow-then-prune strategy for the selection of an optimal decision tree rather than following an apparently simpler stopping rule method. Explain how XOR-type problems can be used to defeat any stopping rule based on a goodness of split criterion for one or more splits.
10. If a training data set is complete (contains no missing values in any predictor), how can a CART tree grown on such data guarantee that it can handle missing values encountered in future data?

References

Bloch, D.A., Olshen, R.A., and Walker M.G. (2002) Risk estimation for classification trees. *Journal of Computational & Graphical Statistics*, 11, 263–288.

Breiman, L. (1995) Current research in the mathematics of generalization. *Proceedings of the Santa Fe Institute CNLS Workshop on Formal Approaches to Supervised Learning*. David Wolpert, Ed. Addison-Wesley, 361–368.

Breiman, L. (1998) *Pasting Small Votes for Classification in Large Databases and On-Line*. Statistics Department, University of California, Berkeley.

Breiman, L., and Friedman, J.H. (1985) Estimating optimal transformations for multiple regression and correlation. *Journal of the American Statistical Association*, 80, 580–598.

Breiman, L., Friedman, J.H., Olshen, R.A., and Stone, C.J. (1984) *Classification and Regression Trees*, Wadsworth, Belmont, CA. Republished by CRC Press.

Breiman, L. and Stone, J. (1978) Parsimonious Binary Classification Trees, Technical Report, Technology Services Corp., Los Angeles.

Cosman, P.C., Tseng, C., Gray, R.M., Olshen, R.A., et al. (1993) Tree-structured vector quantization of CT chest scans: Image quality and diagnostic accuracy. *IEEE Transactions on Medical Imaging*, 12, 727–739.

Cover, T. and Hart, P. (1967) Nearest neighbor pattern classification, *IEEE Trans Information Theory 13*, page(s): 21–27.

Domingos, P. (1999) MetaCost: A general method for making classifiers cost-sensitive. In *Proceedings of the Fifth International Conference on Knowledge Discovery and Data Mining*, pp. 155–164.

Doyle, P. (1973) The use of automatic interaction detector and similar search procedures. *Operational Research Quarterly*, 24, 465–467.

Einhorn, H. (1972) Alchemy in the behavioral sciences. *Public Opinion Quarterly*, 36, 367–378.

Friedman, J.H. (1977) A recursive partitioning decision rule for nonparametric classification. *IEEE Trans. Computers*, C-26, 404. Also available as Stanford Linear Accelerator Center Rep. SLAC-PUB-1373 (Rev. 1975).

Friedman, J.H. (1999) *Stochastic Gradient Boosting*. Statistics Department, Stanford University.

Friedman, J.H., Bentley, J.L., and Finkel, R.A. (1977) An algorithm for finding best matches in logarithmic time. *ACM Trans. Math. Software*, 3, 209. Also available as Stanford Linear Accelerator Center Rep. SIX-PUB-1549, Feb. 1975.

Friedman, J.H., Kohavi, R., and Yun, Y. (1996) Lazy decision trees. In *Proceedings of the Thirteenth National Conference on Artificial Intelligence*, pp. 717–724, AAAI Press/MIT Press, San Francisco, CA.

Gordon, L., and Olshen, R.A. (1985) Tree-structured survival analysis (with discussion). *Cancer Treatment Reports*, 69, 1065–1068.

Gordon, L., and Olshen, R.A. (1984) Almost surely consistent nonparametric regression from recursive partitioning schemes. *Journal of Multivariate Analysis*, 15, 147–163.

Hastie and Tibshirani's Generalized Additive Models. (1986) *Statistical Science*. 1, 297–318.

Huang, J., Lin, A., Narasimhan, B., et al. (2004) Tree-structured supervised learning and the genetics of hypertension. *Proc. Natl. Acad. Sci.*, July 20, 101(29), 10529–10534.

Kooperberg, C., Bose, S., and Stone, C.J. (1997) Polychotomous regression. *Journal of the American Statistical Association*, 92, 117–127.

Kooperberg, C., Stone, C.J., and Truong, Y.K. (1995) Hazard regression. *Journal of the American Statistical Association*, 90, 78–94.

Messenger, R.C., and Mandell, M.L. (1972) A model search technique for predictive nominal scale multivariate analysis. *Journal of the American Statistical Association*, 67, 768–772.

Morgan, J.N., and Sonquist, J.A. (1963) Problems in the analysis of survey data, and a proposal. *Journal of the American Statistical Association*, 58, 415–435.

Provost, F., and Domingos, P. (2002) Tree induction for probability-based ranking. *Machine Learning*, 52, 199–215.

Quinlan, R. (1989) Unknown attribute values in induction. In *Proceedings of the Sixth International Workshop on Machine Learning*, pp. 164–168.

Stone, C.J. (1977) Consistent nonparametric regression (with discussion). *Annals of Statistics*, 5, 595–645.

Stone, C. (1985) Additive regression and other non-parametric models, *Annal. Statist.*, 13, 689–705.

Ting, K.M. (2002) An instance-weighting method to induce cost-sensitive trees. *IEEE Trans. Knowledge and Data Engineering*, 14, 659–665.

Index

A

C

D

E

F

G

H

I

N

T

U

V

W

9781420089646